FACULTY OF ARTS
Charles University

Created for eternity:
the greatest discoveries of Czech Egyptology

MIROSLAV BÁRTA

LADISLAV BAREŠ
JAROMÍR KREJČÍ
MOHAMED MEGAHED
LENKA VARADZINOVÁ
(editors)

Forewords
TOMÁŠ ZIMA
Rector of Charles University

ZAHI HAWASS

Charles University
Faculty of Arts
Prague 2019

This book was published with support of the Programme for the Development of Fields of Study at Charles University, no. Q11: Complexity and Resilience: Ancient Egyptian Civilisation in Multidisciplinary and Multicultural Perspective, and the non-investment subsidy No. MŠMT-906/2019-6, VEG2019/1.

Reviewers:
Wolf B. Oerter
Pavel Onderka

AUTHORS:
Katarína Arias (KA)
Ladislav Bareš (LB)
Miroslav Bárta (MB)
Dana Bělohoubková (DB)
Helena Březinová (HB)
Filip Coppens (FC)
Veronika Dulíková (VD)
Jiří Janák (JJ)
Lucie Jirásková (LJ)
Jaromír Krejčí (JK)
Renata Landgráfová (RL)
Mohamed Megahed (MM)
Jana Mynářová (JM)
Martin Odler (MO)
Marie Peterková Hlouchová (MPH)
Květa Smoláriková (KS)
Břetislav Vachala (BV)
Lenka Varadzinová (LV)
Miroslav Verner (MV)
Hana Vymazalová (HV)
Dorotea Wollnerová (DW)

First published (in Czech) 2018 by Charles University, Faculty of Arts
Cover designed and text typeset by Oleg Man
Printed and bound in Czech Republic by SERIFA, s. r. o., Jinonická 80, 150 00 Praha 5

For more information visit: https://cegu.ff.cuni.cz
Our Facebook page: https:www.facebook.com/egyptologieffcuni
Our You Tube channel: https:www.youtube.com/user/egyptologieffcuni

ISBN 978-80-7308-927-6

Foremen of workers – brothers Talal and Ahmad el-Kereti – cooperated with the Czechoslovak and later Czech Institute of Egyptology for more than 35 years. They were instrumental for many significant discoveries published in this book. Photographer captured them during a break in the archaeological excavation of Kaaper's mastaba, Abusir South, which took place in 1991

Contents

Abusir – the flagship of Czech Egyptology

Foreword by Tomáš Zima

In 2019 Charles University, its Faculty of Arts, and the Czech Institute of Egyptology are celebrating the hundredth birthday of Czech Egyptology. It is an important centenary not only for us, but for archaeology globally. For many years now Czech Egyptologists have been among world leaders in the field, making major breakthroughs (most recently the discovery of the tomb of the priest Kaires) – and helping to set new international research trends.

Above all, the discoveries and research work of Czech Egyptologists in the pyramid fields of Abusir have for decades been an integral part of world cultural heritage. Less well-known, but comparably significant, are their excavations in Saqqara, in the El-Hayez Oasis (part of the Bahariya Oasis), on the territory of ancient Nubia and in the Sudan. At all these sites, and often in extremely challenging climatic, social, cultural and political conditions, the achievements of our colleagues over the decades have been extraordinary, and are "display cabinets" not only for Charles University but for the whole Czech Republic. It says much that in recent years the Czech Egyptological expedition has been the biggest Czech scientific multidisciplinary expedition active beyond the borders of our state.

This book presents the most important discoveries of Czech Egyptologists and the range and variety of their activities.

I am very glad to have had the chance to get to know the work of Czech Egyptologists not only as a reader of their expert articles, monographs and popularising books, but at their research sites in Egypt. In Abusir and in Saqqara I learned at first hand how challenging their research is and came to appreciate the sheer commitment and labour behind their "sensational" finds, so often reported in the world media. I am also pleased to have got to know the work of the "founding fathers", professors František Lexa and Zbyněk Žába, and their successors – professors Miroslav Verner, Ladislav Bareš and currently Miroslav Bárta and his team.

For the future, I wish the Czech Egyptologists all the vigour, enthusiasm, and also resilience that they need for their work. I believe that we can look forward to more discoveries that will enrich our knowledge of the world and the dynamics of its history across several thousand years of human society.

Tomáš Zima
Rector of Charles University

Foreword
by Zahi Hawass

I am extremely pleased to provide a few words for this celebration of 100 years of Egyptology at Charles University in Prague. The past century has witnessed the careers of great Czech Egyptologists who have written their names in gold in the history of the field by teaching many students who then went on to make their own contributions, by writing many outstanding scholarly works and popular books, by translating many important texts, and by making many major archaeological discoveries. These discoveries have headlined in newspapers all over the world and captured the hearts of people at home in the Czech Republic.

Undeniably, these discoveries have changed our understanding of ancient Egyptian history. That is why, when I visit the site of Abusir – which I have called "the land of the forgotten pyramids" – and look toward the peaks of its monuments, I feel as though the name of Charles University is shining in the sky like a constellation.

Charles University's own Egyptological history began 100 years ago, in 1919, when František Lexa joined the faculty and gave the first lectures on the subject here. Their truly great work began some decades later, in 1960, when the Czech Institute of Egyptology chose Abusir as the main focus of the university's excavations. For this reason, no one can really call Abusir "the land of the forgotten pyramids" anymore. Thanks to years of Czech excavation and scholarship, the site has become renowned for its pyramids, in which some pharaohs of the Fifth Dynasty and high-ranking courtiers of the Old Kingdom (Third through Sixth Dynasties) were buried.

Zbyněk Žába initiated Charles University's work in Abusir by excavating one of the most important tombs of the Old Kingdom, the mastaba of Ptahshepses. This private monument, created for King Nyuserre's vizier and son-in-law, has enriched our knowledge of the administration during the golden age of the Old Kingdom. Another leading Czech Egyptologist who has dedicated his life to the site is my friend Miroslav Verner, whose many impressive discoveries in Abusir include the pyramid of Raneferef and the first evidence for how the pyramid was constructed.

I have seen that one of Verner's students, Miroslav Bárta, has brought back the "magic" of Abusir again when he took over his professor's work. Bárta has found a number of Old Kingdom tombs that I have visited, but his most important discovery is a wooden boat of the Third Dynasty. This came as a surprise to all of us as Egyptologists because the boat belonged to a private individual, rather than a king, and also because of its large size. Bárta has formed wonderful relationships with the many Egyptian scholars who aid the Czech Institute of Egyptology in Abusir, and he has become a close friend of mine.

There is one particular story I must mention for this centennial celebration, and it is about the Czech Institute's discovery of the tomb of Iufaa, who was an "overseer of palaces" in about

500 BC. At the time, I was Director of the Giza Plateau. Verner, who was supervising the excavation, came to inform me about his remarkable find: Iufaa's tomb was completely intact.

I went to see the tomb – it was huge, an incredible discovery! I called Farouk Hosni, who was then the Egyptian Minister of the Culture, to deliver this exceptional news. He told me, "Do not open the sarcophagus until I arrive with the press."

I owe special thanks to Charles University, and particularly to Miroslav Verner and Miroslav Bárta because they took three of my Egyptian students to study at Charles University, and they all came back well-prepared to help their country with excellent education and training in the field of Egyptology.

I do hope that the fine Egyptologists of Charles University will continue their vital conservation and restoration work of the site of Abusir, which is a jewel between Khufu's Great Pyramid at Giza to the north and Djoser's Step Pyramid at Saqqara to the south.

I believe that the best gift that Egypt could possibly present to the people of the Czech Republic is an exhibition of statues and other objects found at Abusir to celebrate these past 100 years of Egyptology at Charles University. This will magnificently demonstrate the cooperation and friendship that our two countries have enjoyed through this century – and will enjoy for another hundred years, at least.

Zahi Hawass
Giza, June 2019

Introduction

MIROSLAV BÁRTA

The book that you hold in your hands has emerged, metaphorically speaking, over nearly sixty years, and the journey that led to it has taken a whole century. In 2019 we mark the centenary of the first Czech lectures on ancient Egyptian civilisation at Charles University in Prague, and for roughly six decades now there has been an ever increasing need to present to the public the ever larger assemblage of finds made during the archaeological projects of the Czech (prior to 1993 Czechoslovak) Institute of Egyptology in Egypt and in the Sudan. They are the fruits of the systematic labour and tireless efforts of several generations of Czech Egyptologists to understand and deepen our knowledge of a civilisation whose story ended long ago.

Our aim in this book is not to offer a purely academic study. Instead we want to show all who are interested in ancient Egypt and the Sudan a path to their understanding, using Czech discoveries in North-East Africa. These finds come from the institute's concessions and projects of the institute on the territory of ancient Egypt and Nubia.

The first part of the book is devoted to the pyramid field in Abusir, where the institute launched its systematic research programme in 1960 with the documentation of the mastaba of the vizier Ptahshepses. Together with the excavations themselves, the investigation of this tomb continued until 1974 and conservation and reconstruction works went on for many years after.

Then in 1976 the institute obtained the concession for research in the whole site of Abusir. This comprises three main areas. One is Central Abusir, which is furthest to the north and closest to the famous pyramid field of the 4th Dynasty kings in Giza. With its four pyramid complexes of the rulers of the 5th Dynasty (Sahure, Neferirkare, Raneferef and Nyuserre), it is an area where apart from the kings themselves, mainly members of the royal family were buried. Extensive new excavations have recently been initiated in the northern part of the site, because it is here that other major monuments important for an understanding of the history of the 5th Dynasty undoubtedly lie.

The area of Abusir South, situated south of the pyramid necropolis, is a place where for practically seven centuries (2700–2000 BC) the court elite built their tombs and family cemeteries. In the New Kingdom it was also the site of the unique temple of one of the greatest rulers in ancient Egyptian history, Ramesses II.

Finally, the cemetery of what are known as shaft tombs in the west of the concession saw a great deal of building and cult activity over several centuries in the 1st millennium BC. Leading Egyptian dignitaries of the 6th and 5th centuries BC were buried there in the vicinity of the mysterious tomb of Udjahorresnet, a controversial figure of the period of the beginning of the Persian occupation of Egypt. The most important of these dignitaries was the priest Iufaa.

< Palm grove in the Botanical Garden in the Dokki district of Giza. Located on the other side of the street is the Czech Embassy in Egypt, for many years the headquarters of the Czech Institute of Egyptology of the Charles University Faculty of Arts

Neighbouring on Abusir is South Saqqara, where since 2010 research has been underway on the pyramid complex of the ruler Djedkare Isesi, the immediate successor of the kings buried in Abusir.

The El-Hayez Oasis (part of the Bahariya Oasis), situated roughly 350 kilometres south-west of modern Cairo in the Egyptian Western Desert, is one of the six great oases of modern-day Egypt. Czech archaeologists began work here in 2003 and by 2010 had completed most of their initial archaeological projects, which involved the discovery of a unique early Christian settlement from the fourth and the beginning of the 5th century AD, and excavation of the remains of much older prehistoric sites from a time when the Sahara was still a fertile green area.

No less momentous were the epigraphic and partially also archaeological expeditions organised by the institute on the territory of ancient Nubia almost immediately after its founding in the years 1961– 65. Under the patronage of UNESCO, these projects were part of an international response to the need to protect and document the monuments in the large area that was to be irreversibly drowned by the waters of the new High Aswan Dam. The results of this part of the institute's work included finds of dozens of important historical inscriptions, documentation of the rock shelter decorated with paintings in Korosko, the rediscovery of a vanished temple in Tafa and the documentation of the Roman fortress in Qertassi, as well as research on the tumulus cemetery in Wadi Qitna and Kalabsha South.

Since 2009 the institute has also been conducting excavations in two archaeological concessions in the Sudan. The first is located close to Khartoum on the Sixth Nile Cataract (the Sabaloka region), where the main finds have been prehistoric sites and other signs of the development of Neolithic civilisation in North-East Africa. By contrast Usli, a site situated close to the contemporary administrative centre of Karima in the north of Sudan, is today widely known for the unexpected discoveries of temples and a royal palace from the 1st millennium BC.

For many years the research projects of the Czech Institute of Egyptology of the Charles University, Faculty of Arts, have been unavoidably interdisciplinary and international in nature. They have been providing answers to many questions about the history and evolution of ancient civilisations and cultures on the Nile, and throwing new light on the development of the natural environment and the way in which people adapted to it, the functioning of various different religious systems, the stories of individuals, and the search for meaning in human life. It is the unique opportunity to combine different kinds of sources at the micro- and macro-levels over long periods of time that makes the archaeology and history of ancient Egypt such a rare and important discipline in the framework of contemporary science and research on the complex societies of the 21st century.

< View across the site of Nyuserre's valley temple to the pyramids of Neferirkare and Nyuserre. Small mounds of waste from past archaeological excavations are visible in the foreground

Satellite image
of Abusir, Saqqara
and Dahshur

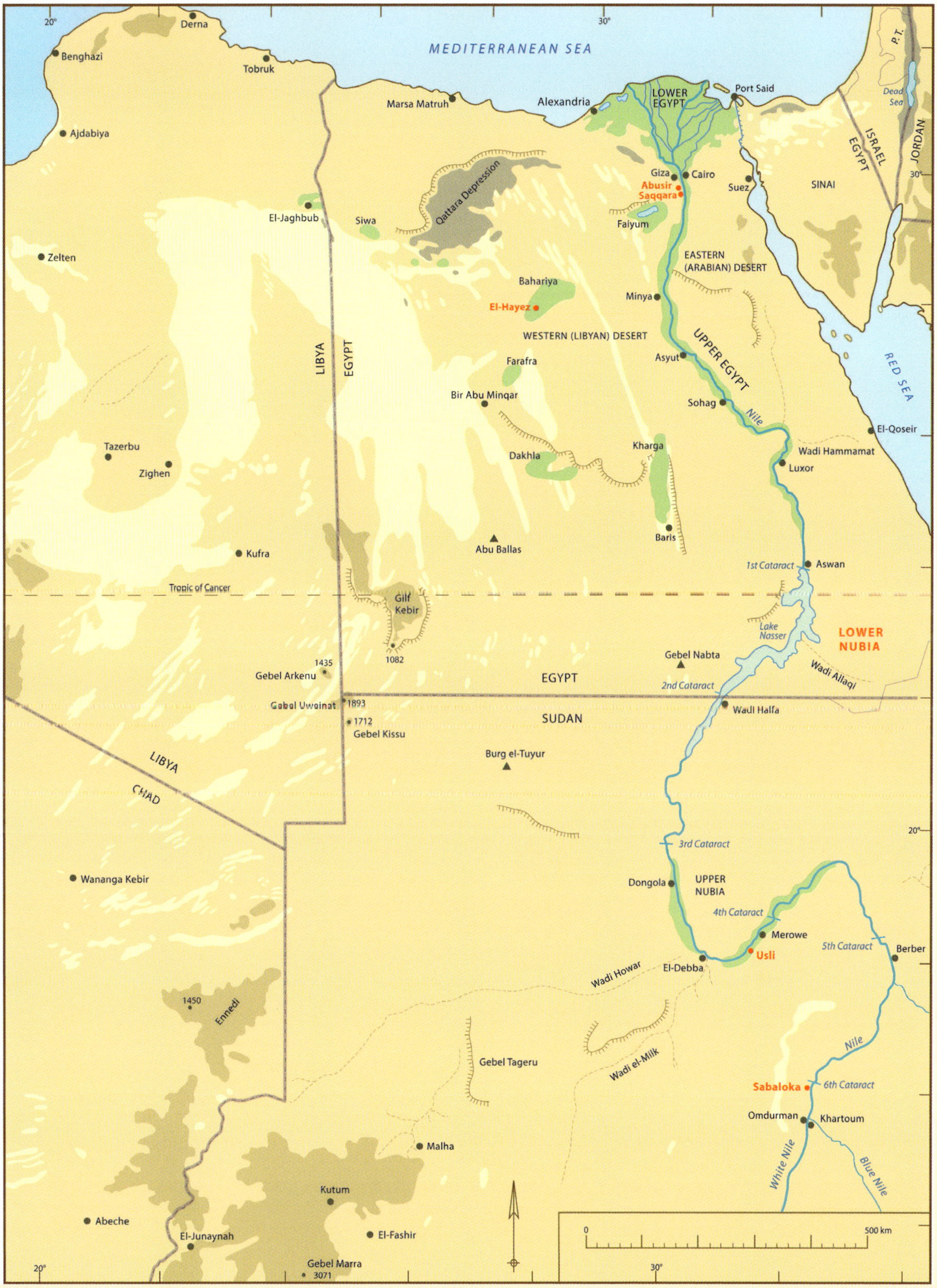

Map of North-East Africa

Abusir pyramid necropolis – in the realm of the sun god

JAROMÍR KREJČÍ

The archaeological research carried out by the Charles University team in Abusir was closely linked with the founding of the Czechoslovak Institute of Egyptology of the Charles University Faculty of Arts. It was in 1958 that Professor František Lexa managed to make a reality of the long-term plan to found the institute. In 1960, even before the start of the rescue work in Nubia, Professor Zbyněk Žába initiated field work in the already known but only partially excavated mastaba of the vizier Ptahshepses, located right in the heart of the Abusir royal pyramid necropolis. After the survey and initial excavation of the large pyramid complexes of the 5th Dynasty kings Sahure, Neferirkare and Nyuserre at the beginning of the 20th century by the German archaeologist Ludwig Borchardt, Central Abusir was a generally known site and considered to have been thoroughly studied. Žába chose it for the Czechoslovak institute on the advice of the distinguished Czech Egyptologist, Professor Jaroslav Černý, and as the next 60 years of research were to show, the choice was an excellent one.

The research in the mastaba of Ptahshepses that took place in the years 1960–74 revealed it to be one of the biggest, and perhaps the most structurally complex non-royal tomb of the Old Kingdom. Indeed, it is remarkable for the use of some elements of royal architecture, such as the saddle construction of the ceiling of the burial chamber. The discovery of the tip of a granite obelisk (an element very closely associated with the solar cult) between the vizier's tomb and Nyuserre's pyramid complex added to the evidence that at the time when the Egyptian rulers were buried here, Abusir was closely linked to the rise of the solar cult. This was also reflected in the building of sun temples, special architectural complexes, close to the royal pyramid necropolis. The rulers buried in Abusir are even sometimes referred to as "the sun kings".

In the later 1970s the then Egyptian Antiquities Organisation granted the then Czechoslovak Institute of Egyptology new territory for archaeological excavations. This archaeological concession included the southern part of the pyramid necropolis. Among the archaeological discoveries made here we should mention the excavation of the pyramid complex of Queen Khentkaus II, and above all the excavation of the tomb complex of King Raneferef with finds of fragments of the scrolls of a large temple archive, a set of royal statues, stone vessels, faience inlays, pottery and much else. In the mortuary temple of this complex the archaeologists found one of the

< The Pyramids of Neferirkare, Sahure and Nyuserre. In the foreground the very dilapidated pyramid of Queen Khentkaus II, and the mastaba of Prince Werkaure

oldest hypostyle halls in the history of Egyptian architecture. They also investigated the pyramid complex Lepsius no. 24 not far from these two complexes. During research on this extensively damaged pyramid they discovered funerary equipment and part of the mummified body of a queen, whose name we unfortunately do not know; it may have been Reputnebu, wife of Nyuserre.

< The pyramids in Central Abusir rising up on the desert plateau above the fields and palm groves of the Nile Valley floodplain

Cemeteries for members of the royal family were also part of the pyramid necropolis. One of these belonged to members of the family of King Djedkare. He himself was buried in South Saqqara, but some of his family members were interred in Abusir. Closer to the central part of the royal necropolis, in the vicinity of the pyramid complex of Khentkaus II, we uncovered the large, extensively destroyed mastaba of Prince Werkaure with an entrance to the underground part leading from the north and a complicated substructure. We find the same type of underground interior in the architecturally unusual double tomb Lepsius no. 25, formed by a pair of mastabas closely adjoining each other.

What is so far the most recent phase of archaeological research in the royal necropolis in Abusir has involved comprehensive excavation of the Nakhtsare's cemetery, a group of four mastabas located south of Raneferef's mortuary temple. The tombs were constructed on a unified plan either during the reign of Nyuserre or not long afterwards. They were for members of the court elite, and we know three of them by name: the Prince Nakhtsare, Kakaibaef and Queen Khentkaus III. The most recent works in the central part of the pyramid necropolis – excavations in the area of tomb of priest and official Kaires and in and around Nyuserre's valley temple show the importance of archaeological research in the royal necropolis.

View of the Abusir pyramid necropolis from the east. The pyramid of Sahure (far right) was the first to be built, and the monumental entrance belongs to the mastaba of the vizier Ptahshepses

Mummy of King Raneferef

Human bones and skin; left hand: l. 18 cm, w. 5.7 cm, bones: max. l. 38 cm (fibula), fragments of skin: max. l. 6 cm, max. w. 5.2 cm. Old Kingdom, 5th Dynasty. Central Abusir – Raneferef's unfinished pyramid (AC 3), discovered 1998. Find no. 15/1/1998.

During archaeological excavation of the burial chamber and antechamber of Raneferef's unfinished pyramid, parts of a mummified male body were found together with fragments of a red granite sarcophagus, bandages and fragments of cartonnage. The whole left hand, right fibula, the complete left clavicle and a few bones (including fragment of a skull) and fragments of soft tissues are the remains of the owner of the pyramid – King Raneferef. This has been established by anthropological examination, radio-carbon dating and the identification of embalming techniques typical of the period of the Old Kingdom. Anthropological analysis supported other evidence found during archaeological research indicating that the king died at the young age of 20–23, after a short reign. He was 167–168 cm tall and, as we would expect, his skeleton shows no signs of heavy work. The find of part of a king's mummy of the Old Kingdom is very important and unusual, the royal pyramids have suffered so much robbery and destruction that very few authentic bodily remains have survived. (JK)

Views into the burial chamber of the Unfinished Pyramid

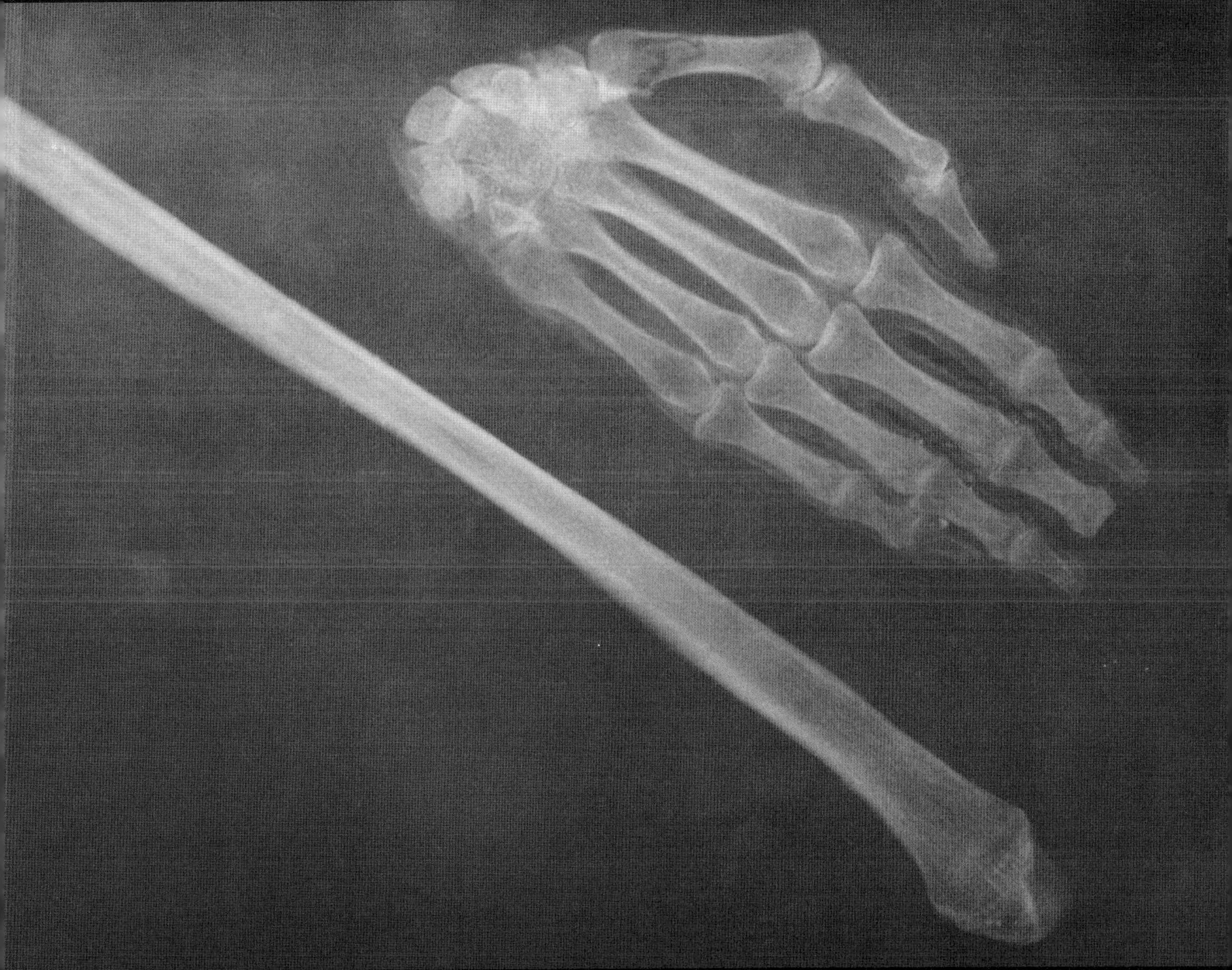

2 Striding statue of King Raneferef with Upper Egyptian crown

Basalt; original h. ca. 85 cm. Old Kingdom, 5th Dynasty, reign of Raneferef. Central Abusir – mortuary temple of Raneferef's pyramid complex (AC 3), discovered 1984. Find numbers 770a/I/84, 809/I/84, 853a,b/I/84, 979/I/84, 1020/I/84, 26k/I/84. Exhibited in the permanent exhibition of the Egyptian Museum in Cairo (inv. no. JE 98181).

The fragments of a striding statue of Raneferef were found in the mortuary temple of Raneferef's pyramid complex in Abusir. The king is depicted in the short, pleated skirt called a *shendjet*, and wears on his head the crown of Upper Egypt. His right hand, resting on his chest, grasps the *hedj* sceptre. The markedly idealised basalt statue with its carefully polished and originally polychrome surface is testimony to the excellent craftsmanship of the ancient Egyptian sculptors and represents Raneferef as a young and self-confident ruler. According to the religious ideas of the ancient Egyptians the king's *ka*, or soul, could be embodied in the statue and thus take part in the rituals that were conducted in the temple every day. The statue is a part of one of the largest and most important sets of royal sculptures from the Old Kingdom hitherto discovered. The place of the discovery is important in itself – the *per tut*, or abode of the statue, the earliest known hypostyle hall in ancient Egyptian funerary architecture. (MV)

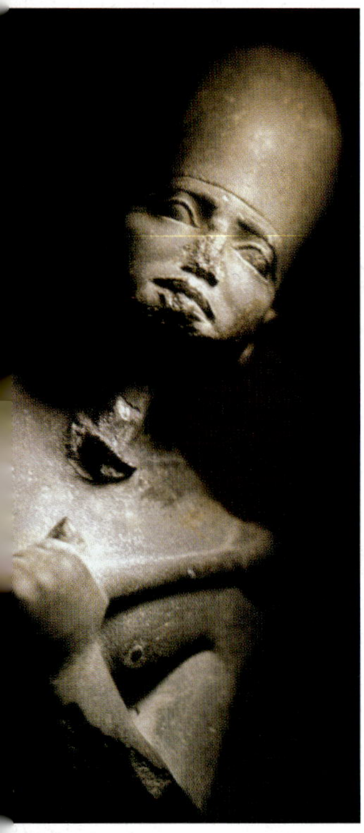

Hypostyle of the mortuary temple of Raneferef

3 Raneferef seated on his throne under the protection of the god Horus

Pink limestone; original h. ca. 35 cm. Old Kingdom, 5th Dynasty, reign of Raneferef. Central Abusir – mortuary temple of Raneferef's pyramid complex (AC 3), separate fragments discovered in the years 1982 and 1984. Find numbers 103a–b/I/82, 771a–d/I/84, 845a–c/I/84. Exhibited in the permanent exhibition of the Egyptian Museum in Cairo (inv. no. JE 98171).

Aesthetically the most beautiful and the most valuable of the statues of Raneferef shows the king sitting on his throne under the direct protection of the sun god Horus. It is exceptional among royal statues of the same period for the way in which the king's body is slightly turned to the right from the belt upwards. His short pleated skirt with triangular front section was much favoured at the time in the royal family. In his right hand, placed on his chest, Raneferef holds the *hedj* sceptre, and his brow was originally adorned by a golden uraeus, the symbol of royal power. Remains of polychromy show that Raneferef had a narrow moustache. The delicately moulded broad necklace was originally decorated with golden leaves. Engraved in the base is the black painted hieroglyphic inscription, "King of Upper and Lower Egypt, Raneferef, may he live forever!" The king's head is protected from the back by the spread wings of the falcon god Horus, "the highest", who holds in his talons *shen* rings, symbols of universal power. The statue expresses the absolute divine and secular power of the Egyptian king, who was regarded as the earthly embodiment of the god Horus. Here the artist has perfectly mastered the anatomy of the human body, and even, unusually for the time, realistically conveyed the characteristic features of the king's physiognomy. What is more, he has breathed "spirit" into the king's sculptural likeness. (MV)

4 Faience inlays from Raneferef's mortuary temple

Egyptian faience; dimensions of selected fragment 6.6 × 4.2 cm. Old Kingdom, 5th Dynasty, reign of Raneferef. Central Abusir – mortuary temple of Raneferef's mortuary complex (AC 3), discovered in 1982. Find number 425/I/82.

Raneferef's premature death meant that his mortuary temple was hastily constructed mainly out of mudbricks and lacked the usual relief decoration. This object is one of more than a thousand fragments of faience inlays that were found in the mortuary temple, and were evidently substitutes for the usual decoration. Made of Egyptian faience, the inlays originally adorned wooden temple furniture, above all the shrines (*naoi*) for the king's statues. The surviving fragments suggest that the shrines were originally adorned with an abbreviated and condensed version of the decorative scheme. Its themes relate mainly to the king himself, and the fragment shown here bears two of Raneferef's five names: the throne name Raneferef inscribed in cartouche and Neferkhau, his Horus name (the legs of a falcon, i.e. the god Horus, are easily discernible on the fragment). Other titles and epithets of the king can be found on the other photograph, where the title *neb iri ikhet*, "Lord of the Ritual Acts" is particularly noteworthy. Apart from the king himself, the inlays often show important Egyptian gods such as Horus or Seth in the roles of protectors of the royal office, Horus of Behdet in the form of a falcon with outstretched wings as Raneferef's protector and the patron goddesses of Upper and Lower Egypt, Nekhbet and Wadjet. A gold strip adhering to one of the fragments shows that the white material filling the gaps between signs and figures was originally covered with gold. (RL)

Part of a set of fragments of faience inlays discovered during excavation of the king's mortuary temple

5 Builders' inscription with a date from the pyramid of Raneferef

Red and black paint on limestone. Old Kingdom, 5th Dynasty, reign of Raneferef. Central Abusir – Pyramid complex of Raneferef (AC 3), western edge of the trench for the descending passage, discovered 1997. Find number Gr.16/I/1997.

The remains of builders' inscriptions in red and black, which are superimposed, are preserved on a limestone block in the core of the pyramid of Raneferef. They were located on the lower western edge of the ditch for the descending passage into the king's posthumous dwelling. The red inscription, today almost illegible, is probably the oldest. It includes a row of horizontally placed V signs along the bottom of the block. This was evidently an instruction for the block to be smoothed off at the level of the signs. There are two inscriptions in black on the block, one faded and the other more prominent. In the more prominent inscription we find the repeated remnants of a date relating to the "first occasion (of livestock census, i.e. collection of taxes)". Under the Old Kingdom tax was usually collected once every two years, and so the date comes from the second year of Raneferef's reign. The first year of a reign, directly following the accession of a king to the throne, was not a full year and was indicated by the term, "uniting of the two lands", i.e. the symbolic reunification of Upper and Lower Egypt in the person of the new ruler. The date shows that construction of Raneferef's pyramid started immediately after his ascent to the throne. (MV)

Northern section of the building trench of the unfinished pyramid with descending corridor

6 Decree of King Djedkare on appointment to an office

Papyrus; w. 29.5 cm, h. 14.8 cm. Old Kingdom, 5th Dynasty, reign of Djedkare. Central Abusir – mortuary temple of Raneferef's pyramid complex (AC 3), discovered in 1982. Collections of the Grand Egyptian Museum, Giza, inv. no. GEM 3223 (JE 97348).

The remains of a papyrus archive discovered in Raneferef's pyramid complex are undoubtedly among the most significant finds of Czech Egyptology. These are unique texts telling us much about the everyday operations of mortuary complexes and giving us glimpses behind the veil that for millennia has hidden the administrative and economic aspects of the royal mortuary cults of the Old Kingdom. They are eloquent testimony to the painstaking bureaucratic routine of the ancient Egyptian scribes. This fragment of a papyrus scroll is one of the better preserved. It carries part of the text of a royal decree by which King Djedkare appointed two dignitaries receivers of part of the offerings from Raneferef's pyramid complex. Similar texts show the close links of the mortuary cults to the economic management of the state. (HV)

Northern storerooms of the king's mortuary temple – place of the find of fragments of the papyrus archive

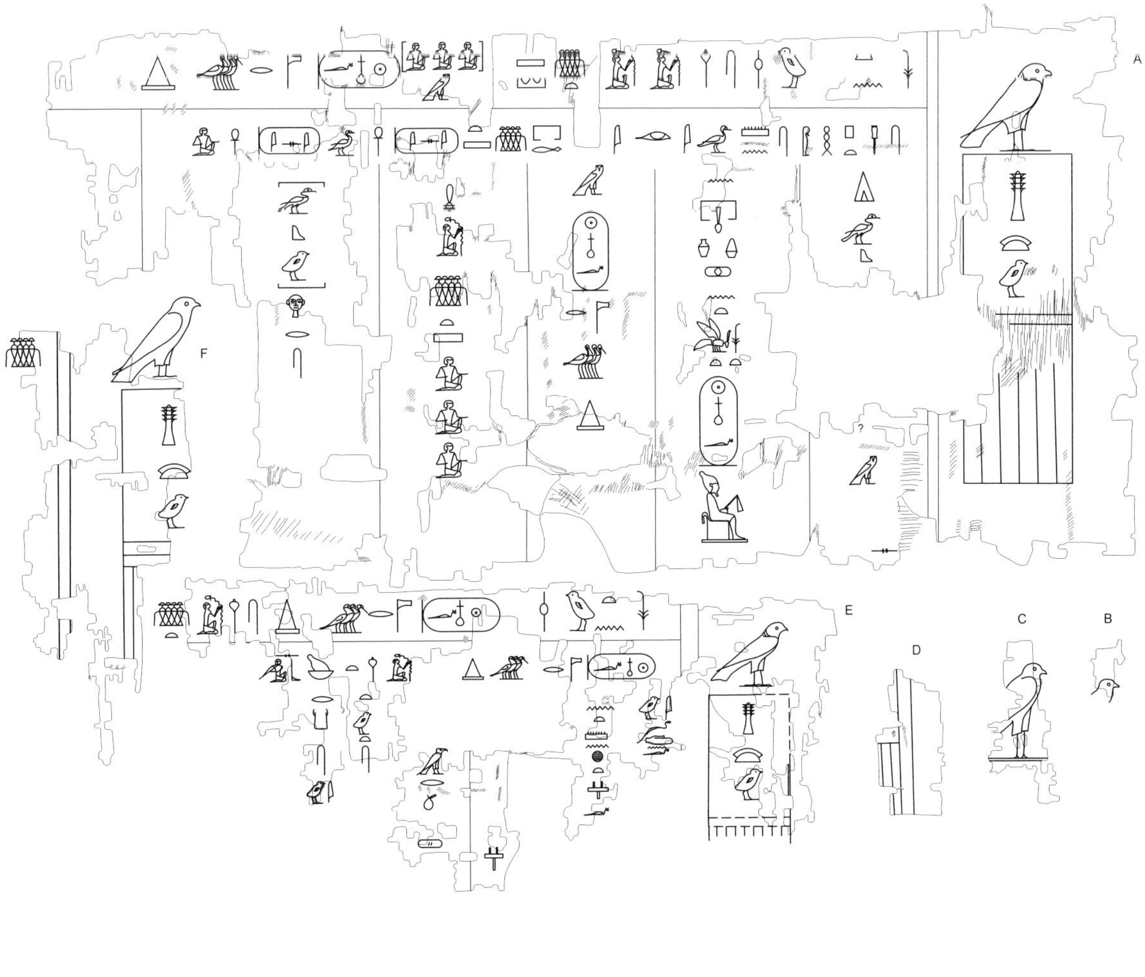
A
F
E
D
C
B

7 Inventory of Raneferef's cult equipment

Papyrus; w. 4.3 cm, h. 14.3 cm. Old Kingdom, 5th Dynasty. Central Abusir – mortuary temple of Raneferef's temple complex (AC 3), discovered 1982. In the collections of the Grand Egyptian Museum, Giza, inv. no. GEM 3223 (JE 97348).

Records relating to the temple equipment form an interesting part of the surviving papyrus archive. Here we find inventories of cult objects, many of them made of valuable materials – gold, silver or Asian copper, rare types of wood and various kinds of stone quarried faraway in the desert. The text also contains detailed notes on the wear-and-tear and damage to individual objects that inevitably resulted over many decades of use. The inventory is eloquent proof that the priests responsible undertook regular thorough inspections of the different storerooms of the mortuary temple. The text reproduced here contains a catalogue of objects kept in the "storeroom of cloth", listing various types of wooden chests, vessels, sticks, wooden symbols of a heron and a hippopotamus, garments and other things. For each kind of equipment a figure is given for the number of such objects found in the storeroom at the time of the record. According to this list the storeroom of cloth contained a total of 206 objects of various kinds. (HV)

Raneferef's unfinished pyramid and western part of his mortuary temple

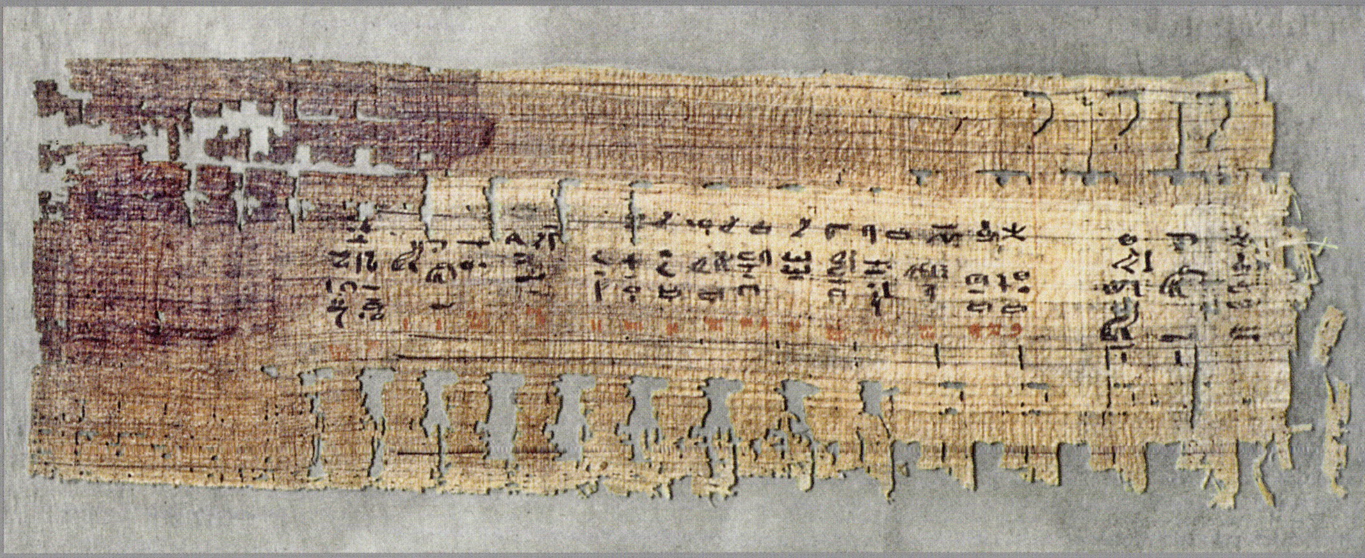

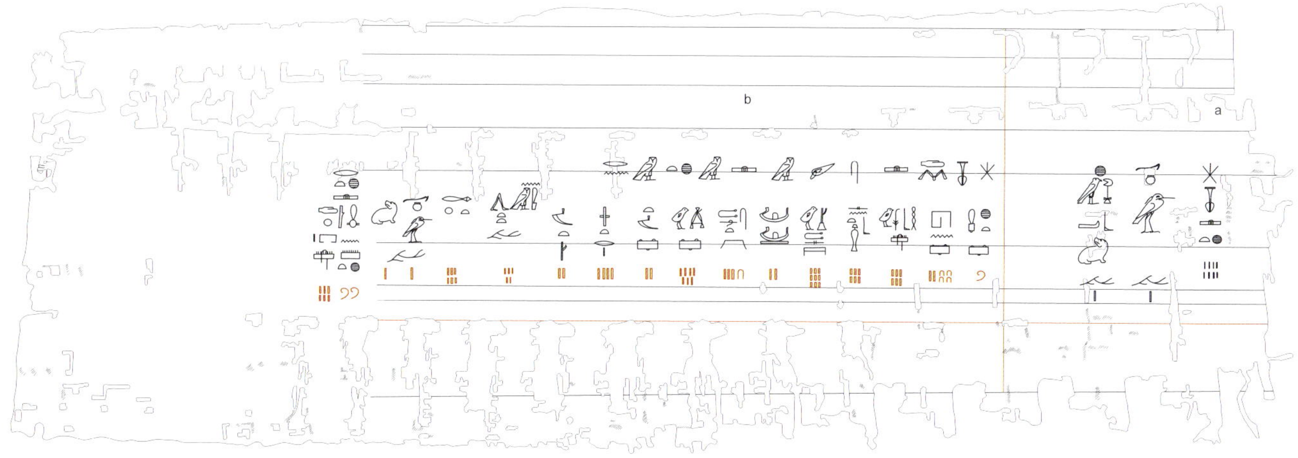

A
b
a

8 Accounting record of rations for employees of Raneferef's pyramid complex

Papyrus; w. 49.8 cm, h. 14.4 cm. Old Kingdom. 5th Dynasty. Central Abusir – mortuary temple of Raneferef's temple complex (AC 3), discovered 1982. In the collections of the Grand Egyptian Museum, Giza, inv. no. GEM 3223 (JE 97348).

Roughly half the papyrus archive consists of book-keeping records that testify to careful control of resources. Many are records of supplies received by Raneferef's mortuary temple, mainly from the royal residence, but also for example from the temple of Ptah and other important economic institutions of the state at the time. This particular record, on the other hand, lists allocations distributed to employees of the temple as remuneration for their services. The vertical columns represent individual employees, who were receiving 1 to 2 loaves of bread and 1 to 2 jars of beer every day, as shown by the figures filled in on the horizontal rows. This table covers the first half of an unknown month. (HV)

Fragment of the relief decoration of the mastaba of the vizier Ptahshepses with picture of a beer jar

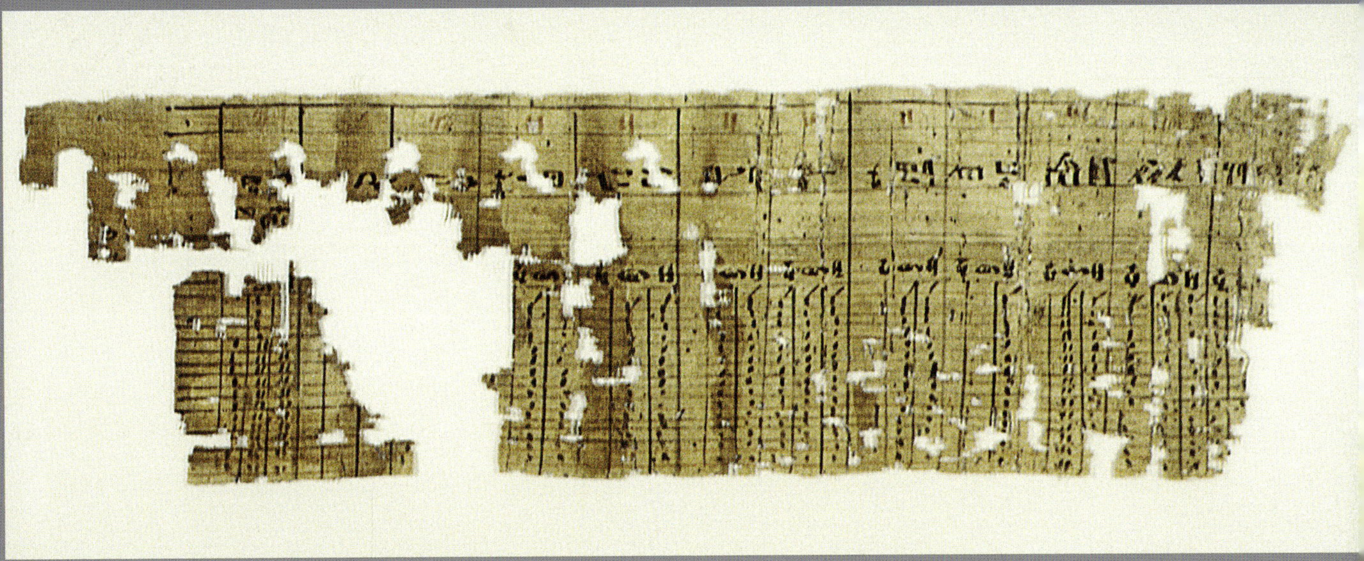

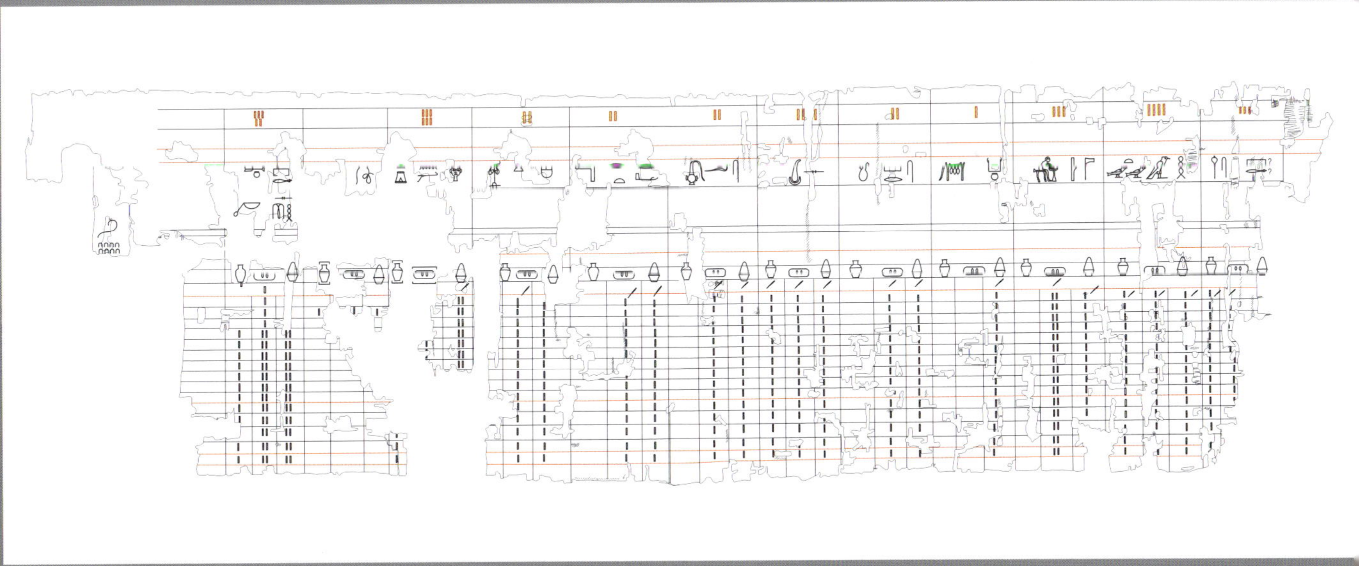

9 Seal imprint bearing the name of King Shepseskare

Clay; 5.1 × 4.6 cm. Old Kingdom, 5th Dynasty, reign of Shepseskare. Central Abusir – mortuary temple of Raneferef's pyramid complex (AC 3), discovered 1985. Find no. 824b, k, II, x/I/94.

The remains of an inscription surviving on a fragment of a clay seal found in Raneferef's mortuary temple mentions the Horus name, Sekhemkhau, of King Shepseskare. This obscure ruler of the 5th Dynasty is known only from the Saqqara List of Kings, in a position immediately after Neferirkare, and on seals from Abusir, six of which have been found in different parts of the oldest section of Raneferef's mortuary temple. We do not know whether Shepseskare left any monument behind him. There is some speculation that the unfinished building of a pyramid abandoned immediately after the start of earthworks north of Sahure's pyramid may have belonged to him. (MV)

It is possible that Shepseskare ordered the building of a pyramid in the area north-west of Sahure's pyramid, but construction was soon abandoned

10 Stone vessels with royal names from Raneferef's mortuary temple

Diorite; vessel 432: h. 9 cm, w. 9 cm, thickness 0.8 cm; vessel 342: h. 5 cm, diameter of edge 17 cm, diameter of bottom 5 cm. Old Kingdom, 5th Dynasty, reign of Raneferef and Menkauhor. Central Abusir – rooms CE and CI, in the central part of Raneferef's mortuary temple, discovered 1982. Find nos 432/I/82 and 342/I/82.

Highly significant finds from Raneferef's mortuary temple include the set of stone vessels (some in fragments), adorned with the names of two rulers of the Old Kingdom – Snofru and Menkauhor. As regards Snofru, the founder of the 4th Dynasty who became a popular historical figure even before the end of the Old Kingdom, such inscriptions were quite frequent practice. Even so, the vessels from the temple of Raneferef represent the largest collection of this kind. We encounter Snofru's name in this set in two main forms: either in the form of his Horus name, Nebmaat, or his throne name – "King of Upper and Lower Egypt" – Snofru. The fact that the finds of these vessels were made close to the innermost stone shrine of the temple, and that the royal names were engraved into the vessels, shows that they played an important part in Raneferef's mortuary cult. In this way, Snofru participated in the cult as a good, acknowledged king and thus confirmed the divine essence of Raneferef as ruler of Egypt. (JK)

Stone vessels at the moment of discovery

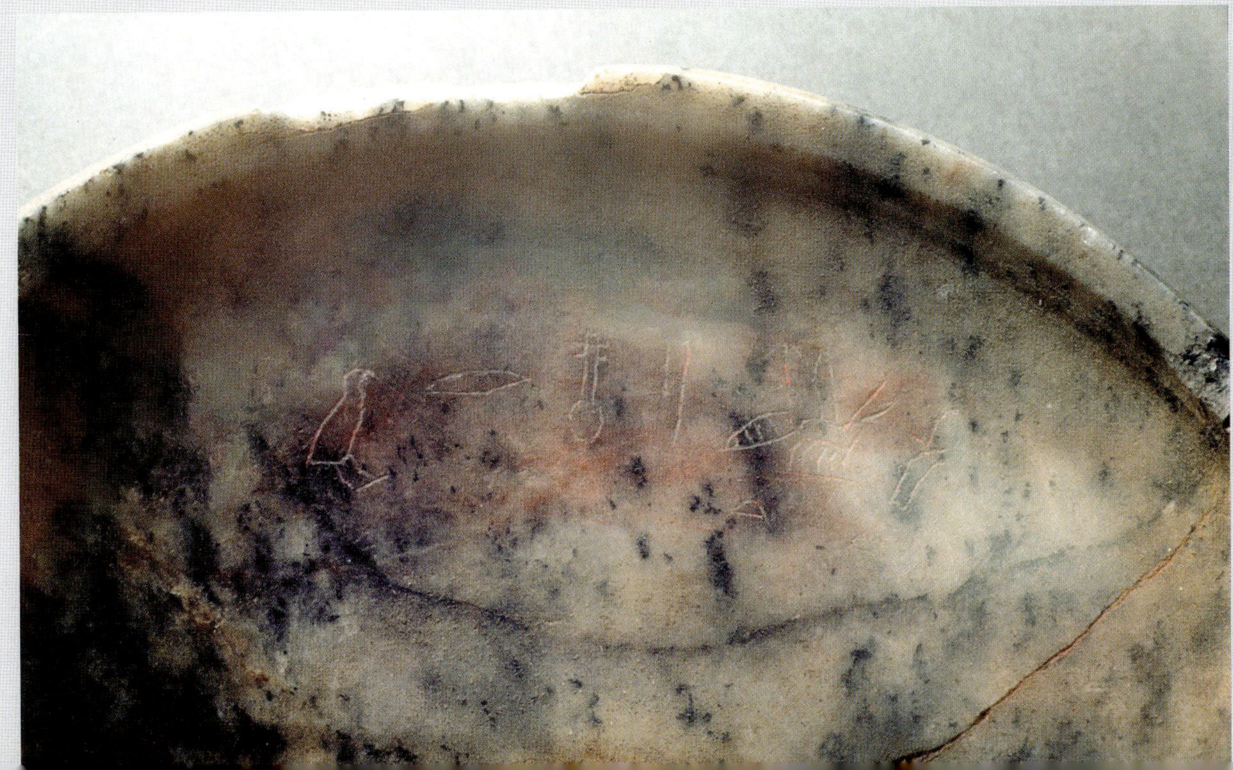

11 Kneeling Asian captive

Wood; h. 15.5 cm. Old Kingdom, 5th Dynasty, reign of Raneferef. Central Abusir – mortuary temple of Raneferef's pyramid complex (AC 3), discovered 1984. Find nos 773b–c/84. In the permanent exhibition of the Egyptian Museum in Cairo (inv. no. JE 98182).

The wooden figurine depicts a kneeling captive with his elbows bound together behind his back. The sharply carved features of the face indicate his Asian origin as does his pointed chin and long shoulder-length curling hair held in place by a broad headband knotted at the back. The peg on the crown of his head shows that the figurine was originally part of a larger object, evidently the royal throne or a piece of furniture. Kneeling captives with the features of Asians, Nubians and Libyans represented enemies of Egypt, the external evil that according to the Egyptian world-view the ruler had to overcome in order to ensure the order of the world. The symbolic conquest of this evil was expressed by the depiction of captive enemies on the inner soles of the ruler's sandals, the bases of the throne or footstools, or the floor of the throne hall. (MV)

12 Ostrakon with the name of Sahure's palace, *Wetjes-neferu-Sahure*

Pottery; fragment a1: 20 × 10.8 cm, fragment a2: 17.3 × 12 cm. Old Kingdom, 5th Dynasty. Central Abusir – mortuary temple of Raneferef's pyramid complex (AC 3), discovered 1982. Find nos 531/I/82-a1, a2.

Hieratic inscriptions, some of them concerning supplies of fat (beef tallow) from the slaughterhouse of Sahure's palace, *Wetjes-neferu-Sahure*, "Sublime is the Beauty of Sahure", are preserved on fragments of vessels found in the mortuary temple of Raneferef. The tallow was probably used for lamps, and the temple staff may have also consumed it or used it in the preparation of food. The palace was one of several built by Sahure, and may even have been his favourite. Eloquent evidence is to be found in some scenes on blocks from the causeway to Sahure's pyramid complex in Abusir, which has been under excavation since the mid-1990s. They depict an enthroned Sahure in the garden of this palace, surrounded by members of the royal family and high-ranking officials, accepting gifts brought from the distant land of Punt by the ships of an Egyptian expedition. There is much to suggest that the palace, still not archaeologically identified, was located close to the pyramids of Abusir. (MV)

Sahure enthroned at a banquet in the royal palace; relief from the decoration of the causeway of his pyramid complex

13 Animal figurines from the mortuary temple of Raneferef

Clay; 1st figurine: l. of body 6 cm, h. 3.8 cm, w. 3.4 cm; 2nd figurine: l. of body 6.9 cm, h. 3.3 cm, w. 2.3 cm, head with horns: h. 3.7 cm, w. 2.80 cm. Old Kingdom, 6th Dynasty. Central Abusir – room R of the priests' dwelling complex, hypostyle hall in the mortuary temple of Raneferef's pyramid complex (AC 3), discovered 1982. Find nos 217/I/82 and 275a/I/82. In the National Museum – Náprstek Museum of Asian, African and American Cultures, inv. no. P 7009 and P 7111.

Two stylised animal figurines, depicting cattle, were found in the mortuary temple of Raneferef's pyramid complex. Both animals have thick bodies, four legs and a tail, and an animal head with horns was found separately. These figurines were found in one of the rooms of a complex of dwellings of the temple priests, which grew up secondarily in the area of the hypostyle hall, and so we might speculate that they were toys, although they might have been ritual or votive objects. Similar animal figurines have been found at various sites throughout Egypt and they are, in general, hard to interpret. (DW)

Abusir boys playing

14 Pillar from the mortuary temple of Khentkaus II in Abusir

Limestone; h. 185 cm.
Old Kingdom, 5th Dynasty.
Central Abusir – mortuary temple of the pyramid complex of Khentkaus II (AC 14), discovered 1976.

The pillared court of the mortuary temple of the pyramid complex of the royal mother Khentkaus II in Abusir was devastated by stone robbers especially in the Ramesside period. Only a single pillar has survived in its place – in the north-western corner of the court. It is made of limestone and was painted in red to give the impression that it was carved from the more precious red granite. On its east side there are remains of a hieroglyphic inscription with parts of her titles, and at the end of the inscription there is a depiction of Khentkaus sitting on a throne. In her right hand she holds the *wadj* sceptre in the form of a papyrus stem with a crown of leaves, in her left hand the *ankh*, symbol of life, and on her brow there is a uraeus. The attacking cobra, the uraeus, was a supreme symbol of the monarch at the time, and so shows Khentkaus's unusually high social status, which is also evidenced by other titles preserved on other antiquities, above all the title "mother of two kings of Upper and Lower Egypt". It seems likely that in a dynastically difficult situation she guaranteed the legitimacy of the succession of two of her sons (possibly even twins), Raneferef and Nyuserre, whose father was King Neferirkare. The ascent to the throne of two brothers one after the other presented a problem because it did not correspond to the mythical Osirian tradition and state dogma asserting that the succession should always be from father to son. (MV)

The mortuary temple of the queen's pyramid complex during archaeological excavation; the pyramid of Khentkaus's husband Neferirkare can be seen in the background

15 Description of statues of Queen Khentkaus II

Papyrus; a: w. 5.5 cm, h. 5.6 cm; b: w. 5.1 cm, h. 5.3 cm. Old Kingdom, 5th Dynasty. Central Abusir – mortuary temple of Khentkaus II. Discovered in 1978. In the collections of the Grand Egyptian Museum, Giza, inv. no. GEM 37122 (JE 94319).

In the pyramid complex of Queen Khentkaus II, the Czechoslovak expedition found a unique record of cult equipment that was itself destroyed or stolen long ago. This text, which was part of the temple archive, is an account of the statues of the queen on which the ancient rituals of regeneration were once performed. For each statue the record mentions the material from which the eyes and eyebrows, and sometimes the sceptre and other attributes, were made. Some statues were kept in shrines made of imported wood and decorated with depictions. The description is accompanied by sketches of individual statues. On one of these papyrus fragments it states that the sketched statue had "eyebrows and eyes of onyx", while another of the statues listed was kept in a shrine, and was wrapped in linen and adorned with a necklace. (HV)

The pyramid complex of Queen Khentkaus II, overall view from the apex of the pyramid of Neferirkare

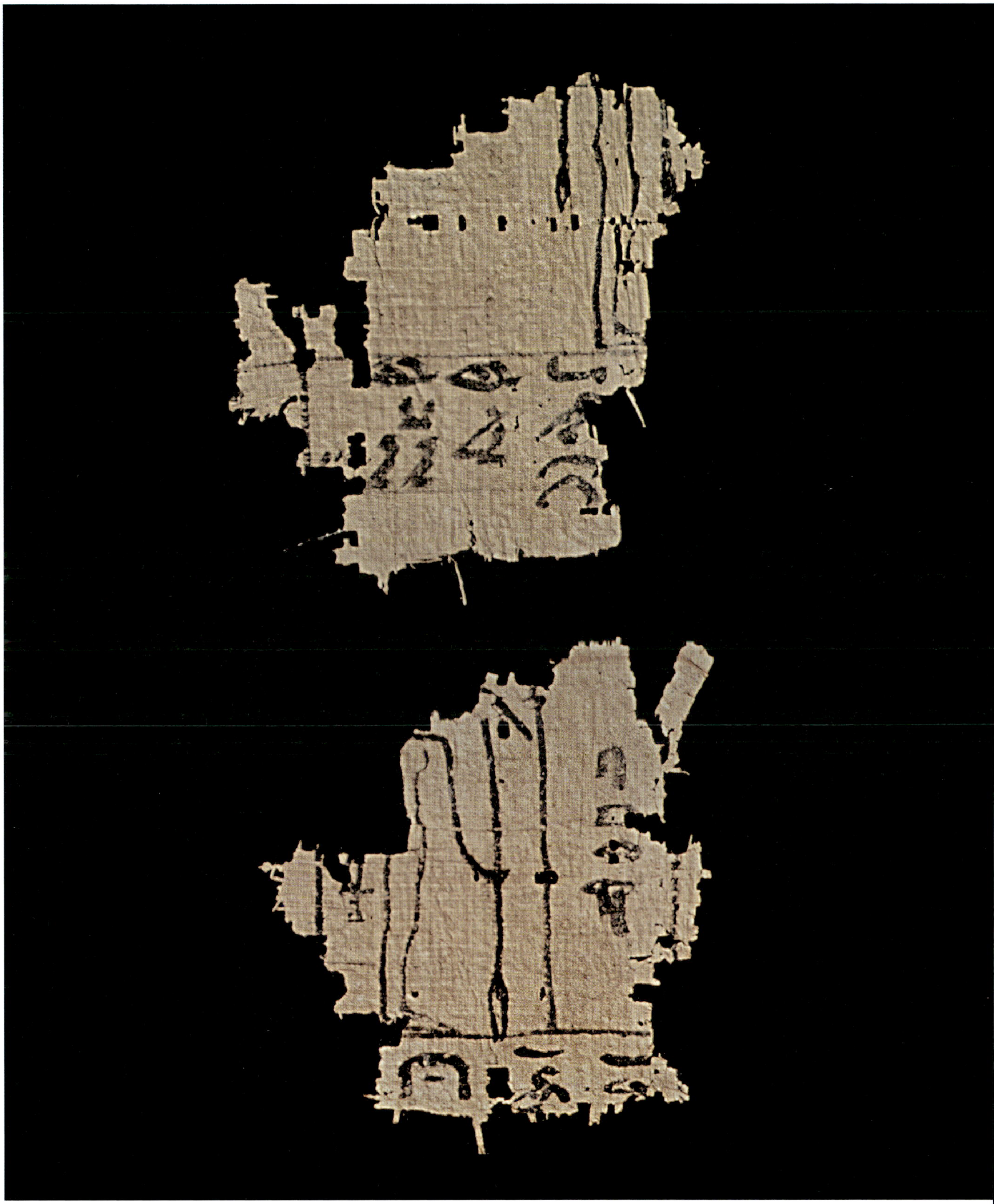

16 Abusir pyramidia

1. Red granite; original h. ca. 145 cm. Old Kingdom, 5th Dynasty. Mastaba of Ptahshepses (AC 8), discovered 1974. 2. Basalt; sides of the base 46 cm, angle of inclination 60°, original h. ca. 40 cm. Old Kingdom, 5th Dynasty. Central Abusir – mortuary temple of Raneferef's pyramid complex (AC 3), discovered 1984.

The fragment of the pyramidion of a red granite obelisk was found by the south-western corner of the mastaba of Ptahshepses. Traces of verdigris on the surface show that the tip of the obelisk was faced with copper plate (probably gilded). Judging by the size of the fragment of the pyramidion, the obelisk was originally at least ten metres in height. The place where it was found suggests that it probably stood by the north-eastern corner of the mortuary temple of Nyuserre's tomb complex. Why it was placed there, however, and whether it might have come from another older, perhaps unfinished building, remains an open question. A basalt pyramidion was found in the ruins of Raneferef's mortuary temple. The surfaces on the sides and openings for fastening show that this pyramidion was also originally faced in what were probably gilded copper plates. In view of its dimensions and the angle of the sides it is probable that it comes from the pyramid (or perhaps cult pyramid?) of an unknown queen; the pyramid is known simply as Lepsius no. 24. (MV)

A journalist from Czechoslovak Radio reporting on the find of a pyramidion at the mastaba of Ptahshepses

17 Builders' inscription from the pyramid Lepsius no. 24

Red ink on limestone; h. 10 cm, l. 81.4 cm. Old Kingdom, 5th Dynasty. Central Abusir – pyramid Lepsius no. 24 (AC 22), west wall of the construction trench. Discovered 1994. Find no. Gr. J/6/94-Z.

Widespread tomb robbing and the activities of stone robbers devastated the tombs of members of the royal family in Central Abusir. On the other hand, the ruined state of these monuments has facilitated study of the building techniques used in their construction. One aspect of those techniques was the recording of technical data and instructions directly on the masonry of the tombs in the form of builders' inscriptions. This inscription was preserved on the western wall of the building trench for the burial chamber in the pyramid Lepsius no. 24, which belongs to an anonymous queen. The inscription, relating to the horizontal construction line drawn below, indicates that the line was to be found "3 cubits above the foundations", i.e. 3 Egyptian cubits (1.56 m) above the level of the floor of the burial chamber which had been built into the construction trench. The triangle angled downwards shows the point to which this information related. The western wall of the construction trench (like its other walls) was covered by a network of such horizontal building lines, with vertical lines indicating the construction axes. Among the builders' marks we also find personal names, such as vizier Ptahshepses, who oversaw the construction of the queen's pyramid, or else the names of quarries from which the building blocks had been supplied, or the anticipated name of the pyramid complex, which was "Both pyramids are vigilant". The name of the building referred to the fact that the whole complex included not just the burial pyramid but a satellite pyramid as well. It is one of the first indications, and possibly the very earliest evidence, of this practice in the case of pyramid complexes of queens. (JK)

The Pyramid Lepsius no. 24

18 Model of a goose or duck from the tomb of Nakhtsare

Travertine; l. 26 cm, w. 15 cm, h. 14.5 cm. Old Kingdom, 2nd half of the 5th Dynasty. Central Abusir – Nakhtsare's cemetery, found at the bottom of the vertical shaft of the tomb of Nakhtsare (AC 25) in 1994. Find no. 16/Q/94.

The soul of the deceased was supposed to live a blissful life in the next world. The performance of magical sacrificial rituals, but also offerings that were part of the funerary equipment of the deceased placed directly in the burial chamber, were needed to ensure this future. Apart from real food and drink, the Egyptians started bringing models of offerings to the deceased in their tombs as a substitute for the real thing quite early in their history. This example from the tomb of Prince Nakhtsare, probably the son of the ruler Raneferef, is a model of a plucked goose or duck (unfortunately we cannot tell which species), made of travertine – Egyptian alabaster. After its magical metamorphosis into real poultry it was supposed to provide the deceased with sustenance during his eternal posthumous life. Together with the other objects from this group of finds (another three models of geese or ducks and models of joints of meat and bread loaves), the model is one of the best examples of this magical practice from the Abusir cemetery. (JK)

Overall view of the mastaba of Nakhtsare

19 Miniature vessels from the tomb of the courtier Kakaibaef

Pottery; the minimum dimensions of the miniature vessels: diameter 2 cm, h. 1 cm; larger red-slipped miniature vessels: h. cca 8 cm, max. diameter cca 3.5 cm. Old Kingdom, 2nd half of the 5th Dynasty. Central Abusir – Nakhtsare's cemetery, refuse layer north-east of the entrance to the tomb of Kakaibaef (AC 29), discovered in 2013.

Miniature vessels are among the most characteristic classes of Old Kingdom pottery. Because the ancient Egyptians believed that they substituted for large vessels, they come in many different types. The most frequently found are bowls and cups, but other shapes were also included, such as vases, jars, stands, etc. They were used most extensively in the mortuary cult, where they were placed in front of the deceased's false door and employed during offering rituals. This is why we often uncover up to hundreds of miniatures in the area of chapels or in their immediate vicinity. They were traditionally wheel-made, which allowed fast mass production of pieces from a single block of clay. In the tomb of the official Kakaibaef several thousand miniature vessels were found in the refuse layer near the entrance to the tomb. They are exceptional not only in their quantity, but also in the quality of clay and surface treatment. They include not only the traditional small miniatures, but also larger miniatures covered in high quality red slip. We can assume that these small-sized vessels were used in the offering chapel of the tomb during the mortuary cult of the deceased and were later disposed of near the entrance to the chapel, where they were found after nearly 4,500 years by the Charles University expedition. (KA)

A cluster of the miniature vessels at the moment of discovery

Most of the miniature vessels were found in the north part of the open court in front of the mastaba of Kakaibaef

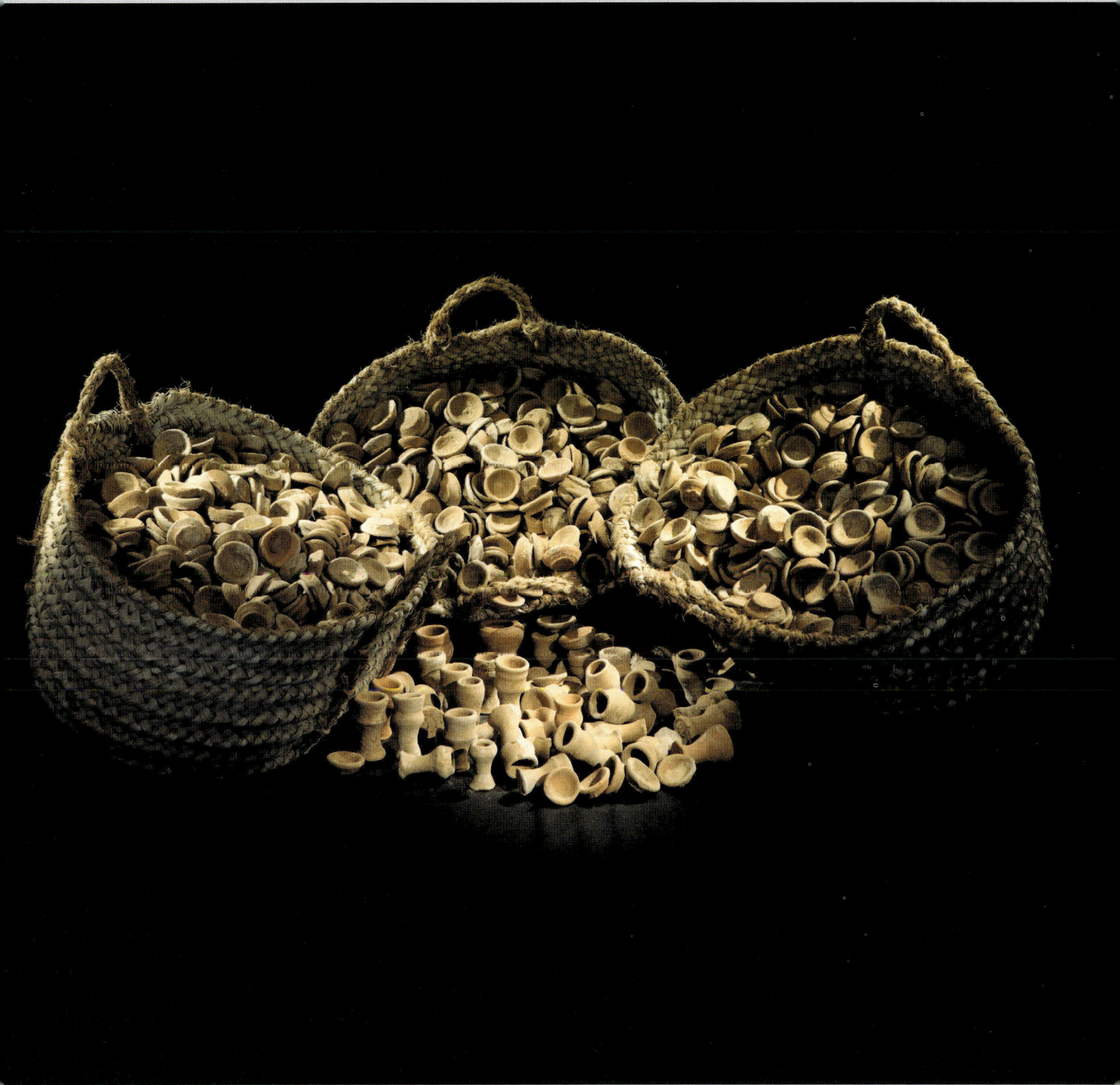

20 Builder's inscription with name of Queen Khentkaus III

Red ink on limestone base: h. 16.30 cm, l. 49.50 cm. Old Kingdom, 5th Dynasty. Central Abusir – Nakhtsare's cemetery, south wall of the burial chamber of tomb AC 30. Discovered 2014. Find no. Gr. 27/AC30/2014.

Over the course of several thousand years the buildings in the royal cemetery in Abusir were very extensively damaged, especially the tombs lying on its southern edge. Their decoration, including false doors with the names and titles of the owners of tombs has in most cases not survived. This applies to mastaba AC 30, but quite a large amount of builders' inscriptions are preserved on the walls and floors of the buildings. Among them is this inscription, which states the title and name of "mother of the king, Khentkaus III", who was most probably buried in this mastaba. Up to 2014 nothing was known about this person, and so excavation of the inscriptions meant an important advance in our knowledge of the royal family of the 2nd half of the 5th Dynasty. The owner of the tombs also bore the title, "royal wife". It is probable that her husband was King Raneferef, who was buried in the nearby unfinished pyramid, but the name of her son, who later sat on the throne of Egypt, remains a mystery. (JK)

Overall view of the mastaba of Queen Khentkaus III

21 Ritual *pesheskaf* knife from tomb AC 31

Flint; l. 16.8 cm, w. 2.7 cm, h. 1.1 cm. Old Kingdom, 5th Dynasty. Central Abusir – Nakhtsare's cemetery, communication passage between the burial chamber and vertical shaft in tomb AC 31, discovered 2016. Find no. 271/AC31/2016.

Despite extensive damage to the building by tomb robbers and stone robbers, we have managed to find a considerable amount of the original funerary equipment during excavation of tomb AC 31, the southernmost mastaba in the cemetery of Nakhtsare. The quality of these finds showed that the female owner of the tomb, whose skeletal remains were also discovered, was one of the court elite, but unfortunately she has not yet been identified. One of the most important finds in this tomb, and indeed in this whole section of the royal cemetery, is this ritual flint knife, which in the standard of its craftsmanship is comparable to knives found during excavation of the pyramids of Neferirkare and Raneferef. The *peseshkaf* knife was used by a priest during the ritual of the opening of the mouth to renew the senses of the deceased. The find of the ritual knife was complemented by the nearby find of a travertine model of a vessel of the *henut* type, which was also used during this ceremony. (JK)

The *pesheskaf* knife at the moment of discovery

Overall view of tomb AC 31

22 Wooden stand from tomb AC 31

Wood; h. 16.3 cm, upper surface: 9.5 × 9.9 cm. Old Kingdom, 5th Dynasty. Central Abusir – Nakhtsare's cemetery, tomb AC 31, connecting passage between the burial chamber and vertical shaft, discovered 2016. Find nos 182a–e/AC31/2016, 255/AC31/2016.

You might think that wooden objects in the funerary equipment of the deceased would be well preserved in the dry desert environment of the Abusir necropolis. Unfortunately the reverse is true, but the results of the excavation of the tombs in Nakhtsare's cemetery are the exception. In some of these tombs there have been finds of wooden objects (not including the secondary wooden coffins): mainly the handles of mirrors, parts of chests and various stands. One is a stand for a stone model vessel (unfortunately of unknown type), as we can see from the shallow circular depression 4.4 cm in diameter on the upper surface. Because tomb robbers tried to remove this stand from its original position in the burial chamber, it was found dismantled in the connecting passage leading to the vertical shaft. It has been reassembled by conservation experts. The set of wooden objects found in Nakhtsare's cemetery is exceptional in the context of archaeology of the period of the 5th Dynasty. (JK)

The separate parts of the stand at the moment of discovery

23 Sacrificed calf from tomb AC 31

Mummified parts of the body of a calf (head, limbs). Old Kingdom, 5th Dynasty, Central Abusir – Nakhtsare's cemetery, tomb AC 31, vertical shaft, discovered 2016. Find no. 198a/AC31/2016.

The excavation of mastaba AC 31 has brought finds that throw light not just on the material culture of the court elite, but also on interesting aspects of funerary customs. Evidence of the ritual associated with the interment of the body of the owner of the tomb to eternal rest was discovered in the vertical shaft of the tomb, on a layer of building waste lying on the bottom. Parts of a sacrificed calf (its head and four limbs) were found together with pottery vessels – *bedja* bread moulds, stands and other types, and fragments of wood or charcoal. It is interesting and rather unusual that part of the body of the animal had been mummified as an important part of the burial ritual supposed to secure for the deceased an eternal and blissful life in the hereafter. References to this custom are to be found in the Pyramid Texts and in the later guides to the Hereafter. Evidence of this ritual has also been found in two other tombs in Nakhtsare's cemetery – in the mastaba of Queen Khentkaus III and of Prince Nakhtsare – and also in the mortuary temple of Raneferef and in tombs in Abusir South. (JK)

Substructure of tomb AC 31. The vertical shaft connected by a short passage with the burial chamber is visible in the lower part of the photograph

24 Set of copper models of tools and vessels from tomb AC 31

Copper or arsenical copper; chisels: max. l. 8 cm, max. w. 6 cm; adzes: max. l. 6.5 cm, max. l. 1.5 cm; axes: max. l. 4.4 cm, max. w. 3.5 cm; saws: max. l. 11.4 cm, max. w. 1.3 cm; circular bowls: max. diameter 5.3 cm, max. h. 1.5 cm; rectangular bowls: max. l. 6.1 cm, max. width 1 cm. Old Kingdom, 5th Dynasty. Central Abusir – Nakhtsare's cemetery, tomb AC 31, burial chamber and communication passage with vertical shaft, discovered 2016. Find nos: chisels – 151/AC31/2016, 209/AC31/2016, 233/AC31/2016a–c, 270/AC31/2016, 274/AC31/2016, 275/AC31/2016; adzes – 78/AC31/2016, 130/AC31/2016, 169/AC31/2016, 233d/AC31/2016, 244/AC31/2016, 248/AC31/2016, 315/AC31/2016, 317/AC31/2016; axes – 268/AC31/2016, 276/AC31/2016; saws – 250/AC31/2016; circular bowls – 156/AC31/2016, 159/AC31/2016, 165/AC31/2016, rectangular bowls – 113/AC31/2016, 245/AC31/2016, 277/AC31/2016, 296/AC31/2016.

Copper model tools and vessels were a usual part of the funerary equipment of the Old-Kingdom social elite. The tools include the blades of chisels, adzes, axes and saws: the essential tool kit for ancient Egyptian carpenters and stonemasons. Instead of the blades of full-size and functional tools only their miniaturised models were placed in funerary equipment. Referring mainly to men's work, the model tools might seem at odds with the results of the anthropological analysis of the skeletal remains found in the burial chamber, which show that the owner of the tomb was a woman (unfortunately we do not know her name). In fact while the models might not refer to something that the owner would have used in her life and would need to use in the afterlife as well, they nonetheless represent symbols of her economic power as a member of the court elite: she was able to order and fund craftwork, for example either on the tomb itself or on its particular parts (such as a false door or an offering basin). The set of models from tomb AC 31 is also important for the fact that it represents a complete set of the different types of models in mid-5th Dynasty. The copper assemblage also included circular and rectangular bowls, the former representing the ritual of the funerary repast, and the latter being miniaturised offering basins. (MO)

Some of the copper models were discovered by the entrance to the burial chamber of mastaba AC 31

25 Storage jars from the funerary equipment of the lady buried in tomb AC 31

Pottery; h. 42.5–44.5 cm, max. diameter: 25.5 –29 cm. Old Kingdom, 5th Dynasty. Central Abusir – Nakhtsare's cemetery, tomb AC 31, burial chamber and vertical shaft, discovered in 2016. Find nos. 114–116/AC31/2016.

Vessels of various types were a usual part of the funeral equipment of the deceased. Their precise number, quality and the representation of different types in a set varied, depending on the social status of the owner of the tomb and his or her economic power. In the case of the lady buried in tomb AC 31 it is evident that this was a continuation of a tradition identified in the tombs of other members of the royal family at Central Abusir. While ordinary officials were often given only beer jars, higher officials were equipped with finer vessels made of Marl clay, which was denser, harder, and due to higher water-proofing more efficient in the storage of liquids. Most of them were never filled with actual beer or wine, but with Nile mud serving as an imitation of real liquids for practical reasons. The storage jars found in the primary floor layer in the burial chamber of tomb AC 31, however, are very capacious ovoid vessels with distinct tall necks and pointed bases, and originally probably contained real offerings. In some of them, we found a powdery organic substance together with various seeds, beetles, tiny animal bones and pieces of charcoal, later covered by mud. Only future planned analyses will show whether these are the actual remains of fluids, burnt offerings, or the vessels were used to store other organic substances; in either case, this find is unique. (KA)

The location of the pottery vessels, parts of the funerary equipment and skeletal remains of the owner of tomb AC 31 at the time of discovery

26 Sculptural portrait of the vizier Ptahshepses

Quartzite; h. 23 cm, w. 20 cm, depth 12 cm. Old Kingdom, 5th Dynasty. Mastaba of Ptahshepses (AC 8), discovered in 1961 in the area of the pillared court. Find no. C 948c. In the permanent exhibition of the Egyptian Museum in Cairo (inv. no. JE 98796).

In the context of the Egyptian archaeology of the Old Kingdom the mastaba of the vizier Ptahshepses is exceptional both for its size and its relief and sculptural decoration, which combines with the architecture of the tomb to form an integrated aesthetic whole. Only fragments of the sculptural decoration have survived, but it has been possible to reconstruct twelve statues that were originally placed in the tomb. One of them was an engaged statue made of quartzite depicting the owner of the tomb. Its head is the best preserved part. This slightly damaged fragment realistically portrays an older, tired man with bags under the eyes and wrinkles around full lips emphasised by their protruding line. The eyes are almond-shaped and elongated. The face had a beard, but most of it has not survived, and on the head there was a smooth wig, which is something we rarely encounter in statues from the Old Kingdom. The statue was either part of the false door set in one of the chapels of the extensive tomb, or of a naos which may have been placed in the pillared court. The use of quartzite, a very hard mineral, shows the high status of the owner of the tomb. (JK)

The pillared court of the mastaba of Ptahshepses during excavation

Fragment of quartzite statue of Ptahshepses in the place where it was found

27 Sarcophagi of Ptahshepses

Red granite and white limestone; the sarcophagus of Ptahshepses: l. 294.5 cm, w. 149.5 cm, h. 110 + 63 cm; the sarcophagus of Khamerernebty: 253.3 cm, w. 114 cm, h. 90,3 + 34 cm. Old Kingdom, 5th Dynasty. Mastaba of Ptahshepses (AC 8), burial chamber, discovered 1968.

Ptahshepses's exceptionally high social position is indicated not only by his extensive tomb with its very complex ground-plan and unusual architectural elements, but also by the pair of superbly executed sarcophagi intended for the bodies of the owner of the tomb and his wife, Princess Khamerernebty. For a commoner, the use of granite, the quarrying of which was a royal monopoly and under the strict control of the king's office, was a mark of great royal favour, and a sign of Ptahshepses' strong position at the court. The large dimensions of the sarcophagus intended for the tomb's owner and the high quality of the craftsmanship of both sarcophagi are also worth noting. The smaller one clearly belonged to Khamerernebty, and while its lid was broken by tomb robbers, the damage enables us to study its construction. The inside of the main lower part of the sarcophagus, like that of the larger one, was faced in very high-quality white limestone. The burial chamber in which both sarcophagi were found is also architecturally very interesting. The great width of the chamber (4.59 m; it thus exceeded the width of the burial chambers of the Egyptian kings of the time), made it impossible for the ceiling to be constructed by the usual flat method. The solution was to use an unconventional element, a saddle ceiling. But a saddle ceiling above burial chambers was usually reserved only for the pyramids of kings (and in one case for a queen and in another for a prince). (JK)

Khamerernebty's sarcophagus was moved by robbers into the niche intended for canopic jars; in the photograph Abusir workmen are dragging it back into the burial chamber

28 Statue of the royal advisor Kaires

Red granite, polychromy; base 41 × 23 cm, h. 73 cm. Old Kingdom, 5th Dynasty. Tomb of Kaires (AC 33), discovered in burial chamber no. I in 2018. Find no. 79/AC33/2018.

The statue was found in the burial chamber of the dignitary Kaires, probably in its original position (*in situ*) by the east wall of the sarcophagus, with its face turned to the east. This is one of the few examples showing that the burial chambers of high officials might contain a statue or statues of the owner. The statue had been broken into two parts but still bears traces of the original polychromy – yellow on the kilt and belt, black on the chair, green on the inscriptions, red on the eyes and blue on the pectoral. Some of the dignitary's titles are preserved on the base. Kaires was "a keeper of the secrets of the king, a keeper of the secrets of the House of Life and the Morning House, the overseer of all royal works, a priest and overseer of the *wab* priests in the pyramid complexes of kings Sahure and Neferirkare", and "a priest of the goddess Hathor". Kaires' titles, the site of his tomb in close proximity to the pyramid of Neferirkare, as well as its architecture including basalt pavement in the chapel and the entrance (the exclusive right of the ruler), show that he was an individual of quite extraordinary status in his time. (MB)

View of the site of the tomb of Kaires in the very heart of royal Abusir

Moment of the discovery of the statue in the burial chamber of Kaires

29 Statue of Princess Hedjetnebu

Wood; original h. ca. 81.5 cm. Old Kingdom, 5th Dynasty. Central Abusir – cemetery of Djedkare's family, discovered 1987. Find no. 8/K/87. In the permanent exhibition of the Egyptian Museum in Cairo (inv. no. JE 99438).

The statue of Princess Hedjetnebu was found in her tomb in the cemetery of Djedkare's family in Abusir. It depicts the princess standing with her arms hanging down by the sides of her body, which is painted yellow. This colour is characteristic for women and children and may reflect the fact that they spent less time outside in the sun. The princess wears a long white dress with wide shoulders, adorned in the upper part with red, green and white horizontal stripes and black zigzag lines. On the top side of the pedestal of the statue there is a carved hieroglyphic inscription that reads, "honoured before the Great God, his (the king's) own (daughter), Hedjetnebu." The statue originally stood in the serdab adjoining the offering chapel, from where the princess represented by the statue could watch the ceremonies taking place in the chapel through a slit. (MV)

The statue of Hedjetnebu at the time of its discovery

30 Princess Khekeretnebty watching the bringing of offerings

Pigments, stucco; w. 1.52 m, h. 1.26 m. Old Kingdom, 5th Dynasty. Central Abusir – Cemetery of Djedkare's family, vestibule of the tomb of Princess Khekeretnebty, discovered 1976.

Not only the building of tombs, the bringing of offerings, the performance of magical rituals and the mummification techniques maintaining the physical integrity of the body, but also the decoration of the cult areas of the tombs with reliefs and statues was necessary to ensure the eternal life of the deceased in the next world. One of the few pieces of evidence for this practice to have survived in the Abusir pyramid field is the painted decoration of the vestibule in the tomb of the royal daughter Khekeretnebty. The whole breadth of the only decorated, west wall of the room is filled with a scene showing the princess sitting on a chair and supervising the bringing of offerings and sacrificial animals necessary for her mortuary cult. The royal daughter is dressed in a robe that is close-fitting at the shoulders, and has a long wig and headband. In her right hand she holds a lotus flower, which she is smelling. Above the figure is a hieroglyphic inscription giving her titles and epithets, such as "king's daughter of his body", "his beloved" and her name Khekeretnebty. The bringing of offerings is depicted to her left in four registers. Here we see men bringing antelopes (one of them an oryx) and two bulls, striding bearers of baskets with offerings and also a man holding a papyrus scroll. It has no writing on it but is symbolic of lists of offerings. As the remaining red outline and mostly unpainted areas show, the scene was never finished. (JK)

Vestibule and offering chapel of the tomb of Khekeretnebty

31 Set of travertine models from the tomb of Khekeretnebty

Travertine; h. of jars 6.7–8.6 cm, diameter of bowls 4.3–6.2 cm. Old Kingdom, 5th Dynasty. Central Abusir – cemetery of Djedkare's family, burial chamber of tomb of Khekeretnebty. Discovered 1976. Find nos 83–124/B/76. Some pieces are in the collections of the National Museum – Náprstek Museum of Asian, African and American Cultures (inv. no. P5567–5583, P5590–5593).

During the Old Kingdom, sets of model stone vessels, most often consisting of somewhere between 70 and 90 pieces and made in travertine and limestone, were parts of the funerary equipment supposed to provide for all the basic needs of the deceased in his or her eternal life in the netherworld. At the magical symbolic level they would offer a constant supply of food and drink, and perfumed ointments. This incomplete set of nine little vases and 34 bowls from the tomb of Princess Khekeretnebty is exceptional because the bodies of the vessels are adorned with hieratic inscriptions in black ink describing three kinds of tall vessel – the *aperet*, *djuyu nefer* and *abesh*. The reason for marking the vessels with the names of their types may have been the high degree of stylisation of shapes that in the 2nd half of the 5th Dynasty meant that their appearance no longer corresponded to the original pottery types. (LJ)

Documentation of parts of Khekeretnebty's funerary equipment started in the tomb itself

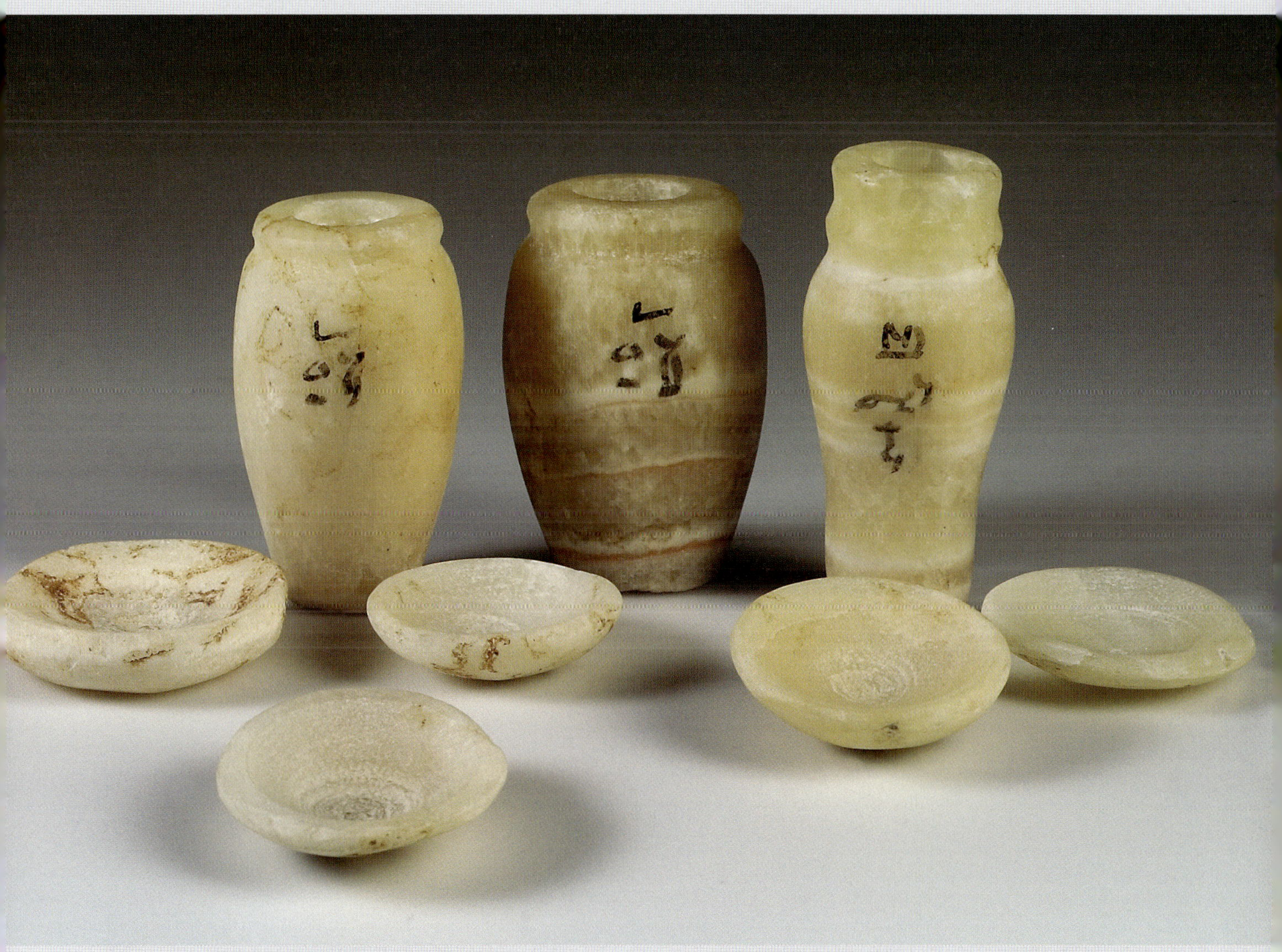

THE PYRAMID NECROPOLIS

32 Textile with inscription from the tomb of Princess Khekeretnebty

Linen; w. of strip of fabric 7–8 cm, l. of inscription 18.7 cm. Old Kingdom, 5th Dynasty. Central Abusir – cemetery of Djedkare's family, burial chamber of tomb of Khekeretnebty, discovered 1976. Find no. 169a/B/76.

Several fragments of linen, some bearing traces of an inscription written in black ink, were found in the mastaba of Princess Khekeretnebty in the cemetery of Djedkare's family in Central Abusir. On one fragment, which was lying close to the princess's sarcophagus, we read, "the king's subordinate Kehef, (his) helper, director of the weavers of Khenem. Royal (cloth, width) 1.3 (rolls)". Inscriptions on textiles could take various forms and above all have different meanings. We know instances of maker's marks, owner's marks or marks of the quality of the fabric. The specific function of the inscriptions from the mastaba of Princess Khekeretnebty is not entirely clear. We might speculate that the two names and titles denote the original owners of the fabrics who donated them for the princess's funeral ritual. The use of these fabrics need not in fact be connected with the buried princess's body itself, however, but could be part of her funerary equipment. (DW)

Khekeretnebty's burial chamber

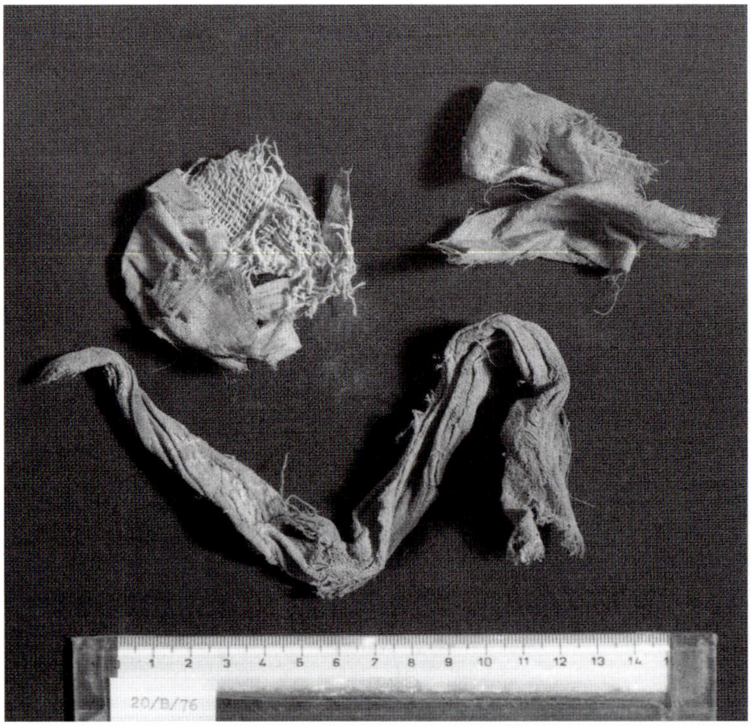

Scraps of bandaging found during research on the princess's tomb

33 Tisethor's false door

Limestone; h. 151 cm, w. 66 cm. Old Kingdom, 5th Dynasty. Central Abusir – cemetery of Djedkare's family, discovered 1976. Find number 193/B/76.

The small burial chamber for Tisethor, very probably the daughter of Princess Khekeretnebty, was created by a secondary structural alteration to the north part of Khekeretnebty's tomb. The storage chamber in the part of the same tomb above ground was then turned into Tisethor's offering chapel. A false door, through which during rituals Tisethor's *ka* could come from the other world to accept offerings, was set into its west wall. The decoration of the door follows the usual scheme: Tisethor sits in a panel in the upper section at an offering table surrounded by abundant offerings. Under the panel on the lintel and frame doors are inscriptions that are partially carved and partially only rendered in black paint with the funerary formulae and title, "King's ornament, his beloved and honoured, Tisethor". The inscriptions on the door frames mirror each other and contain the wish, "An offering that Osiris gives that there may be (made) invocation offerings of bread, beer and cakes at every festival. Lady, honoured before the Great God and before the King, King's ornament, Tisethor". On both sides of the door the inscriptions end with a standing figure of Tisethor. (MV)

Tisethor's false door stood at the west wall of the offering chapel

34 Sarcophagus of Faaf

Limestone: l. 265 cm, w. 110 cm, h. 100 cm. Old Kingdom, 5th Dynasty. Central Abusir – cemetery of Djedkare's family, discovered 1978.

Faaf, of the beautiful name Idu, built his tomb beside the tomb of Princess Khekeretnebty and Princ Neserkauhor in the cemetery of Djedkare's family in Abusir. Discovered in the burial chamber was a large, only roughly worked limestone sarcophagus of the chest type. Despite the stonework, a hieratic inscription relating to the intended recipient and made shortly after the breaking off of the block in the quarry is still decipherable on the front of the sarcophagus. From the inscription it is clear that Faaf was a scribe and tutor to the royal children, and a priest in the pyramid complexes of Raneferef and Khentkaus II, and in Nyuserre's solar temple. The date, given as "the year after the 17th occasion of the census of cattle, 1st month of the summer season, 23rd day", is very valuable for the reconstruction of the chronology of Djedkare's reign. Since the census of cattle (collection of taxes) usually happened every two years, it can be deduced that Faaf acquired the limestone block for his sarcophagus roughly around the 34th year of Djedkare's reign. This is important evidence for the length of this ruler's reign. (MV)

Faaf's burial chamber

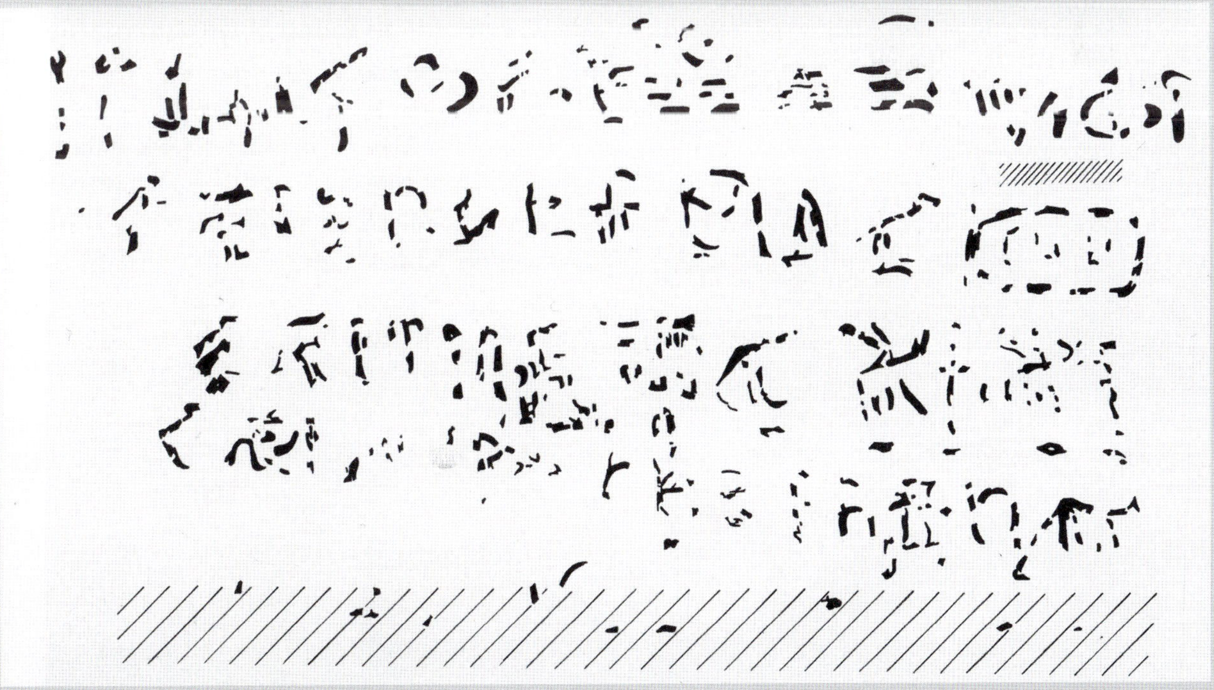

35 | Decorated coffin of an unknown beauty

Wood (not specified); 2.04 × 0.59 × 0.62 m. Third Intermediate Period. Central Abusir – mastaba of Werkaure (AC 26), corridor room no. 2, discovered 2008. Find no. 38/AC26/2008.

The area of the royal cemetery in Central Abusir was used not only in the Old Kingdom but also in later periods, when it was a burial place for the poorer inhabitants of the surrounding settlements in the 1st millennium BC. In many cases the body of the deceased was placed in a wooden coffin. This richly decorated wooden coffin was found in the superstructure of the tomb of Prince Werkaure, built in the 2nd half of the 5th Dynasty. It is a double anthropoid container. Only the lid is decorated, especially in the area of the head. The face is painted orange and hemmed by a wig with blue and white stripes. Above the face is a depiction of a hawk, here inaccurately representing a vulture with outstretched wings, upside down. The vulture was usually associated with the protective goddess Nekhbet. Inside was the body of a woman who died at the age of 30–40. Unfortunately her name remains unknown. This object is the only completely preserved coffin from the mastaba of Werkaure. (MPH)

The coffin with the remains of an unknown woman at the time of discovery. A torpedo shaped vessel, evidently one of the few items in the funerary equipment of the deceased, was found beneath the head section

36 Fabric with depiction of the god Horus

Linen, distemper; 35 × 30 cm. Third Intermediate Period. Central Abusir – mastaba of Werkaure (AC 26), discovered 2008. Find no. 38_M_J.

During archaeological excavation in the substructure of Werkaure's mastaba, a fragment of linen in tabby weave was found among the very damaged mummies interred in the underground access corridor to the burial chamber. Preserved on its reverse side was a painting consisting of a thin layer of different coloured distemper in black, white, red, blue and brown. It depicts the head of a falcon on a black and brown background. The woven fabric was part of the textile bandaging of the mummified body of the deceased – it comes from one of the secondary interments that took place during the 8th and 7th centuries BC below and above ground in Werkaure's tomb (from the period of the 5th Dynasty) and in the area east of it. The original function of the painted textile is not clear, and this type of find is not very usual in Egyptian archaeology of the 8th and 7th centuries BC. The motif of the falcon depicted on the cloth refers to Horus, the ancient Egyptian god of the sky, sun and light, but also a deity closely bound up with the royal office. (HB and DW)

Passage no. 7 in the substructure of Wenkaure's tomb filled with damaged mummified remains and waste building material

37 Faience pendant in the form of *wedjat* eye

Egyptian faience; l. 2.7 cm, h. 2.3 cm, w. 0.8 cm. Third Intermediate Period. Central Abusir – area east of the mastaba of Werkaure (AC 26), on site of secondary burials, discovered 2006. Find no. 4/AC26/2006.

As well as pottery, stone vessels, offerings or their models, funerary equipment included personal adornments, jewellery and amulets. Gold, electron and various types of semiprecious stone were used in their manufacture but the most lavishly employed material was Egyptian faience. This pendant is a case in point. It was very probably part of a necklace of one of the deceased buried close to the tomb of Werkaure – but roughly seventeen centuries after its completion. The pendant shows the eye of Horus, the *wedjat*, and so refers to the mythical battle between Horus and Seth, during which Horus lost an eye, but with the help of other gods got it back. This is why the *wedjat* was a symbol of healing for Egyptians, but also symbolised protection, perfection and power. The *wedjat* is one of the most frequent amulets encountered in Egyptian archaeology. (JK)

Eastern part of the superstructure of the tomb of Werkaure

38 | Wooden figurine of a woman from the mastaba of Werkaure

Wood: l. 18.5 cm, max. w. 6.2 cm, h. 2.3 cm. Third Intermediate Period. Central Abusir – area of the burial chamber of the mastaba of Werkaure (AC 26), found in 2008. Find nos: figurine 75/AC26/2008, vessel 76/AC26/2008.

From the time of the Middle Kingdom figurines of naked women were often placed in tombs, and these are known as "concubine" figures in Egyptological literature. The small wooden figurine of a woman, found in the pillaged and devastated burial chamber of the mastaba of Prince Werkaure, is of this type. The figurine represents a naked woman with emphasised pubic area and above all hips and thighs. Its triangular face has only rudimentary features. On the head it has a simple short wig. The arms have not survived although the holes where they were fixed to the shoulders are visible, and the feet are also missing. Figurines of concubines appear almost exclusively in the funerary equipment of women. Their main function was the protection of women in erotic life and also in pregnancy and menstruation. Unfortunately, the mummified and embalmed bodies of the deceased interred in the underground part of Werkaure's tomb during the 8th and 7th centuries BC were later destroyed by stone robbers. This means that we cannot assign this interesting find to a specific person, but we can assume the owner to have been a woman. Discovered together with the figurine was a small but finely executed pottery model of a red vessel. It is very probable that it formed a set with the figurine. (JK)

Construction trench for the substructure of Werkaure's mastaba during excavations

Cemeteries in the shadow of the Step Pyramid – Abusir South

MIROSLAV BÁRTA

The cluster of cemeteries that today we call Abusir South in line with their location on the modern map of Egypt has a distinctive position in the history of the Abusir pyramid field. The whole of the southern half of the Czech archaeological concession is dominated by the central mound on which most of the Old Kingdom tombs here were built. Other slopes running east down from the upland plateau of the Western desert to the Nile Valley were also densely built up. Yet because this area lies between the Abusir pyramids to the north and the even more famous pyramids of Saqqara to the south, dominated by the Step Pyramid of the legendary King Djoser, it was entirely

View from the south, from Djoser's Step Pyramid, on the whole site of Abusir; Abusir South is in the centre of the shot

overlooked until the beginning of modern excavations in 1991. Up to the middle of the last century what is known as the Lake of Abusir existed on its eastern edge. In Antiquity this was the main entrance gate into its cemeteries, while just a little further east stood the capital city of the first unified state of ancient Egypt and the Old Kingdom. The city was called the White Walls, and it was later known as Mennofer or Memphis.

The tombs in Abusir South are a record of the course of the development of the ancient Egyptian state from the 27th to the 22nd centuries BC. Archaeological excavations have led to the discovery of tombs and tomb complexes belonging to several different social classes of people employed at the royal court, in the temples, mortuary complexes and in state service in general. This makes them unique testimony to the history and evolution of the state, religious beliefs and art of ancient Egypt. Among the oldest tombs here are Hetepi's mastaba from the reign of Djoser, which has one of the earliest known relief decorations, and the tomb known only as AS 54 which belonged to an anonymous official from the end of the 3rd Dynasty and where archaeologists found the first fully preserved wooden boat from ancient Egypt. They also include the tomb of Kaaper, a border guard and priest of the frog goddess Heqet, the family cemetery of the highest physician in the land Shepseskafankh and other members of his family such as the royal daughter Sheretnebty, the overseer of granaries and treasuries Nefer, and the solar priest Neferinpu. Finally from the 6th Dynasty, the very end of the Old Kingdom, comes the tomb of the vizier Qar and his sons, for example. In many respects these monumental buildings, often with surviving decoration and large sets of finds of pottery, metal and stone tools, blocks covered with reliefs and inscriptions, statues and much else, rank among the best art and craft works ever created in Egypt of the 3rd millennium BC.

Finally we should not forget to mention one of the most recent and unexpected discoveries in this area, which is the temple of Ramesses II built in the 12th century BC on the eastern edge of Abusir South, north of the Lake of Abusir. It was probably intended to strengthen the legitimacy of the monarch through the association with the solar cult.

> The central low mound in Abusir South where the most important tombs of officials dated to the Old Kingdom are concentrated

39 | Hetepi's offering scene

Limestone. Old Kingdom, 3rd Dynasty. Abusir South – tomb of Hetepi (AS 31), discovered in 1999.

The mastaba of Hetepi can be dated approximately to the reign of King Djoser, the builder of the Step Pyramid in Saqqara. This scene was found on the north wing of the facade of Hetepi's chapel, which was otherwise undecorated. It is a canonical offering scene in which the deceased owner of the tomb receives ritual offerings that were believed to be essential for his sustenance and well-provided existence in the afterlife. The main offerings include loaves of bread on the offering table and beer jars under the table. Other offerings are placed around them and above Hetepi's head there are two lines of hieroglyphic inscription with his name and titles. These indicate that Hetepi occupied high-ranking positions at the court and served as a priest of the goddess Bastet among others. (MB)

Workmen inside Hetepi's chapel

> Detail of the exceptionally finely rendered face of Hetepi

40 Stone bowl with name of King Huni

Magnesite; h. 9 cm, rim diameter 19.2 cm. Old Kingdom, 3rd/4th Dynasty. Abusir South – tomb AS 54, shaft I, discovered in 2010. Find number S123/AS54/2010.

In what seems so far to be the only burial chamber in the anonymous tomb AS 54, and at its entrance, archaeologists found the fragments of at least 133 stone vessels. Only one of them bore an inscription, and this is the *nswt bjtj* name of the king Huni – *nswt-H(nj)*. Huni is a relatively little-known ruler, the last in the line of the kings of the 3rd Dynasty. This made the find of the bowl, which Huni himself may well have given to the unknown high-ranking dignitary, all the more important. The mastaba AS 54 is the largest tomb yet found in Abusir South and as the dominating feature of the vicinity was set on the summit of the low elevation looking down onto the Abusir wadi and the cemetery in North Saqqara on its opposite bank. (LJ)

< View into what is so far the only burial chamber found in mastaba AS 54, where the bowl bearing the name of King Huni was found in scattered fragments. The fragment with the engraved name was discovered close to two stone walls that had been built for an unknown reason after the robbery of the tomb and devastation of the funerary equipment of the deceased

Detail of the king's name, which was engraved in the upper section of the internal surface of the bowl by a sharp pointed object, using the technique of pricking

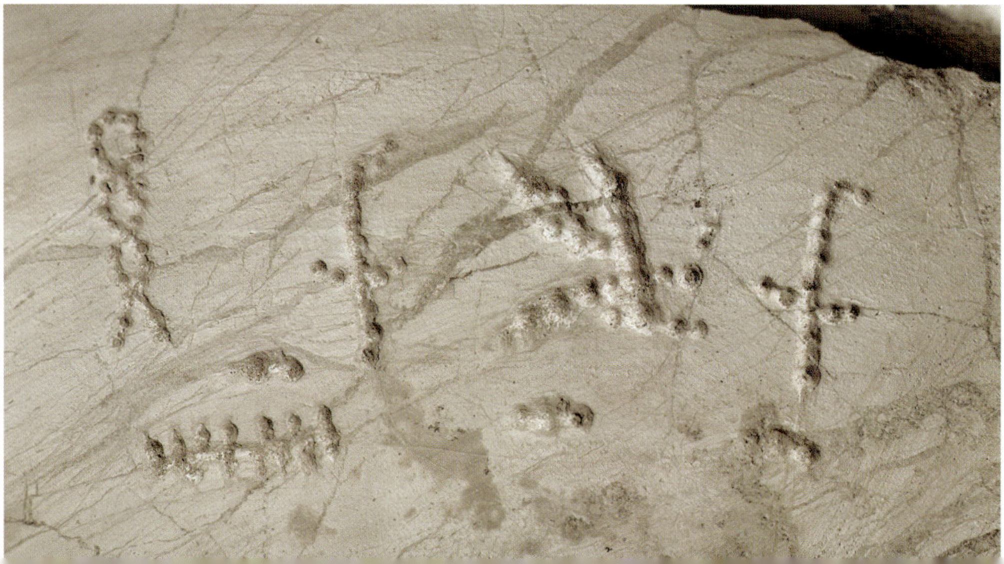

41 Meidum bowl from the anonymous tomb AS 54

Pottery, covered in polished red slip; rim diameter 12 cm, max. diameter 13.5 cm, h. 9.5 cm. Old Kingdom, 3rd Dynasty. Abusir South – anonymous tomb AS 54, room in front of the chapel, excavated in 2010. Ceramic number 15.AS54.2010.

So-called Meidum bowls are amongst the most beautiful ancient Egyptian ceramic vessels. They are named after the place of their initial discovery, during excavations in the pyramid field in Meidum, but later archaeological work showed that these were far from the earliest examples and that they could be found throughout the whole Egypt. Their quality and treatment distinguishes them at first glance from other pottery of the Old Kingdom. They were usually made of high quality materials, most often very fine Nile or Marl clay, and were given their characteristic finish by a highly polished red slip. In the course of the Old Kingdom, the shape of the Meidum bowls changed quite strikingly, with the relatively deep small pots of the 3rd Dynasty gradually evolving into very wide shallow bowls. These changes make them a useful aid to the chronological determination of associated finds and archaeological contexts. Their surface treatment also changed over time, from the typically light orange colour of the early Old Kingdom to dark "bordeaux" red at its end. In the anonymous tomb AS 54 we found a beautiful example of an early Meidum bowl in the debris of the room in front of the chapel. It was discovered fully intact in the south-east corner and has the shape characteristic for the 3rd Dynasty, namely an S-shaped rim, sharply bent shoulder and quite deep body. It was very probably used for bringing offerings during the regular cult in the chapel. (KA)

East part of tomb AS 54, which belonged to an unknown dignitary probably from the reign of King Huni, with a view of the chapel and other cultic areas

42 Wooden boat

Wood; l. 17 m, w. 2.2 m, d. 0.60 m. Old Kingdom, 3rd Dynasty. Abusir South – south of tomb AS 54, discovered in 2015.

The wooden boat made of local varieties of timber, and above all acacia wood, was discovered south of the tomb AS 54 dated to the end of the 3rd Dynasty, probably the reign of King Huni. Unfortunately the name of the owner has not survived, but the architecture of the tomb, its dimensions and the existence of this exceptional boat, all indicate that he must have been one of the highest ranking dignitaries of his time. This is the first completely preserved boat known to archaeologists from so early a period of Egyptian history. The find enables us to reconstruct in detail the techniques employed in the construction of boats of this type and date – all the structural elements have survived, including evidence of joining using lashings and pegs. It is absolutely exceptional for a boat burial to be part of the architecture of a non-royal tomb in this period. (MB)

In the course of two archaeological seasons the unique boat was protected from the weather by a tent construction

Detail of the entirely preserved boat construction

43 Limestone stela with offering scene and two engaged statues

White painted limestone; h. 1.09 m, w. 0.46 m, l. 18.5 cm. Old Kingdom, 5th Dynasty, probably the reign of Neferirkare. Abusir South – tomb of Nyankhseshat (AS 104), discovered 2018. Find number 1/AS104/2018.

The high-ranking official Nyankhseshat had his tomb built at the beginning of the 4th Dynasty. In the first half of the 5th Dynasty a limestone stela with an offering scene and two engaged statues was inserted into the mudbrick eastern wall of this tomb. The limestone slab belonged to the dignitary Sekhemka and his wife Henutsen and depicts the couple sitting opposite each other at an offering table loaded with loaves of bread. In the middle is a list of sacred oils and below it are the engaged statues of Sekhemka and Henutsen with traces of the original colours. In front of the stela was discovered a limestone basin on which offerings were presented to the deceased to enable them to live forever. The stela was set up to commemorate the deceased. The high quality of the craftsmanship suggests that the object may have been produced in a royal workshop. (MO, MPH)

Detail of Henutsen's face

< The stela belonging to Sekhemka and his spouse Henutsen is shown here at the moment of its uncovering. It was set into the mudbrick masonry of the east wall of tomb AS 104

44 | Ears and beard from the burial chamber of Kaaper the Younger

Clay with imprints of textile; ears, right: l. 6.2 cm, w. 3.9 cm, max. thickness 1.9 cm; left (incomplete): l. 4.6 cm, w. 3.3 cm, max. thickness 1.4 cm; beard 4.2 × 3.8 × 2.5 cm. Old Kingdom, 5th Dynasty, probably the reign of Nyuserre. Abusir South – tomb of Kaaper the Younger (AS 61), discovered in 2010, investigated in 2016. Find number 32/AS61/2016 (ears), 35/AS61/2016 (beard).

Although the burial chamber of Kaaper the Younger was robbed in antiquity, the archaeologists managed to find rare evidence of the funeral customs of the time inside it. The right and left ear, both life size, and the beard were modelled in clay. While the ears are faithful representations of real human organs, the beard is stylised, with horizontal indentations copying the line of the chin in a way that was also common in relief decoration. The upper edge of the beard is shaped so as to fit precisely on the chin of the deceased. The prints of textile on the surface of the ears and beard suggest that both were originally parts of the face mask with which the actual face of Kaaper the Younger was covered in the burial pit of his burial chamber. A textile face mask with stiffened ears discovered in the mastaba of the high-ranking dignitary Weserkafankh, who was a contemporary of Kaaper, is a parallel find. Remnants of funerary equipment also include faience beads, gold leaf and fragments of a wooden staff, which was a symbol of Kaaper the Younger's rank and prestige, since he had been the "elder of the court" (VD)

The superstructure of the mastaba of Kaaper the Younger was built from limestone blocks, but the outer layer was stripped by stone robbers in antiquity. The west wall of the tomb adjoins an extensive mastaba from the reign of King Huni. On the other sides Kaaper's mastaba is surrounded by tombs made of mudbricks

45 Statue of Nefer

Limestone. Height of statue: 40 cm, base: 33 × 21.5 × 5 cm. Old Kingdom, 5th Dynasty. Abusir South – tomb of Nefer (AS 68d), serdab located east of the chapel, discovered 2012. Find number 149b/AS68d/2012.

One of the four statues of the official Nefer and his wife found in the serdab immediately behind the entrance to his rock cult chapel. This sculpture shows the highly placed Nefer as a scribe, in typical cross-legged posture. Nefer is dressed in a short kilt, has a wig on his head and on his lap an unrolled papyrus scroll on which there are written prayers guaranteeing his life in the afterlife and a list of the most important offerings for the maintenance of his cult. Scribes were the backbone of the ancient Egyptian state. Dignitaries in the state bureaucracy often also served as priests, and this was the case of the Abusir Nefer. (MB)

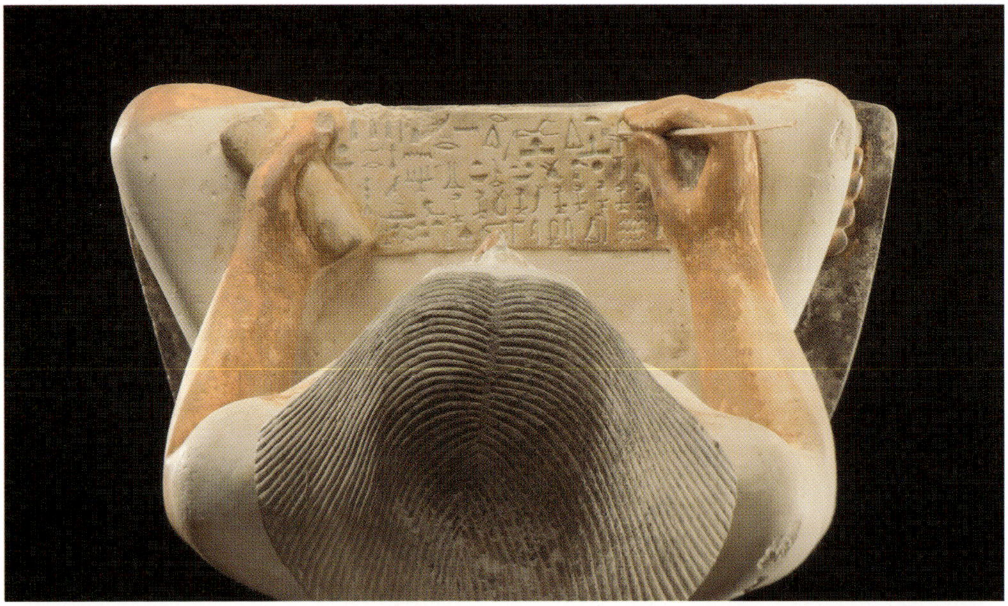

The scribe Nefer holds on his lap a papyrus scroll with offering formulae and a list of offerings provided as part of his mortuary cult

Statues of the official Nefer *in situ* in the serdab

ABUSIR SOUTH

46 | Nefer's false door

Limestone, low relief with polychromy; h. 2.13 cm, w. 0.98 cm. Old Kingdom, 5th Dynasty, reign of Nyuserre. Abusir South – chapel, rock tomb of the dignitary Nefer and his wife Neferethathor, discovered *in situ* in 2012. Find number 164/AS68d/2012.

This stela has survived in its entirety including the original polychromy. It consists of a lintel bearing the text of a prayer, a central panel with list of offerings and on the sides figures of Nefer and his wife Neferethathor seated at table with loaves of bread, and a smaller lintel with list of religious feasts and columns of text giving the titles of the owner of the tomb and his wife. At the foot of the stela stands the official Nefer in the embrace of his wife. Nefer was the overseer of the scribes of the royal documents, the overseer of the treasury and granaries, and priest in the solar temple of the ruler Nyuserre. Neferethathor was in charge of royal properties and also a priestess of Hathor, Lady of the Sycamore. This is one of the most beautiful false doors to have survived from the Old Kingdom. (MB)

The corridor chapel where the cult of Nefer, his wife and whole family was performed. Visible in the floor are the openings of the shafts leading down into the individual underground chambers

> Nefer's false door contains inscriptions and titles relating to Nefer himself and to his wife Neferethathor. Even the original colours have survived almost undamaged

ABUSIR SOUTH

47 | Offerings above the burial of a child in the tomb of the dignitary Nefer

Bone, ceramic, wood, mudbricks; dimensions of burial niche with offerings: 1.28 × 0.9 × 0.8 m. Old Kingdom, 5th Dynasty, probably the reign of Nyuserre. Abusir South – tomb of Nefer (AS 68d), discovered 2012, shaft of the child excavated in 2014. Find numbers 403–408/AS68d/2014.

In 2014 a rare sight met the eyes of the archaeologists during final work on the excavation of the rock tomb of the high-ranking dignitary Nefer. While excavating the last – smallest and shallowest – of the four shafts, they found undisturbed filling layered with animal offerings, which meant that they could expect an intact burial at the bottom. In the west wall of the shaft at a depth of 2.60 metres and behind the untouched mudbrick blocking wall they then found a niche with offerings placed over the burial of a child. The human remains were of a boy of about twelve, probably the son of the tomb owner. His body was adorned with a bead necklace, and placed on its left side in the burial pit, which had been filled up with yellow sand sealed with a layer of Nile mud. The burial pit had been covered in limestone slabs, on which the offerings were set: the head of a calf, a white painted wooden box with two mud bricks equipped with a seal bearing the name of King Nyuserre, a large ceramic (what is known as "imported") vessel and eleven smaller pots that originally contained various grains and fruits. (VD)

Burial pit with the burial of a child, whose body had been covered with yellow sand and sealed with a layer of Nile mud

ABUSIR SOUTH

48 | Double statue of an ancient Egyptian dignitary

Limestone: max. h. of statue 37 cm, base: 19 × 12 × 5 cm. Old Kingdom, 5th Dynasty. Abusir South – burial chamber of the tomb of Nefershepes, discovered 2012. Find number 17/AS67/2012.

The limestone double statue was found in the burial chamber of the official Nefershepes in Abusir South. Nefershepes' tomb was built in the reign of Nyuserre and belonged to a dignitary who held the post of overseer of scribes of the gang of workmen at the royal court. The circumstances of the discovery of this sculpture are surprising; it was found in the underground part of the tomb, south of Nefershepes's sarcophagus. This is highly unusual because statues were usually placed in the above-ground parts of tombs. All the same, it is probable that this statue was placed here as part of the funerary equipment (see also no. 28). The statues show the official in two different attitudes: striding and standing with feet together. The most recent studies suggest that the appearance of such double statues in the reign of Nyuserre was related to a new conception of the journey to the netherworld. (MB)

View of the tomb of the dignitary Nefershepes from the south-west

< Labourers at work – pulling out a heavy stone block using a technique a thousand years old

< The burial chamber almost ten metres below the surface concealed a limestone sarcophagus. The double statue of the owner of the tomb lay just to the south of it

ABUSIR SOUTH

49 Models of burial boats

Wood; boat a: l. 64 cm, w. 17 cm, h. 16 cm; boat b: l. 64.3 cm, w. 10.3 cm, h. 12.2 cm; boat c: l. 50 cm, w. 13.5 cm, h. 9 cm. Old Kingdom, 5th Dynasty. Abusir South – structure AS 69 above the tombs of Princess Sheretnebty and the dignitary Nefer, discovered in 2012.

Located above the rock cut chapels of Princess Sheretnebty and the dignitary Nefer is a tomb that seems to have been connected with the chapels. Hidden in this tomb was a small structure containing burials of model boats with oars. This was a very unusual find, since such models were usually placed directly inside burial chambers, or in serdabs in the tomb chapels but these three models were buried separately, and moreover each represents a different kind of craft. This makes it difficult to determine their meaning, although the placing of the models with their prows towards the west suggests that they were associated with ancient Egyptian beliefs about the journey to the next world. (MM)

Models of boats buried with their prows facing west in a small structure originally concealed in the interior of the tomb

Removal of the boats from the place of the find before transport to a secure storage place

50 | Naos with three high relief figures

White limestone; naos: h. 139 cm, w. 126 cm, thickness 29 cm, figures: h. 103.3 cm, w. 23.5–31 cm, thickness 11–15.5 cm. Old Kingdom, 5th Dynasty. Abusir South – corridor in the tomb complex of Princess Sheretnebty, discovered in 2012.

Two naoi flanking the entrance to the rock-cut chapel of the dignitary Nefer show three high relief figures standing side by side. The most prominent is the central female figure, which undoubtedly depicts Princess Sheretnebty. Both male figures on each side most likely refer to Nefer, the owner of the easternmost rock cut tomb in the tomb complex. Nefer is depicted in a festive kilt, once with a short and once with a shoulder-long wig. Another two naoi were placed by the entrance to the neighbouring chapel of Princess Sheretnebty. These are larger than Nefer's but not so finely elaborated, and contain a figure of a man and a man with his boy child respectively. These figures most likely depict the husband of Princess Sheretnebty and their eldest son. There may once have been another naos in the complex with a figure of the princess herself. (HV)

By placing the female figure between two male figures the ancient artist emphasised her as the central focus of the sculpture

51 Reconstructed bead collar necklace

Faience; beads of various sizes, for example wave-shaped spacer components 6.0–6.4 × 1.2 × 0.6 cm. Old Kingdom, 5th Dynasty, probably the reign of Nyuserre, Abusir South – rock tomb of Nefer (AS 68d), discovered in 2012, shaft 3 excavated in 2014. Find number 395/AS68d/2014.

Faience bead jewellery adorning the bodies of the deceased was a common part of the funerary equipment of officials, priests and their families in the period of the Old Kingdom. Although most of the tombs were robbed in antiquity, bead jewellery was not of great interest to the robbers and was often ignored. In 2014 an intact shaft with burial chamber (shaft 4) was found in the rock tomb of the high-ranking dignitary Nefer. The sarcophagus contained the skeletal remains of an adult man whose identity remains unknown. On the day of the burial a wooden staff was laid in the sarcophagus next to the deceased and his body was adorned with faience bead jewellery, predominantly turquoise, light blue or brown in surface coloration. Subsequent analysis enabled researchers to identify the composition pattern of the same types of beads in the necklace, armlets and ankle circlet. Typologically there are seven identifiable kinds of faience bead (tubular, small rounded, droplet-shaped, bloom-shaped) or component (semicircular terminal, wave-shaped spacer, terminal spacer). Parallels have been used to partially reconstruct the collar necklace from the cluster of beads found by the right arm. (VD)

Limestone sarcophagus with the skeletal remains of an adult man, whose body was adorned with bead jewellery

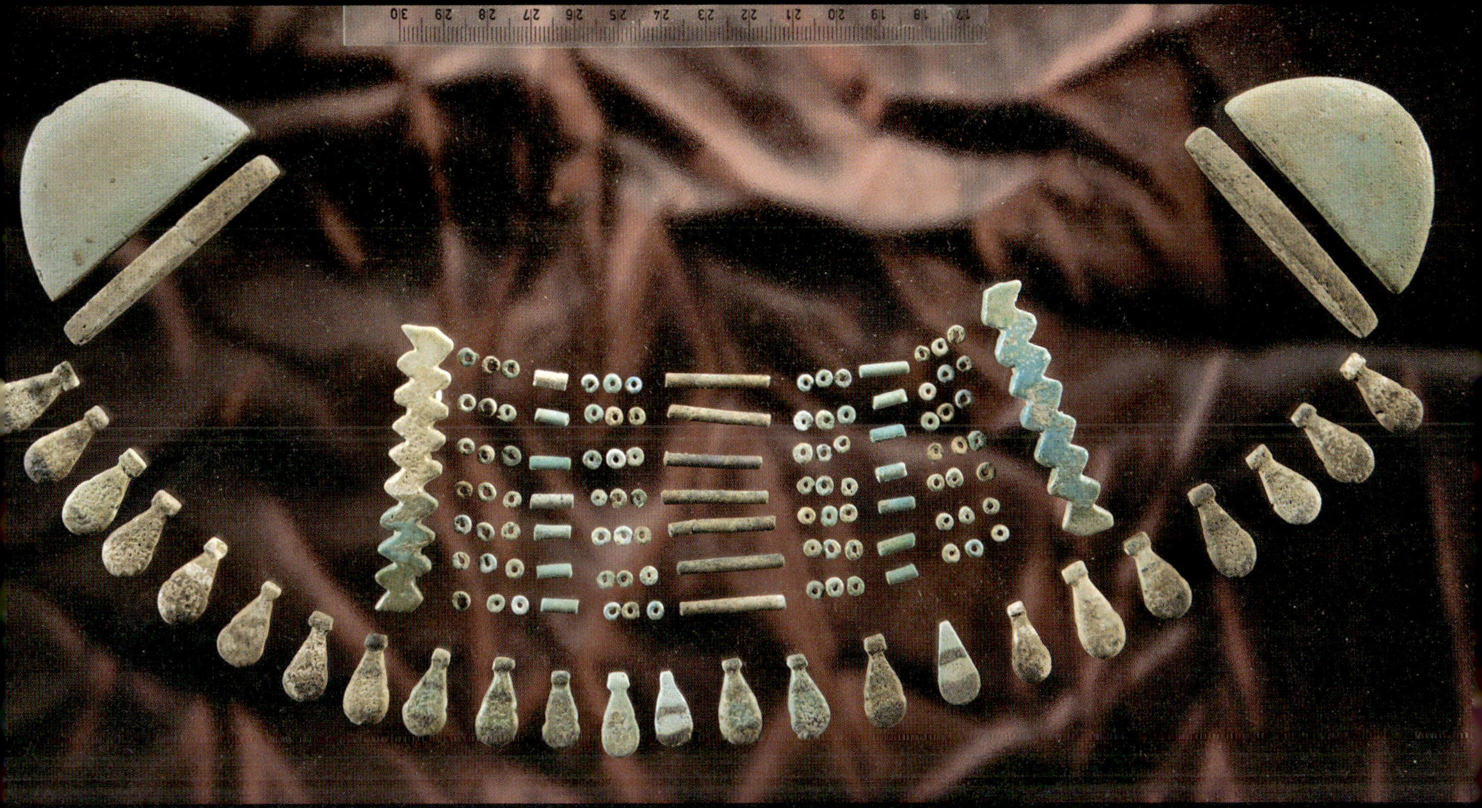

52 Fragment of relief decoration from the tomb of the inspector of hairdressers Ankhires

Limestone with polychrome decoration in low relief; 78 × 34 × 29 cm and 15 × 19 × 29 cm. Old Kingdom, 5th Dynasty, probably the reign of Nyuserre. Abusir South – tomb of Ankhires (AS 98), discovered in 2016. Find number 42+44/AS98/2016.

Although stone thieves seriously damaged the decoration of the superstructure of the tomb of Ankhires, inspector of the hairdressers of the royal palace, dozens of surviving fragments enable us to get an idea of its execution and the appearance of the interiors. The block illustrated here shows a scene from Ankhires' household. The four seated figures probably represent Ankhires' children. The first of these is a man with folded arms, wearing a long close-fitting robe. The next two are also men, scribes with writing implements in front of them, and above them the inscription: "... of the inspector of hairdressers of the Great House (royal palace) of Ankhires in his house. When he was..." which is unique for the expression "in his house". No formulation of this kind had been documented in any excavated Old Kingdom tomb. The figure of the tomb owner had presumably been depicted at the beginning of the scene, his other titles indicating that he worked in intimate proximity to the king, caring for his hair and headdress. He had thus touched the living god. The grandeur of Ankhires' tomb reflected his prestigious social position. (VD)

Detail of scribe with writing implements, and seated in the position typical of the profession

53 *Kherep* sceptre from the tomb of the inspector of hairdressers Ankhires

Wood, black ink; l. 36.5 cm. Old Kingdom, 5th Dynasty, probably the reign of Nyuserre. Abusir South – tomb of Ankhires (AS 98), discovered in 2016. Find number 82/AS98/2017.

An almost completely preserved wooden *kherep* sceptre was discovered in the serdab of the mastaba of Ankhires. Although it was broken when found, conservation work restored it in its full length and brought out the faded hieroglyphic inscription written in black ink on the upper part of the sceptre: "Inspector of hairdressers of the Great House, Ankhires". The text identifies the tomb owner and gives his most important title. A second very similar sceptre was found in the serdab but only one hieroglyph survives from its inscription. The two sceptres were originally grasped in the hands of statues representing Ankhires. In ancient Egypt sceptres and staffs were symbols of social status and power. This is why they were also placed in the tombs of officials and could not be omitted in relief or sculptural depictions of the deceased. (VD)

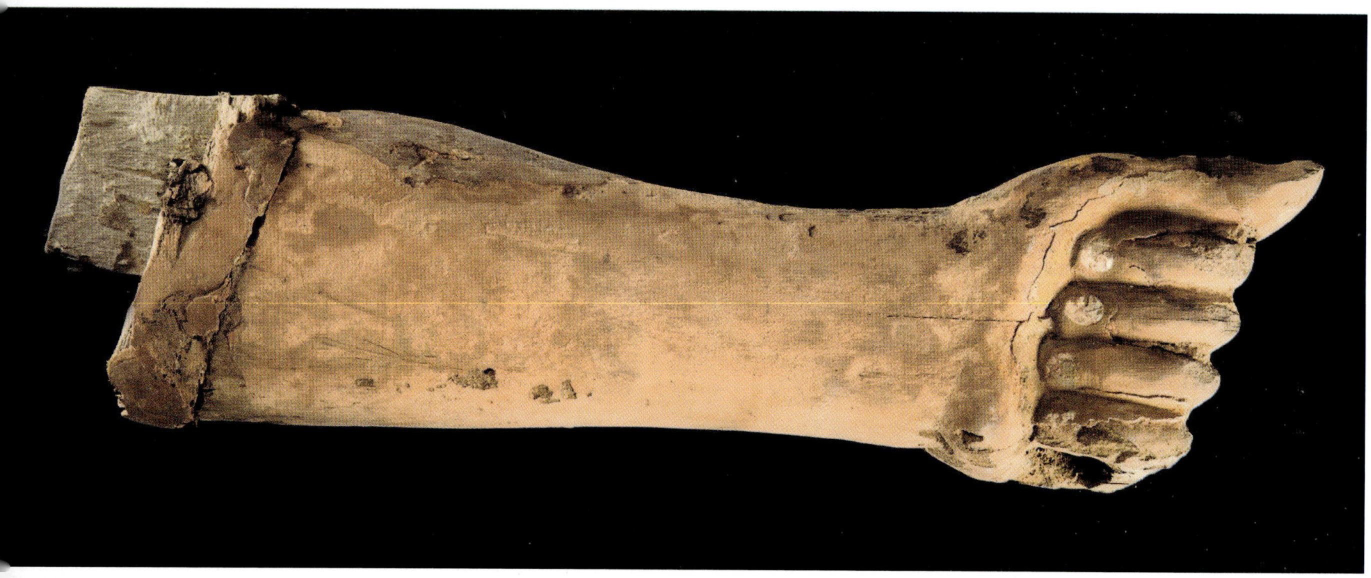

The hand of one of Ankhires' statues found in the serdab together with the sceptre

0
2.5
5 cm

54 | Statue of Princess Sheretnebty with son

Polychromy on limestone; h. 37.5 cm, w. 12.5 cm, thickness 20.2 cm. Old Kingdom, 5th Dynasty. Abusir South – serdab in the tomb chapel of Princess Sheretnebty, discovered 2012. Find number 215-5/AS68c/2012.

The serdab, a closed niche for statues, in the rock-cut chapel of Princess Sheretnebty and her family contained the remains of more than ten statues in wood and limestone. While the wooden statues had almost entirely disintegrated in the course of time, the limestone statues survived in relatively good condition. This sculpture was found broken in three pieces. It depicts the princess herself, sitting in a dignified pose on a chair in a long white gown and shoulder-long wig over her real hair. Her small son, depicted naked and with a typical child's side lock falling onto his shoulder, is standing by her left side. (HV)

The discovery of one larger part of the statue of the princess and her son in the debris of the serdab

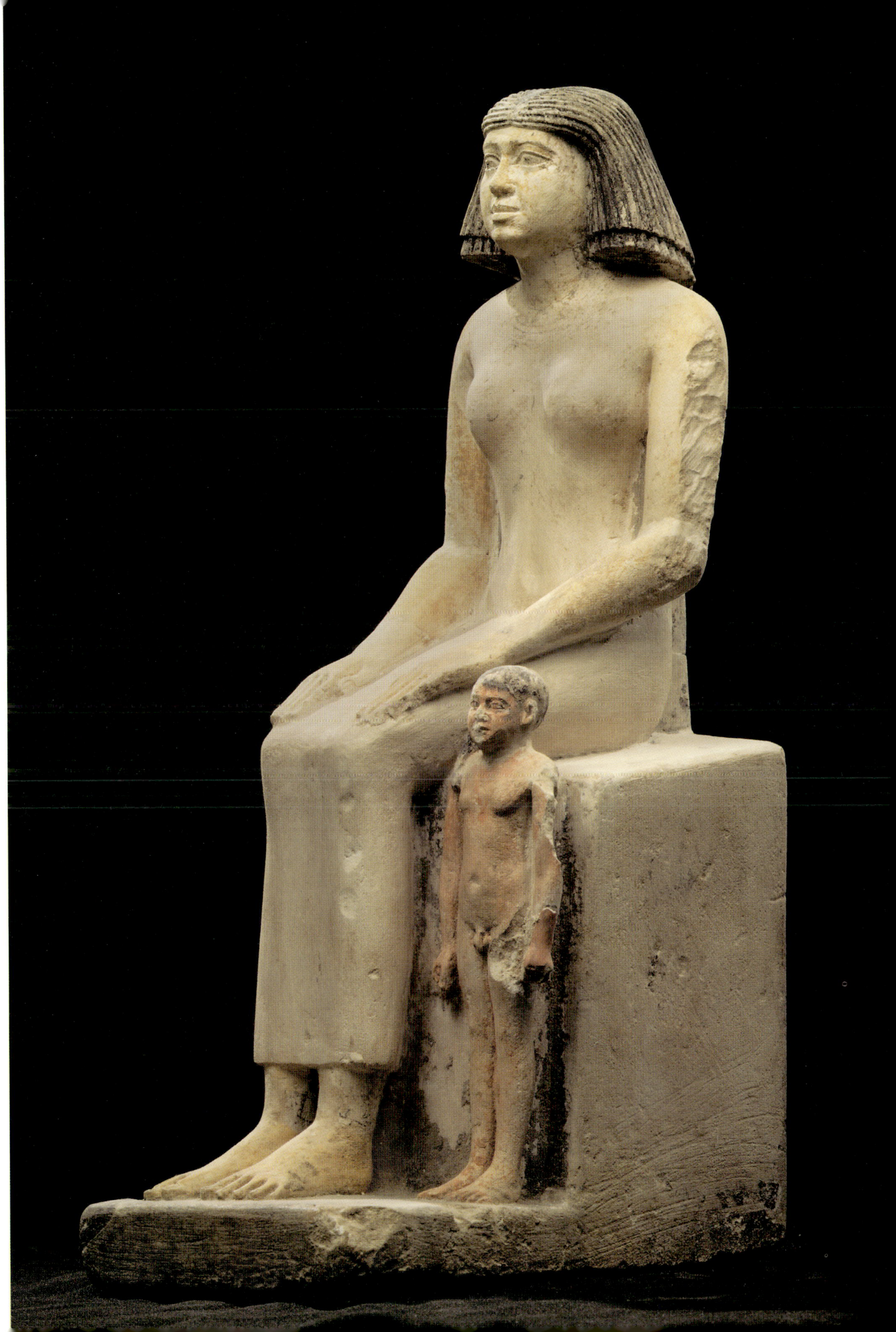

ABUSIR SOUTH

55 | Statue of Sheretnebty and her husband

Polychromy on limestone; h. 62 cm, w. 38 cm, thickness 41 cm. Old Kingdom, 5th Dynasty. Abusir South – serdab in the tomb chapel of Princess Sheretnebty, discovered 2012. Find number 215-I/AS68c/2012.

The largest sculpture found in the serdab in the rock-cut chapel of Princess Sheretnebty shows a seated couple. There is no doubt that this statue represents Sheretnebty herself and her husband. The man is depicted in a typical pose, seated with one palm resting on his thigh and the other closed in a fist. He is dressed in a festive kilt and short wig, and wears a broad collar on his chest. The princess, sitting on his left side, embraces him with her right arm around his waist. Her elegant white gown is deep cut and goes down to her ankles, and her broad collar bears traces of green and blue pigment. Her own hair peeps out from under the wig. The faces of both figures are finely modelled, but some parts of their bodies are less skilfully rendered. The unnatural length of the princess's right arm, for example, suggests the limited experience of the artist who planned the composition. (HV)

ABUSIR SOUTH

56 | Fragments of the false door of Princess Sheretnebty

Limestone; dimensions of illustrated fragments h. 56.5 cm, w. 22.5 cm. Old Kingdom, 5th Dynasty. Abusir South – burial chapel of Princess Sheretnebty, discovered in 2012. Find numbers 47/AS68/2012, 155/AS68/2012, 230/AS68/2012.

The false door of Princess Sheretnebty was destroyed long ago by ancient tomb robbers, but some of its fragments have been found in the courtyard and corridor of the tomb complex and also in the princess's chapel. The door was decorated in sunken relief and bore the usual image of the princess in front of an offering table with bread and inscriptions giving her name and titles. While the inscriptions on pillars in the shared courtyard name her only as the beloved daughter of the king, her false door carried a more complicated title, revealing that Sheretnebty received offerings from the pyramid complex of King Nyuserre. This evidence confirms that Sheretnebty was Nyuserre's daughter and through her marriage had served her father's policy of gaining the loyalty of a powerful family of officials. The princess's false door was quite roughly worked, indicating that the artists had to work quickly. The princess's burial shaft remained unfinished and her burial seems to have been hasty and modest. She evidently died unexpectedly. (HV)

The largest of the four rock chapels in burial complex AS 68, which belonged to Princess Sheretnebty and her family

Niches for false doors and a square opening broken into the blocking wall of the serdab are visible in the west wall of the chapel

57 Funerary equipment of the husband of Princess Sheretnebty

White and grey limestone, ceramic, copper; l. 245 cm, w. 114 cm, h. 111 cm. Old Kingdom, 5th Dynasty. Abusir South – burial chamber in the westernmost shaft in the tomb chapel of Princess Sheretnebty, discovered in 2013. Find nos. 291/AS68c/2012, 300/AS68c/2012, 58a–l.AS68c.2012.

The burial of Princess Sheretnebty's husband was one of the most magnificent discovered in Abusir South. Of the more than 30 burials in the princess's tomb complex it had the deepest shaft, the largest burial chamber and one of the best executed white limestone sarcophagi, which undoubtedly came from the royal workshop. On the floor of the chamber lay canopic jars, the remains of offerings of meat and ceramic vessels, some of them ritually broken during the burial. Small finds in the hole cut by the ancient tomb robbers in the wall of his sarcophagus confirm that the body of the deceased was originally wrapped in fine linen and adorned with jewels and beads. It is an irony of fate that the name of this important man, who had the good fortune to become the king's son-in-law, has not yet been discovered. (HV)

Parts of the burial, including a few small bones and textiles, were left in the debris in front of the sarcophagus by the tomb robbers

Set of ceramic vessels from the funerary equipment of the husband of Princess Sheretnebty; all the red vessels were intentionally broken during the funeral rituals

ABUSIR SOUTH
2013
AS 68C
SHAFT 1
20.10.

58 Statue of the dignitary Iti

White limestone; h. 21.8 cm, w. 7.4 cm, thickness 14.4 cm. Old Kingdom, 5th Dynasty, Abusir South – serdab in the tomb chapel of Princess Sheretnebty, discovered in 2012. Find number 215-3/AS68c/2012.

Only one of the statues in the serdab of Princess Sheretnebty bore an inscription revealing its owner's identity. The other statues were not labelled but undoubtedly represent Sheretnebty and her husband, the main owners of the tomb, while this the smallest preserved statuette belonged to the "overseer of the gang, Iti". His relationship to the tomb owners is not entirely clear. He was probably their close relative and possibly one of their children, and may have been buried in one of the shafts in Sheretnebty's tomb. (HV)

Foreman of the workmen and long-term friend of the Czech expedition, reis Ahmad el-Kereti, examining the freshly discovered statuette of Iti

A hieroglyphic inscription carved into the base of the sculpture reveals Iti's name and position

59 Decoration of the entrance to the rock chapel of Duaptah

Limestone; lintel: max. l. 134 cm, h. 31 cm, thickness 17.5 cm, drum: l. 84 cm, h. 20 cm, thickness 25 cm. Old Kingdom, 5th Dynasty. Abusir South – courtyard of the tomb complex of Princess Seretnebty and Duaptah's burial chamber, discovered in 2012 and 2013. Find numbers 77/AS68c/2012, 270/AS68c/2013.

Only in the westernmost of the four rock tombs that were part of the tomb complex of Princess Sheretnebty, in the tomb of Duaptah, has the original decoration survived. Originally placed above the chapel entrance, the lintel bearing the usual offering formula, title, name and image of the owner of this chapel was found broken in two pieces in the courtyard in front of Duaptah's tomb, while the drum belonging under the lintel had been thrown into Duaptah's burial chamber by ancient tomb robbers. Small fragments of reliefs from the side walls of the entrance that once held up the lintel and drum have also survived. (HV)

The rock-cut chapel of the tomb of Duaptah with two burial shafts hewn into the floor and a simple stone offering table in front of a shallow niche

60 | Stopper with seal imprint from the burial chamber of Duaptah

Unfired clay; max. diameter 5.6 cm, max. h. 2.5 cm; diameter of opening 1 cm. Old Kingdom, 5th Dynasty, reign of Djedkare. Abusir South – tomb complex of Princess Sheretnebty, burial chamber of Duaptah, discovered 2013. Find number 270/AS68a/2013.

Although Duaptah's burial was robbed in antiquity, small remnants of objects from the funerary equipment were preserved in the chamber. Among the scattered remnants in the half-open sarcophagus archaeologists found beads and small pieces of gold foil, evidently part of the lost adornments of the body of the deceased. In the south part of the chamber lay pottery vessels and animal bones that remained from offerings of meat. Beside them wooden objects had once been placed, but these had long ago turned to dust. A clay stopper with seal imprint, which once fastened the tied ends of a string, evidently came from a wooden chest. This seemingly unglamorous find has enormous importance for Egyptologists, because the inscription imprinted on the stopper dates Duaptah's burial to the reign of King Djedkare. (HV)

Duaptah's burial chamber after removal of debris

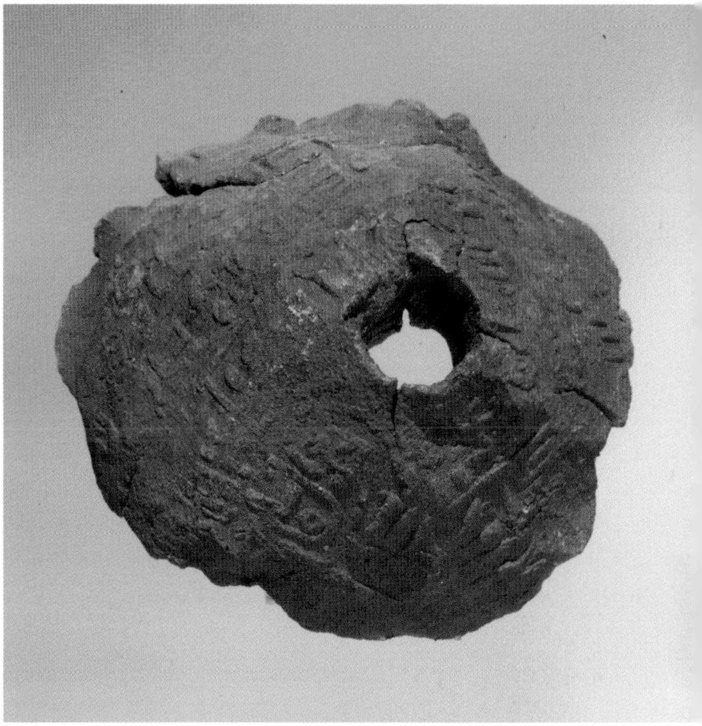

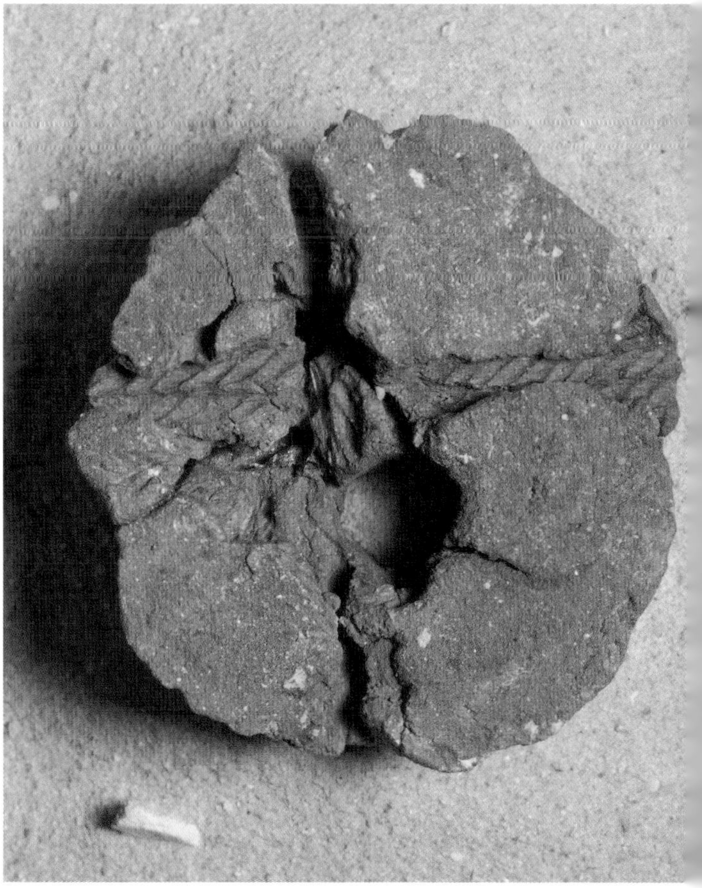

61 Hieratic inscription in the tomb chapel of the dignitary Shepespuptah

Red pigment on limestone; the longest inscription: l. 3.1 m, h. 15 cm. Old Kingdom, 5th Dynasty. Abusir South – west wall of Shepespuptah's rock chapel in the tomb complex of Princess Sheretnebty, discovered in 2012. Find Number Gr2/AS68b/2012.

A few inscriptions in hieratic script were found on the walls of the rock-cut chapel of the dignitary Shepespuptah, which is situated in the tomb complex next to the chapel of Princess Sheretnebty. The east and west walls of the chapel bear the titles and name of the owner, recording his high social position. Shepespuptah's duties included responsibility for the redistribution of offerings for the royal mortuary cults, which indicate that he held in his hands a large part of the economic production of the country. Another inscription on the blocks of the casing indicates that there was an inspection in the tomb at the end of the reign of Djedkare, which confirms the dating of the tomb to the late 5th Dynasty. Shepespuptah's physical remains found in his burial chamber show signs of serious health problems, and are reminders that wealth and power are no guarantee of an easy life. (HV)

Overall view into the courtyard of the tomb complex AS 68

62 | False door of Shepseskafankh

Limestone; w. 1.60 m, h. 3.60 m. Old Kingdom, 5th Dynasty. Abusir South – tomb of Shepseskafankh, discovered in 2013.

The false door of the official Shepseskafankh still stands in his cult chapel. Its upper lintel is missing but it is otherwise complete. Its decoration is unfinished, and so parts of the inscriptions and figures of the owner of the tomb are only outlined in red with black corrections, which was the usual practice before the stonemasons began their work. It seems that the owner of the tomb died prematurely or unexpectedly and the seventy days allowed for burial of his body were not enough for the craftsmen to be able to finish all the work. This allows us to study the different stages of the work and techniques of the ancient Egyptian craftsmen. Shepseskafankh was the overseer of (all) the physicians of Upper and Lower Egypt, physician of the royal palace, priest of the king and the gods Hathor, Khnum and Heqa. He was both the highest physician in the land and the keeper of secrets of the king. It should be noted that several other physicians were buried in this small family cemetery. (MB)

Access corridor and cult chapel in the tomb

< Shepseskafankh's false door – detail: this part of the inscription shows the craftsman's procedure in decoration – first the inscriptions were outlined in red, and then corrected in black. Only then did the master stonemason start work

63 False door of the priest Neferinpu

Limestone; 1.17 × 2.62 × 0.20 m. Old Kingdom, 5th Dynasty, reign of Nyuserre and Djedkare. Abusir South – Tomb of Neferinpu (AS 37), discovered 2007. Find numbers 1 and 2/AS37/2006 and 67/AS37/2007.

This false door consists of three large blocks of limestone, and two years of research were needed before it could be reassembled. Originally it stood in the corridor chapel of the tomb of a priest of several deceased Abusir kings, the sun god Re and the goddess of truth Maat; Neferinpu held a total of sixteen different offices and positions at court and in the royal funerary temples. The false door consists of a lintel with the prayers for Neferinpu's life in the afterlife and his seated likeness; the middle section (central panel) has on its sides the motif of the false door as entrance to the netherworld and here the owner is depicted sitting in front of a table with offerings of bread loaves and other offerings; the lowest part of the door contains most of his titles and standing figures. (MB)

View of the chapel of Neferinpu, which contained a total of four cult places. The lower part of Neferinpu's false door survived *in situ*

64 Burial of a mouse in the sarcophagus of the priest Neferinpu

Animal bones; l. ca. 7 cm. Old Kingdom, 5th Dynasty, reign of Djedkare. Abusir South – burial chamber of the tomb of Neferinpu. (AS 37), discovered 2007. Find number 50/AS37/2007.

In addition to Neferinpu's own bodily remains and some objects of funerary equipment a mouse burial was found in his sealed sarcophagus. The mouse had originally been wrapped in cloth and laid beside the knee of the deceased with its head towards the south. This find has no parallel from the Old Kingdom, but from later records it appears that the mouse may have been connected with the journey of the deceased to the other world, with the revival of the senses after the last judgment and with the god Khentiirty, who stood at the side of the sun god Re during his mythical battle with the demon Apophis. (HV)

First views into the opened sarcophagus of the priest Neferinpu

65 | Canopic jars from the tomb of the priest Neferinpu

Limestone; h. 22.5–25 cm. Old Kingdom, mid-5th Dynasty, reign of Nyuserre. Abusir South – tomb of Neferinpu (AS 37), discovered 2007. Find numbers 4–7/AS37/2007.

Starting in the 4th Dynasty, four jars that were practically identical in form and size, and usually made of limestone with flat lids, became essential parts of burials of high officials. They contained the mummified organs of the deceased: lungs, liver, stomach and intestines. Each had a different patron god, one of the four sons of Horus. Such jars were found in the burial chamber of the sun priest Neferinpu. They were placed south of his sarcophagus in a wooden cabinet with two clay seals (see no. 66). By the time of the discovery the cabinet had already disintegrated. It is noteworthy that the jars were empty. This may indicate that while Neferinpu acquired the jars to demonstrate symbolically that he was rich enough to afford costly mummification, his body was in fact never mummified. (MB)

Neferinpu's canopic jars were placed south of his sarcophagus, originally in a wooden cabinet that disintegrated in the course of the millennia

5/OO/07
6/OO/07
7/OO/07
CM

ABUSIR SOUTH

66 | Seal impressions from the burial chamber of Neferinpu

Clay; diameter 9 cm, h. 3.6 cm. Old Kingdom, 5th Dynasty, reign of Nyuserre and Djedkare. Abusir South – tomb of Neferinpu (AS 37), discovered 2007. Find number 35/AS37/2007.

Two seals made of Nile mud were originally placed on the wooden cabinet for the canopic jars that were part of the mummification ritual and traditionally contained the mummified organs of the deceased (see no. 55). Although the cabinet gradually disintegrated completely over time, the limestone jars and seal impressions survived to be found during archaeological excavations. The mud impressions show the Horus name of the ruler Djedkare and some of Neferinpu's titles: priest of the goddess Maat, guardian of the mystery, *wab* priest of the king and funerary priest in the pyramid complex of *Nyussere*, as well as a title associated with the god of wisdom Khnum. (MB)

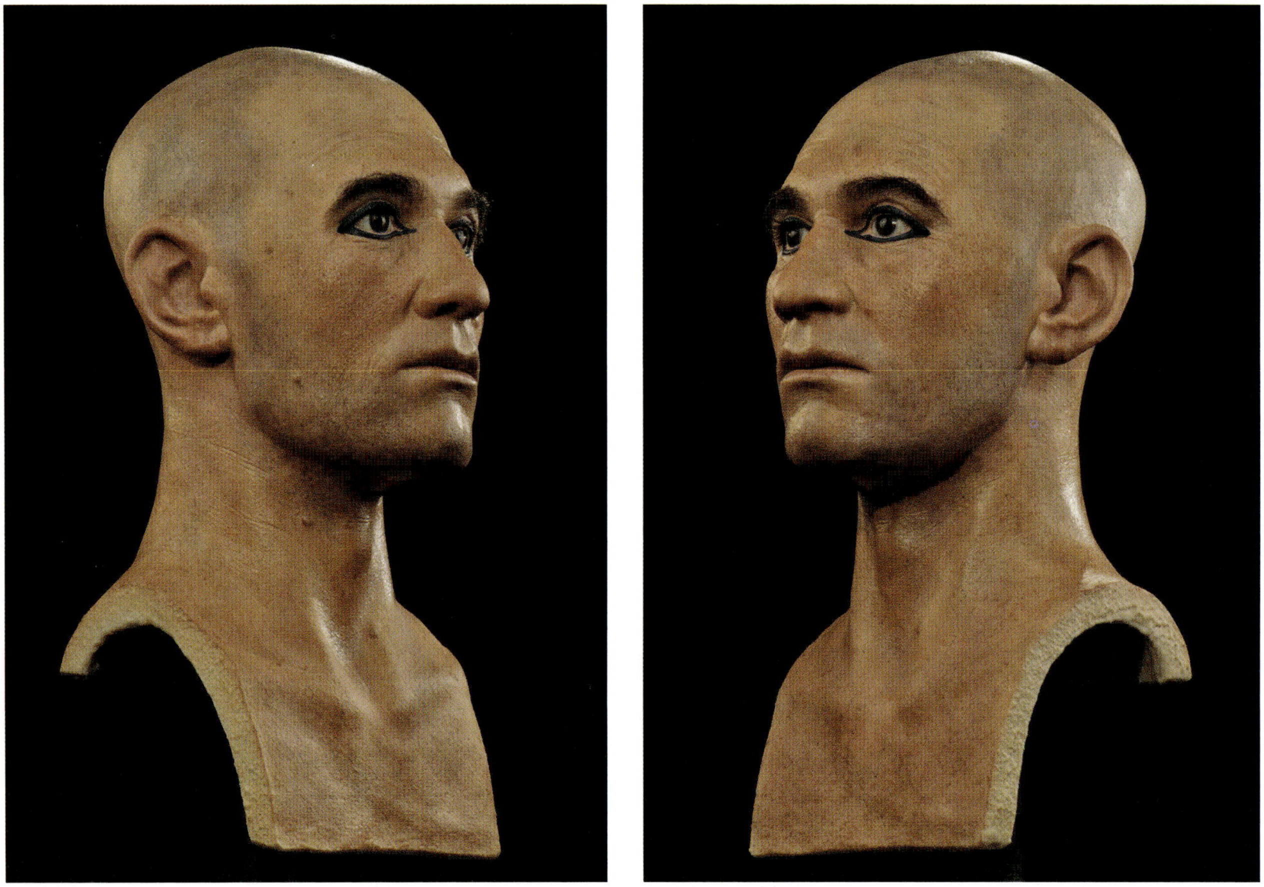

Reconstruction of Neferinpu's appearance. This was what the ancient Egyptian priest living 4,400 years ago probably looked like

67 Beer jar as a gift for the afterlife

Pottery; h. 35–41 cm, rim diameter 9.5–11.5 cm, max. diameter 18–21 cm. Old Kingdom, 5th Dynasty, reign of Djedkare. South Abusir – tomb of Neferinpu (AS 37), discovered 2007. Find numbers 3/AS37/2007, 10/AS37/2007 to 18/AS37/2007.

Beer jars are among the most common types of find in Old Kingdom cemeteries and Abusir is no exception. Usually we find dozens or even hundreds of these jars, often in combination with other vessels and objects, not only in the tombs but also in the areas around them. In the case of some poorer burials, beer jars are often the only recorded type of artefact. They were placed in the burial chambers of lower and middle-ranking dignitaries as substitutes for beer for the deceased in the afterlife. In the intact chamber of the priest Neferinpu we uncovered a total of ten complete and sealed beer jars, laid beside the limestone sarcophagus. Because the Egyptian week consisted of ten days, we can assume that the deceased was assigned one beer per day in the afterlife. The beer jars were also part of regular offering rituals in the above-ground parts of the tombs and we encounter both intact vessels placed in the cult niches as well as deposits of jars close to the entrances to the tombs. In almost all cases we can say with certainty that these offerings were purely symbolic, since these jars were not filled with real beer but with Nile mud, representing beer at a ritual level for all eternity. (KA)

The sealed beer jars of priest Neferinpu were placed west of his intact sarcophagus and were found together with a set of miniature limestone vessels

68 Copper mirror from the tomb of Neferherptah

Presumably arsenical copper; h. 19.9 cm, w. 18.5 cm, thickness 0.3 cm. End of the 5th Dynasty or 6th Dynasty. Abusir South – tomb of Neferherptah (AS 65), discovered 2010. Find number: 54/AS65/2010_c.

Tomb AS 65, belonging to the physician Neferherptah, had been damaged and thoroughly robbed. This made it all the more surprising that a mirror with the remains of a wooden handle and traces of textile used to wrap the object should have been found in shaft 1. In the Old Kingdom mirrors were made usually of arsenical copper and the largest corpus comes from Giza; the find is an isolated one in Old Kingdom tombs in Abusir. Mirrors were sometimes part of the funerary equipment of women, but also of men of the social elite of the 6th Dynasty. In the case of tomb AS 65, we can presume that the mirror belonged to Neferherptah's spouse. Apart from their practical role in body care, mirrors had a religious significance; in some rarely preserved scenes from Old Kingdom tombs we find them appearing in dance rituals dedicated to the goddess Hathor. (MO)

A mirror was found in the burial chamber of the southernmost shaft 1 in the tomb AS 65

The mirror was found after the removal of the first layers of human bone fragments and mud deposits

69 Relief of the dignitary Ankhiemaptah and his wife

Limestone; h. 42 cm, w. 98 cm, thickness 29 cm. Old Kingdom, early 6th Dynasty. Abusir South – unfinished shaft in the corridor of the tomb complex of Princess Sheretnebty, discovered in 2012. Find number 372/AS68/2013, GEM 10064.

A block adorned with sunken relief was found in one of the unfinished shafts in the corridor in front of the rock cut chapel of Princess Sheretnebty. It shows a couple sitting side by side. The hieroglyphic inscription in front of the pair contains the then usual offering formulae, titles and name of the owner Ankhiemaptah and his wife Neferhekenhathor. The place of the find suggests that the husband and wife may have been buried in one of the six shafts in the chapel of Sheretnebty. The artistic style of the reliefs nonetheless indicates that they lived slightly later than the princess, and may have belonged to the generation of her children or grandchildren. Ankhiemaptah was overseer of a gang of craftsmen, just like the dignitary Nefer, to whom the neighbouring rock-cut chapel belonged. (HV)

Shallow shaft with wedged blocks, one of them bearing inscriptions and relief of the dignitary Ankhiemaptah

ABUSIR SOUTH

70 | Stand for offerings *in situ* in front of Kaisebi's false door

Pottery, covered in red slip and fine white plaster; max. h. 51.5 cm, rim diameter 23 cm, base diameter 23.5 cm. Old Kingdom, early 6th Dynasty. Abusir South – chapel of the tomb of the dignitary Kaisebi (AS 76), discovered in 2015. Find number 9/AS76/2015.

A beautiful testimony of ritual activity was found in the chapel belonging to the dignitary Kaisebi. A tall stand was uncovered *in situ*, i.e. in its original place of use, in front of Kaisebi's lavishly decorated false door. At the time of the discovery it was missing about a fifth of its height, but further fragments were found in the debris of the room and it proved possible to restore the stand to its full height. It is exceptional not just from the point of its dimensions (it is more than half a metre tall), but also for its quality and overall craftsmanship. It was covered with highly polished red slip and subsequently coated with a white plaster during ritual activity, similarly to the walls of the chapel and the false door itself. It is very rare to find a stand of this kind in such a well-preserved condition and especially in its original archaeological context, because usually we uncover only scattered sherds of such vessels. In most cases they were part of what is known as the permanent equipment of the chapel. Such a stand would be kept in the chapel for repeated cultic practice and would be probably replaced only when damaged. Bowls, platters or trays of offerings for the deceased were placed on the stand. (KA)

View of the chapel of the dignitary Kaisebi before the excavation

< A moment during the final cleaning of the chapel. The stand was placed right in front of the false door of the deceased 4,500 years ago

71 | Altar of Sankhuptah

Limestone; 0.99 × 0.60 × 0.21 m. Old Kingdom, 6th Dynasty. Abusir South – tomb of Sankhuptah. Discovered in 2007 on the bank of the dried up Lake of Abusir. Find number 1/LA/2007.

This altar from the end of the Old Kingdom is one of the most beautiful of its kind. It was found *in situ* in the small mudbrick chapel of the official Sankhuptah, whose title identifies him as the overseer of granaries. Depicted on the altar as well as Sankhuptah himself are his wives Akhti and Nedjetempet, his eldest son and scribe Nebemtsenenet, his (yet another) eldest son Kaipuptah, his son and scribe Meryreptah, his son Werbauptah and his daughter Khenut. The altar has two rectangular basins for offerings of beer and water, a table with seven sacred oils, bread and basic offerings and a vessel with spouted bowl for ritual cleansing. Together with the accompanying prayers it therefore contains all the elements essential for life in the afterlife. (MB)

The altar was discovered on the shore of the Lake of Abusir, where nobody had expected to find an Old Kingdom tomb

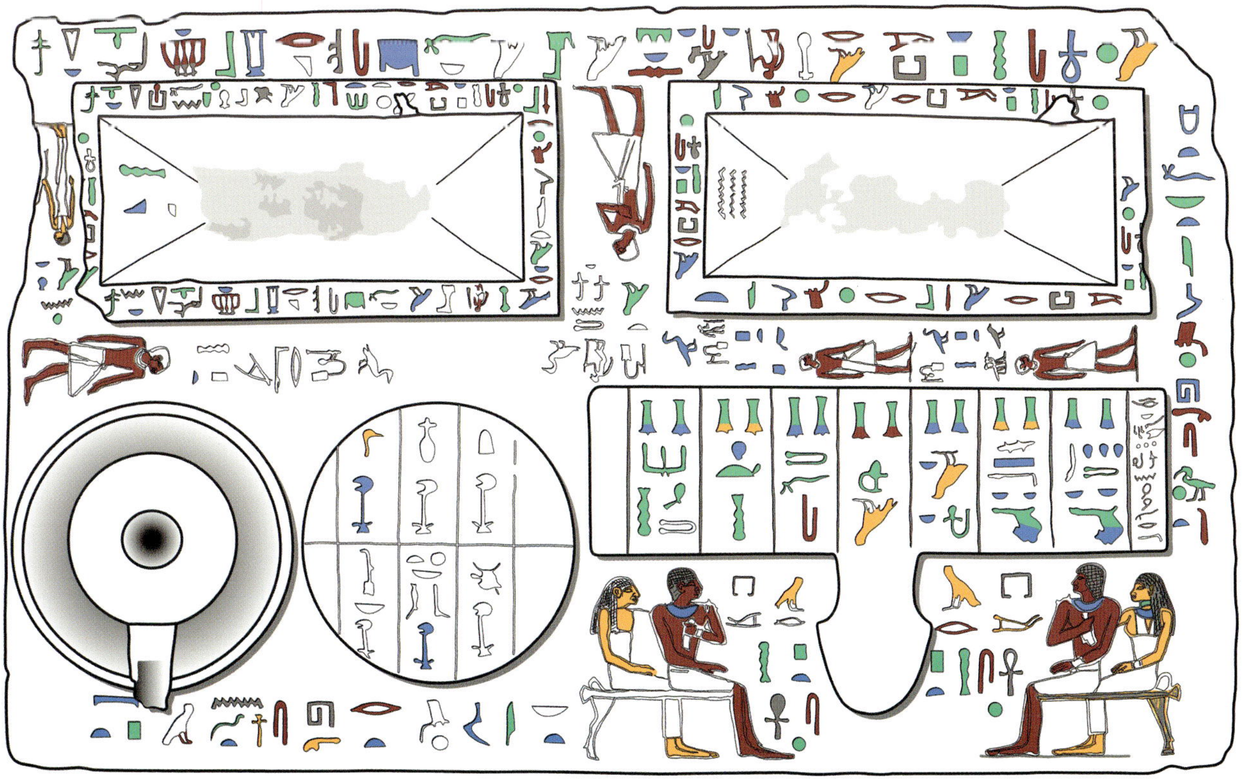

ABUSIR SOUTH

72 Travertine head-rest from Setib's burial chamber

Travertine; h. 18 cm, max. w. 16.2 cm. Old Kingdom, 6th Dynasty. Abusir South – tomb AS 79, discovered 2015. Find number 106/AS79/2015.

The head-rest, made of calcite, was part of the burial equipment of a woman called Setib. It was made of three separate parts: an upper section, stem and base. It bears the engraved inscription: "Revered before Anubis, the One upon his Hill, Setib. Revered before Osiris, royal (female) servant, Setib". In ancient Egypt head-rests served to support the head during sleep, and they were a usual part of burial equipment. For high-ranking people they were most often made of limestone, calcite or wood, while in poorer tombs we can find mudbricks or pieces of stone in the function of head-rest. This particular find was placed close to the head of the deceased Setib, who was interred in a decorated wooden coffin in the burial pit. Fortunately her burial chamber had been only partially disturbed by ancient thieves and so almost all her burial equipment including the jewels that she was wearing have been preserved. Setib's shaft was part of a tomb whose owner was probably Setib's father Khemetnu. (VD)

Setib, holding onto the robe of her mother Kerefet, is depicted with her parents and two brothers

< View into Setib's coffin, adorned with inscriptions, the head-rest is to the left of the skull

ABUSIR SOUTH

73 Musical scene with love song

Limestone; h. 32 cm.
Old Kingdom, 6th Dynasty.
Abusir South – chapel of the tomb of Inti (AS 22), discovered 2000.

A rare musical scene, showing two pairs of seated harpists and singers opposite each other, forms part of the painted decoration of the north wall of the tomb chapel of the judge and priest Inti ("He who achieved [the goals]"). The scene is accompanied by a hieroglyphic inscription containing the tune and the opening words of a song: "I love you, being captivated by your beauty." Given that these opening words mention "captivation, fascination, enchantment" by female beauty, this is most probably a love song sung by the singers depicted. If so, then here we have the very earliest surviving love song in the history of mankind, more than a thousand years older than the famous ancient Egyptian love songs from the Ramesside period, performed by female singers and musicians at banquets and celebrations held in the houses and gardens of wealthy Egyptians. (BV)

View of the north wall of the chapel of Inti during excavation

74 Block with the motif of life in a papyrus thicket

Limestone;
40 × 38 × 18 cm.
Old Kingdom, 6th Dynasty.
Abusir South – burial complex of the judge Inti, surface layers of debris, unknown owner, discovered in 2000. Find number 39/AS22/2000.

The Egyptians thought of tombs as in some sense posthumous dwellings. While the soul of the ruler, the living god on earth, departed after his death to join the gods in the heavens, the netherworld for ordinary mortals could be found inside their posthumous residences. The most important place in the above-ground part of the tomb was the cult chapel, where the mortuary cult of the deceased was conducted. Its walls were decorated with scenes of offering bearers, members of the family and priests making offerings, and scenes from the earthly world that often had a religious context. This was the case in scenes of the deceased sailing through a papyrus thicket, where he was supposed to be resurrected like the god of the underworld Osiris. (MB)

75 Set of vessels from the embalming deposit in the tomb of Inti

Pottery, covered with a red slip; rim diameter of the largest bowl ca. 35 cm, h. 15 cm, of the smaller bowls: diameter cca 20 cm, h. 9 cm. Old Kingdom, 6th Dynasty. Abusir South – burial complex of the judge Inti (AS 22), ritual shaft E, discovered in 2002.

In Abusir, apart from the burial shafts, which could be quite deep and ended in burial chambers or at least a niche for the interred remains (Inti himself was buried in a shaft 22 metres deep), we very occasionally encounter what are known as ritual shafts. They were usually very small and shallow, in most cases around just 1.5 metres deep, but quite rich in their contents: in addition to numerous fragments of pottery we also usually find pieces of textile, organic material, various beetles and sometimes a hard white substance that has been identified as remnants of natron. By far the most frequent ceramic finds in these shafts are high quality red-slipped bowls in various shapes, in exceptional cases complemented by other kinds of vessel (e.g. here we see a *hes* libation jar among the bowls). Several of them contained traces of dark resin on its inner and sometimes also outer surface. The presence of natron and resin indicates a very different function from the usual funerary contexts. According to written sources, these substances were involved in the embalming process together with the bandages, and it is therefore very likely that these vessels and other objects were originally used during the mummification and were later piously interred in these shallow shafts. (KA)

The bottom of the shallow ritual shaft E in the tomb of the judge Inti, which was not used for a burial but for the interment of what is known as an embalming deposit

JJ Shaft E

76 Face mask

Plaster; 23 × 16 cm. Old Kingdom, 6th Dynasty, reign of Pepy I. Abusir South – burial complex of the judge Inti, burial chamber of shaft B, discovered in 2002.

This mask was found in one of the secondary burial chambers built into Inti's burial complex. It belonged to a man. His burial chamber was quite small, with room only for the burial. One interesting feature of the chamber was a brick ceiling in the form of a dome. The burial itself had been entirely destroyed by robbers, but by a miracle the death mask preserving the likeness of the owner survived. The mask was created by wrapping the face of the deceased in bandages, which were then impregnated by a layer of plaster. The face mask was part of the identity of the deceased in the afterlife, ensuring that he did not lose his physical features – the statues or idealised depictions of the deceased on the walls of the tomb served the same purpose. (MB)

View of the architecture of Inti's tomb, dominated by the cult chapel

ABUSIR SOUTH

77 Copper vessels and their miniatures from the burial chamber of Inti Pepyankh

Copper or arsenical copper; *nemset* vessel: h. 17.1 cm. diameter. 13.3 cm; complete spouted jar: h. 22.5 cm, diameter 16.3 cm; complete wash basin: h. 16.5 cm, diameter 33 cm; *heset* vessel: h. 27.8 cm, diameter 7.6 cm; model vessels: max. h. 11.1 cm, max. diameter 10.7 cm. Old Kingdom, 6th Dynasty, reign of Pepy II. Abusir South – burial complex of the judge Inti, tomb AS 22, shaft A and burial chamber, discovered 2002. Find numbers: large vessels 127/AS22/2000_a–d, set of model vessels 130/AS22/2000_a–f, 134/AS22/2002, 135/AS22/2002.

This set of offering vessels from the burial chamber of Inti Pepyankh is one of the masterpieces of the Old Kingdom metalworkers. Copper or arsenical copper sheets were skilfully hammered into the final forms of the vessels. For simpler shapes just one piece of a thick sheet was used, and in the case of complex shapes, spouts were attached on where necessary. Chiselled inscriptions confirm the purpose of the vessels: they were part of the funerary repast, a ritual essential for the posthumous welfare of the deceased. This lavish set contains two pairs of spouted jars and basins, an oval *nemset* vessel and slender elegant *heset*, all of them full-size. This set was complemented by a set of miniaturised vessels made of thin sheet and a copper altar (see no. 79). Written sources testify to the use of the same kind of vessels in the cult of gods and kings, and so this set from a burial chamber also gives us an idea of the ritual equipment of temples at the same period. (MO)

Excavated vessels in their find spot, partially excavated models and altar in upper right corner

Detail of Pepyankh's name and titles engraved around the diameter of the vessel

10 cm

ABUSIR SOUTH

78 | Receptacles for food offerings from the tomb of Inti Pepyankh

Limestone: h. 9.5–21 cm, l. 21.5–48 cm, w. 16.5–28 cm. Old Kingdom, 6th Dynasty. Abusir South – burial complex of the judge Inti, burial chamber of shaft A belonging to Inti Pepyankh, discovered 2002. Find numbers 12/AS22/2002, 1–12.

The preparation of burial equipment was a matter of tremendous importance for ancient Egyptians of all social classes. A proper burial and subsequent mortuary cult carried out by members of the family or professional priests was the guarantee of an individual's posthumous survival, while funerary equipment ensured that all his or her "material" needs would be met in the afterlife. These ten limestone receptacles were found in the burial chamber of Inti Pepyankh in the complex of the priest and judge Inti from the 6th Dynasty. The total of five receptacles for offerings of fowl (goose, duck and pigeons) and another five for pieces of beef, contained the original offerings. Each receptacle had a lower section covered by a lid in the form of the offering concerned. The last two receptacles were round and originally contained rounded breads, another traditional part of ancient Egypt diet (and of modern Egyptian diet as well). (MB)

The receptacles for offerings of meat, fowl and bread were found east of the pillaged sarcophagus, close to the unique copper vessels and altar

79 Copper altar and set of miniaturised and model vessels from the burial chamber of Inti Pepyankh

Copper or arsenical copper; altar: l. 2 cm, w. 23.5 cm, h. 12 cm; miniature bowls: max. h. 9.4 cm, diameter 5.9 cm. Old Kingdom, 6th Dynasty, reign of Pepy II, discovered 2002. Find number: altar 128/AS22/2002, vessels 128/AS22/2002_d–m.

We know of only a few copper altars from the late 6th Dynasty, and the find in Abusir is most probably the biggest and heaviest. The table was made of thick sheet, with circular openings cut into it for the bowls. It has an intricate design. The rectangular top has projections on one long side and both short sides, forming two hieroglyphic signs *hetep* when viewed from above. This was no accident, because the set of copper and stone vessels on the altar (some still in their original places even after 4,300 years!) served for two important rituals: the funerary repast and the ritual of the Opening of Mouth. The bowls and *heset* vessel were used during the funerary repast, and the copper vessel with S-shaped profile, named *hatjes*, and model stone vases in basalt and rock crystal in the Opening of the Mouth. The ancient Egyptian word *hetep* meant offerings, but also the offering altar itself. The altar was supposed to ensure that Inti Pepyankh was well-nourished and content in the afterlife. (MO)

Reis Ahmad and reis Talal el-Kereti carefully uncovering the altar

80 | Scribes' palette

Travertine; case: l. 27 cm, w. 3 cm; broken lid: l. 9 cm, w. 2 cm. Old Kingdom, 6th Dynasty. Abusir South – burial complex of the judge Inti, sarcophagus of the dignitary Inti Pepyankh, discovered 2002. Find number 141/AS22/2002.

Scribes played a very important role in ancient Egypt. They were the pillar of the state administration, with the responsibility for recording harvests and farm animals and collecting taxes, and they were the political and intellectual elite of their time. In the 3rd millennium BC only at most a few thousand people in every generation knew how to read and write. This unique scribes' palette was found in the sarcophagus of Inti Pepyankh in the burial complex of the judge Inti. It consists of a case for reed pens, with a sliding lid. At one end of the case there are two hollows for the black and red powder that produced ink when mixed with water and arabic gum. Similar hollows have survived on a fragment of the lid, and in these the ink would actually be mixed – all the texts would be written in black, with red used to highlight important passages or dividing lines. This artefact had not only a practical but a significant symbolic meaning for its owner, because it indicated his prestigious social position. (MB)

The scribes' instruments were found inside the robbed sarcophagus of the owner

b
c
141-JJ-02
a

81 Set of stone receptacles for cosmetics

Travertine; h. max. 11.4 cm. Old Kingdom, middle of the 6th Dynasty, reign of Pepy I. Abusir South – burial complex of the judge Inti, sarcophagus of the official Inti Pepyankh, discovered 2002. Find numbers 133a–h/AS22/2002.

Despite their relatively small size these travertine artefacts are not miniaturised models but real cosmetic vessels that originally contained aromatic oils and unguents for the needs of the deceased. They were found north of the sarcophagus of Inti Pepyankh and had originally been placed in a wooden cabinet, which had disintegrated by the time of discovery. Cosmetics, perfumes and aromatic oils played an important role in ancient Egypt and their luxury variants were the privilege of the elite of the time, both men and women. In mortuary cult they also fulfilled a significant role in care for the deceased as he or she was initiated into life in the afterlife. The unique shapes of the different examples testify to their different specific functions. (MB)

These receptacles for cosmetics found north of the sarcophagus are another unique set from the burial chamber of Inti Pepyankh

82 | Set of copper model tool blades from the burial chamber of Inti Pepyankh

Copper or arsenical copper; chisels: max. l. 12.1 cm, max. w. 0.8 cm; adzes: max. l. 10.7 cm, max. w. 3.9 cm; axes: max. l. 6.7 cm, max. w. 6.6 cm; saws: max. l. 16.1 cm, max. w. 2.1 cm. Old Kingdom, 6th Dynasty, reign of Pepy II. Abusir South – tomb AS 22, shaft A and burial chamber, discovered in 2002. Find numbers: 125/AS22/2000, 129/AS22/2000, 140/AS22/2002.

The lavish funerary equipment of Inti Pepyankh included a set of model tool blades: chisel and adze blades, axe heads and saw blades, of the kind used by Old Kingdom carpenters and stonemasons. During his lifetime Inti never worked with these tools, as it would have been beneath his dignity. The model set was a symbol of the economic power of the Old Kingdom elite, for only a highly placed man or woman could have ordered and funded craft work. Clearly few people could have afforded a costly stone tomb and rich funerary equipment. A certain level of abstraction was prevalent in the Old Kingdom practice, with full-size functional objects represented by miniaturised model tool blades. If Inti Pepyankh had lived just a few decades later, in the First Intermediate Period, the model of an entire craft workshop would have been placed in his burial chamber with him. (MO)

Detail of the binding of the chisel blades. Corrosion has preserved the cord as well

Batch of copper model tool blades

10 cm

83 Imported vessels for Qar the Younger

Pottery; max. height of vessels 0.53 m. Old Kingdom, 6th Dynasty, reign of Pepy II. Abusir South – tomb of Qar the Younger, south-east corner of the burial chamber, discovered 2000. Find number 86, I–15/AS17/2000.

Wine was imported into Egypt in pots that came mainly from Syria-Palestine. Archaeological discoveries suggest that wine had become one of the most sought-after luxury commodities of the elite at the latest from the end the 4th millennium BC. Finds of similar vessels from the cemeteries in Abydos, Giza, Saqqara and other sites show the importance of imported wine for the expression of social prestige throughout the 3rd millennium BC. These finds include imported vessels in the tombs of high-ranking officials in Abusir, including Qar the Younger (the son of the vizier Qar) – dated to the 23rd century BC. They are mute witness to the role of wine in ensuring a good life in the afterlife in the eyes of the elites of the time. (MB)

Syro-Palestinian amphorae for wine, and their copies, were intended to ensure Qar the Younger's pleasurable life in the afterlife

84 Tablet of the seven sacred oils

Travertine; 16.5 × 8.4 × 1.1 cm. Old Kingdom, 6th Dynasty. Abusir South – burial chamber of the tomb of Senedjemib, discovered in 2001. Find number 122/AS 18/2001.

This beautiful painted tablet of the seven sacred oils was an essential part of the funerary equipment of the judicial official and overseer of the mortuary priests Senedjemib ("He who gladdens the mind"). In addition to a brief formula and the title and name of the owner, the hieroglyphic text mentions precious oils, among which we can tentatively identify mint, pine, cedar and olive oil. The table showing the names of the seven most important oils was supposed to ensure for the owner their abundance in the next world and so his ability to regenerate his body through their use. This was a permanent stone substitute for the oils, their efficacy increased still more by the potency of the number seven. Seven was a number always endowed with symbolic meaning in ancient Egypt, not only in religion and magic, but also in architecture and art. (BV)

View of the sarcophagus in the burial chamber of Senedjemib's tomb

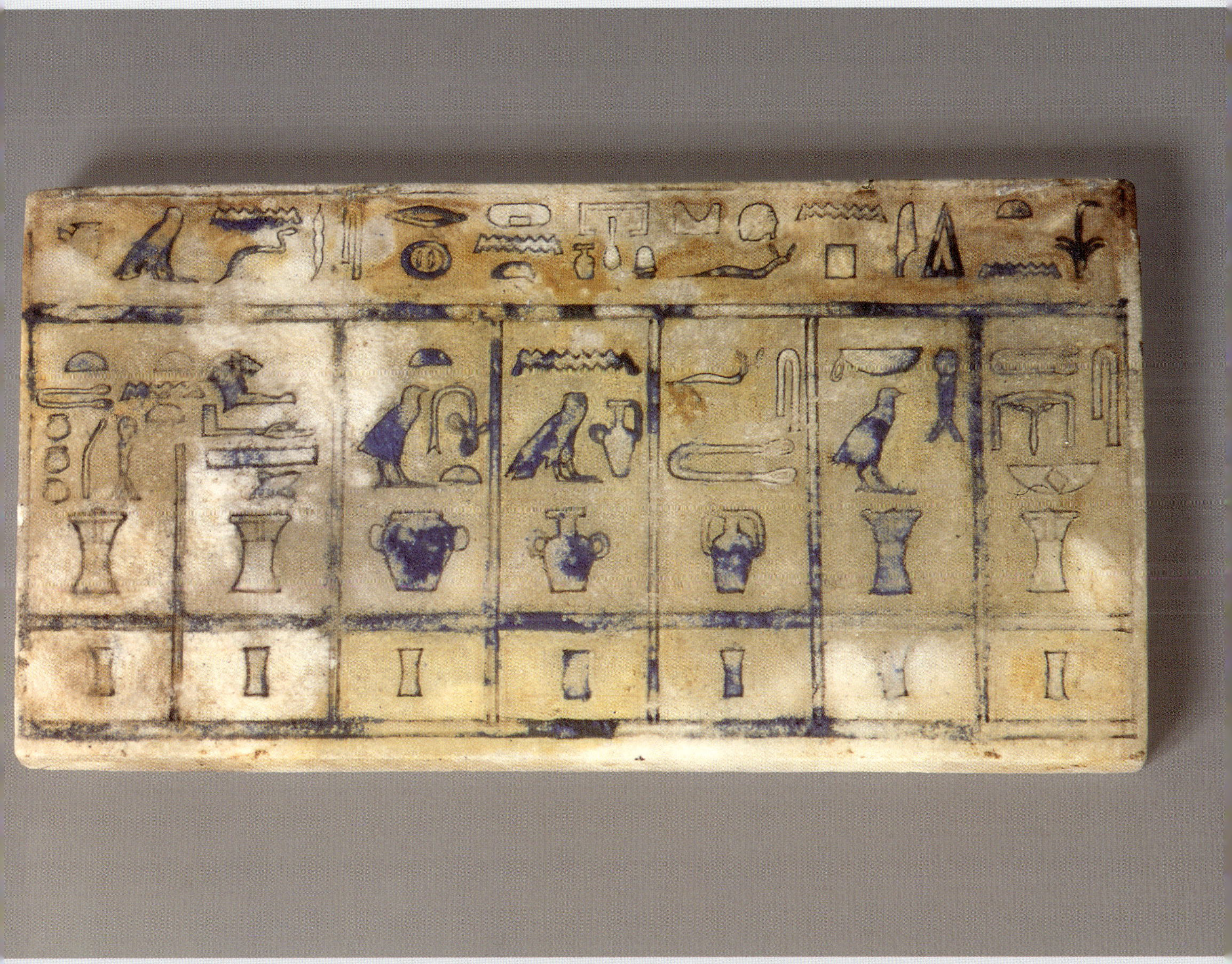

85 Engaged statues of Meryherishef

Limestone; 1.27 × 88 × 27 cm. Old Kingdom, 6th Dynasty. Abusir South – burial complex of the judge Inti, filling of shaft A, discovered 2000. Find number 16/AS22/2000.

A few large limestone blocks with engaged statues and inscriptions belonging to a priest who lived at the end of the Old Kingdom and was called Meryherishef have been discovered in Abusir. On this particular block we see a standing Meryherishef dressed in a short close-fitting kilt and with a wig falling almost to his shoulders. The accompanying inscriptions give his name and titles, the most important of which was the office of priest of the *meret* shrine of the goddess Hathor. These shrines played a prominent role in the cult of the king and the demonstration of his close relationship with the ancient Egyptian gods, in this case the goddess Hathor. Like several others this block comes from Meryherishef's tomb, but the tomb itself has yet to be located. The location of the tomb is one of many still unsolved mysteries of the cemetery in Abusir South. (MB)

Detail of the engaged statue of Meryherishef with elaborately worked wig

86 | Hemshezemtet's lintel with green inscription

Limestone with polychrome decoration in sunken relief; 66 × 36 × 15 cm. Old Kingdom, 6th Dynasty. Abusir South – tomb of Hemshezemtet (AS 82), discovered in 2015. Find number 56/AS82/2015.

The tomb of Hemshezemtet is interesting both for the architectural design and painted decoration of the walls of the chapel (of which only fragments survive), and also for the titulary of its owner. Hemshezemtet's name and titles have been preserved only in one place, in the inscription on the lintel placed above the niche in the funerary chapel of his tomb. The lintel is visually subdivided into two horizontal sections. The upper section contains eight lines of text written in small hieroglyphic signs rendered in sunken relief and filled in green. In a mortuary context the choice of green was no accident. It was associated with the god Osiris and the symbolism of resurrection and was often used in the Pyramid Texts. The lower part of the lintel consists of a framed line of text in larger painted hieroglyphs. The inscription offers a long list of Hemshezemtet's titles, which are mostly related to judicial functions. Some of these titles had never been encountered by archaeologists before, like Hemshezemtet's name, which can be translated as "Servant of the goddess Shezemtet". It is significant that Hemshezemtet was also a priest of the goddess. (VD)

When discovered, Hemshezemtet's chapel was filled with rubble almost up to the ceiling

87 Fan from the tomb of Hemshezemtet

Rush and grass plants (*Juncus cf. maritimus* and *Poacea*); w. 28.4, h. 19.2 cm. Old Kingdom, 6th Dynasty. Abusir South – tomb of Hemshezemtet (AS 82), discovered 2015. Find number 58/AS82/2015.

The hot Egyptian climate meant that fans were a common part of everyday life in ancient Egypt. Fans could vary greatly in materials and size, depending on the social rank of the owner. Palm leaves could serve as simple if not durable fans. At the other end of the scale were elaborately worked fans made of precious materials like gold and ostrich feathers. Probably the best-known finds of this type are the fans from the tomb of King Tutankhamun, from the New Kingdom. Archaeological discoveries of fans from earlier periods are quite rare, but a fan survived in the funerary chapel of the judicial official Hemshezemtet. The fan is semicircular in shape and made of slender sticks woven together and fastened with string. It was evidently originally part of a life-size wooden statue of the tomb owner placed in the niche of the chapel. A fan appears in the relief decoration of the tomb of the vizier Ptahshepses in Abusir, for example, where one of the funerary priests is holding it. (VD)

Also found in the chapel were the remains of a life-size statue

88 | Wooden statue

Wood with polychromy; h. 40 cm. Old Kingdom, probably 6th Dynasty. Abusir South – cult structure (AS 82b), discovered 2015. Find number 24/AS82b/2015.

The statue was the focal point in the intact cult structure, where it looked down from a niche built under the ceiling in the western wall onto dozens of wooden human figurines placed at regular intervals. The identification of its owner and the context of the building in its relationship to the neighbouring tombs is still uncertain. The statue represents a striding naked man with a short wig and with inlaid eyes that give the impression of magical power in its gaze. The right hand, hanging down straight, originally held a sceptre, while the left, bent at the elbow, grasped a long staff. Both objects were symbols of high social status. The surface of the statue was originally covered with white plaster and painted with a reddish-brown pigment, traces of which survive on the back. The proportions of the statue are symmetrical and the body is finely modelled. The feet, parts of the calves and the base have not survived, and neither has the kilt, which was probably made of textile. (VD)

The wooden statue of the tomb owner was placed in a niche in the west wall of the cult structure, and looked down on a crowd of dozens of other wooden human figurines

89 | The oldest ushabti from Egypt

Acacia wood; h. ca. 9–10 cm. End of the Old Kingdom? Abusir South – object AS 82, filling of shaft 2. Discovered 2016. Find number 17/AS82/2015.

Several dozen small male figurines made of acacia wood were found north-west of the cemetery of Shepseskafankh in a complex of shafts investigated in 2015. An arched brick chamber, which contained the set of wooden models and in a niche a wooden figurine of their owner (whose name is unknown, see no. 88) had been built on the bottom of one of the shafts. The figurines had been placed on wooden pedestals, always in groups of roughly ten. It is reasonable to assume that here we have some of the earliest examples of figurines of servants – later ushabti, who were supposed to carry out physical labour for the deceased in the next world and to take care of his needs. All the figurines are dressed in short kilts and close-fitting wigs. Their original polychromy has partially survived. (MB)

View of the surface of the structures with the mouths of the shafts leading to the serdab with ushabti

Interior with ushabti during archaeological documentation

90 Cartouche of Ramesses II

Painted limestone; h. 22 cm, l. 39 cm. New Kingdom, 19th Dynasty. Abusir South – east, Temple of Ramesses II, discovered 2017.

The first rulers of the New Kingdom were well aware of the political, economic and above all religious significance of ancient Memphis. The flowering of the town was reflected in the expansion of the cemeteries used by the inhabitants of the town in the course of the New Kingdom, with the Saqqara necropolis becoming the most prestigious. The cemetery that extended south of the causeway of Unas was used from the middle of the 18th Dynasty up to the reigns of the first Ramesses, when important officials of the royal court and priests found their last resting places here. Although our idea of Memphis in the period of the New Kingdom is closely bound up with cemeteries, both written and archaeological evidence indicates the presence of sacred monuments as well. One is the temple that Ramesses II (who ruled 1279–1213 BC) had erected in Abusir – on the bank of what was known as the Lake of Abusir. Some of the limestone blocks that were parts of the decorative programme of this temple carry elements of the royal titulary. On the block illustrated here it is part of a cartouche with the royal family name (known as the nomen) of Ramesses II, i.e. Ramesses-Meryamun – "Ramesses, beloved by Amun". (JM)

The temple of Ramesses II from the south-east (on the left); the photograph on the right shows its outline

91 | Mask of a cow

Acacia wood; h. 51 cm, w. 28 cm. Late Period. Abusir South – surface find in 2002.

This unique mask was discovered by chance in the surface layer of sand in Abusir South. Its original location is unknown. It is a burial mask made of local acacia wood and originally fastened to the head of a mummified sacred cow. The cow was the personification of the goddess of love and protective goddess of mothers, Hathor, who was worshipped in Egypt from the earliest times. Her cult, like the cult of the other animals considered by the ancient Egyptians to be sacred, such as cats, ibises, bulls, baboons and dogs, reached the peak of its popularity in the Late Period, i.e. in the course of the first half of the 1st millennium BC. In the context of the Saqqara cemeteries of sacred animals, Hathor was regarded as the mother of the bull Apis. Sacred cows were buried in a cemetery in North Saqqara. (MB)

The unique face mask of a cow burial suggests that the discovery of a cemetery of sacred cows can be expected in Abusir

92 | Aryballos-shaped lekythos with a sphinx

Pottery; h. 7. 5 cm, diameter of edge 3 cm; diameter of bottom 5.2 cm. 4th century BC. Abusir South – structure AS 33, sand filling of the shaft, about 1 m below the surface (shaft 21), discovered in 2005. Find number 2/AS33/2005.

This red-figure lekythos has survived intact even though it comes from the secondary sand filling of the shaft in structure AS 33 in Abusir South. Typologically it is an Attic ceramic pot – an aryballos-shaped lekythos with low squat body and small vertical handle. Its entire surface is covered with a lustrous black glaze, from which the motif of recumbent sphinx stands out (female figures, or just their heads with the typical "melon" hairstyle, are much more frequent on such vessels). Originally these little vases were filled with oil for men to anoint themselves with after a bath or sport, or with perfume, in this case part of the cosmetic equipment of Greek women not only in Greece but elsewhere in the chore, because Greeks liked to preserve their *modo graeco* even when abroad. (KS)

View of the south-west corner of mastaba AS 33, clearly showing the outlines of the secondary dug shaft in which the Attic lekythos was found at a depth of roughly 1 m

Group of shaft tombs from the middle of the 1st millennium BC in Abusir West

LADISLAV BAREŠ

For many centuries the ancient Egyptians seem to have ignored the slightly undulating low elevation about 200–300 metres south-west of the group of royal pyramids. It was only at the very end of the 26th Dynasty, sometime between the years 540 and 525 BC, that a group of high-ranking dignitaries at the royal court selected it for the construction of their tombs. We can only speculate about the reasons for the choice of this site. It may have been important that visually it lies on the straight line connecting the biggest Egyptian pyramids in Giza with the oldest pyramid complex in the country, in nearby Saqqara, which belonged to the pharaoh Netjerykhet (Djoser), and represented the head of two shallow valleys running from the east and the south-east. It is also close to older royal buildings, and so a place sanctified by long tradition, and probably also near the cemetery of foreign mercenary soldiers whom these dignitaries commanded. The geological substructure here, formed by a massive layer of hardened mud of the Tertiary Sea, was suitable for the construction of tombs.

The central part of a tomb of this type is a burial chamber built of limestone blocks at the bottom of a large (up to 12 × 12 metres) shaft dug to a depth of up to 25 metres. The shaft was filled in again after completion of the tomb and so access to the burial chamber was via a narrow secondary shaft and then along a horizontal corridor leading directly to the entrance to the burial chamber, and more a tunnel than a passage. Situating the burial chambers far below the surface seems to have been intended as a way of bringing the mummies of their owners as close as possible to the underground kingdom of the dead, ruled by the god Osiris, but also as an attempt to protect them from tomb robbers. At least in some cases the parts of these buildings above ground were grandly constructed and richly adorned, although later almost wholly destroyed.

The oldest tomb in the whole group is clearly that of the famous Udjahorresnet, whose statue in the Vatican Museums, or rather the inscription on it, remains the most extensive Egyptian source for events surrounding the conquest of Egypt by the Persian ruler Cambyses in 525 BC. After the occupation of the country by the Persians, Udjahorresnet, who was originally the commander of foreign mercenaries and admiral of the fleet, became one of the most important local collaborators with the new rulers.

< View into the interior of the main shaft of the tomb of Iufaa, dug into a thick layer of the sediments of the Tertiary Sea. Ancient thieves managed to get down to this level, but fortunately for us they did not get as far as the roof of the burial chamber, only about a metre further down

Only one of the whole group of tombs was never robbed in antiquity. This was the tomb of the priest Iufaa. His burial chamber and parts of his sarcophagi are richly adorned with often unique texts and scenes that were supposed to make his journey to the next world easier and secure him a blessed eternal life.

The burial chamber and double sarcophagus of the general Menekhibnekau likewise contains a quantity of texts and scenes carved in relief. Little remains of his once lavish

View of Abusir West in 2002, with Udjahorresnet's tomb on the right and Iufaa's tomb on the left; at the time of the photograph the excavation of Menekhibnekau's tomb and tomb AW 6 had not yet started

funerary equipment, but the remnants include a unique official seal, for example. In addition to the three large tombs already mentioned there are another two, as yet only partially excavated structures of similar size, and as many as five or six smaller tombs, of which two have now been excavated. One of the smaller tombs, likewise with a decorated burial chamber, belonged to the courtier Padihor.

93 Foundation deposits of the tomb of the admiral Udjahorresnet

Pottery, copper, wood, Egyptian faience. Late Period, 26th Dynasty. Abusir West – shaft tomb of Udjahorresnet (AW I), discovered in 1993. Find numbers 204/H/93 (NW corner), 209/H/93 (NE corner), 213/H/93 (SW corner).

Three sets of foundation deposits were placed into rectangular depressions of roughly the same size in the north-west, north-east and south-east corners of the limestone enclosure wall of Udjahorresnet's huge shaft tomb in the Saite-Persian cemetery in Abusir West (the south-western deposit has not been found). The contents of the separate sets differ slightly but they essentially consisted of a few ceramic miniatures, pieces of copper, little wooden tablets with or without traces of gilding and a set of little faience tablets, some of them bearing the name of King Ahmose II (Amasis) in cartouche – a fact that has been an enormous help in dating the tomb and the whole Saite-Persian cemetery founded by Udjahorresnet. The foundation deposits are an entirely unique find in the context of large shaft tombs from the Late Period. Foundation deposits were placed in the corners of important buildings in the belief that they had the magic power to preserve them for eternity. (KS)

The foundation deposit originally placed in a small hollow under the north-eastern corner of the enclosure wall of Udjahorresnet's tomb, soon after excavation

94 Double sarcophagus of the priest Iufaa

Outer sarcophagus: white limestone; l. 3.8 m, w. 2.3 m, h. of bottom part 1.4 m, thickness of the lid with bevelled side edges 1 m. Inner sarcophagus: basalt; l. 2.2 m, w. max. 0.9 m, inserted into lower part of outer sarcophagus, in a hollow 2.36 m long, max. 1 m wide and 1.04 m deep. Late Period, end of the 26th to beginning of the 27th Dynasty. Abusir West – burial chamber of the tomb of Iufaa (AW 2), discovered in 1996.

The massive double sarcophagus filled almost the entire interior of Iufaa's burial chamber, which lies at the bottom of a huge shaft at a depth of about 20 metres. Only around half a metre of free space remained on both sides of the sarcophagus and there was only about 80 centimetres between its lid and the arched ceiling. The outer sarcophagus is made of two monolithic blocks, and the anthropoid inner sarcophagus (i.e. a sarcophagus in the shape of a recumbent human mummy) lay in a hollow in the bottom block. Sarcophagi of this type, sometimes with yet another wooden coffin inside, were used in the period around the middle of the 1st millennium BC for the interment of the mummified bodies of high-ranking dignitaries. Iufaa was undoubtedly one of this elite group, although he seems to have died after a long serious illness at what would otherwise have been the very beginning of his career. (LB)

The lifting of the lid of the inner sarcophagus was a challenging test of the abilities of all members of the team

95 | Bead net on the mummy of the priest Iufaa

Egyptian faience; tubular beads with a pale blue glaze: l. 1–3 cm, diameter ca. 2 mm; tiny round beads (blue, green, red, black, yellow colour): diameter ca. 1 mm. Late Period, end of the 26th to beginning of the 27th Dynasty. Abusir West – burial chamber of the tomb of Iufaa (AW 2), discovered after the opening of the inner sarcophagus in 1998. Find number 89/R/98.

The mummy of the priest Iufaa was guarded by several layers of protection, both real (i.e. the tomb, the walls of the burial chamber, the double sarcophagus, wooden coffin and linen bandages) and magical. Apart from amulets inserted directly into the bandages around the body of the deceased, the main magical protection was the intricately worked net of faience beads that covered the whole mummy. A gilded face mask, modelled in plaster, was part of this net. While the longer tubular beads of Egyptian faience with pale blue glaze formed the basis of the net, tiny round beads in various colours were used to create the likenesses of gods: the kneeling sky goddess Nut with her winged arms outstretched in a protective gesture, the four sons of Horus who symbolised the four points of the compass, and the traditional maternal goddesses Isis and Nephthys. In the 7th and 6th centuries BC similar nets appear on the mummies of high-ranking dignitaries and also, for example, on the body of Iufaa's sister Imakhetkherresnet, who was buried in one of the secondary corridors of Iufaa's tomb. (LB)

The mummy of Iufaa after the lifting of the lid of the inner sarcophagus

96 Canopic jars of the priest Iufaa

Travertine; h. 38–39 cm (bottom 26.5–29.5 cm, lid 10–12 cm), max. diameter 16.5–18.5 cm. Late Period, end of the 26th to beginning of the 27th Dynasty. Abusir West – burial chamber of the tomb of Iufaa (AW 2), discovered in 1996. Find number 71/R/96a–d.

The basic shape of canopic jars, which were used for the storage of the organs removed from the body during mummification, remained the same from the 3rd millennium BC, but the form of their lids changed over time. Particularly in the 1st millennium BC, the lids were quite often given the form of the heads of what were known as the four sons of Horus: Imsety (associated with protection of the liver) had a human head, Duamutef (protecting the stomach) a jackal head, Kebehsenuef (protecting the bowels) an falcon head and Hapy (protecting the lungs) a baboon head. Further protection was provided by another four selected goddesses associated with the individual canopic jars, i.e. Isis, Neith, Selqis and Nephthys, and short texts on the outer side. Inside the canopic jars the organs were covered in melted resin which, as can be seen, sometimes dripped over the edge. The canopic jars were either left free standing in the burial chamber or – as in Iufaa's case – placed in pairs in two decorated wooden chests. (LB)

Detail of one of Iufaa's canopic jars. It was originally supposed to contain his lungs, and so entrusted to the protection of the god Hapy and the goddess Nephthys, whose name is repeated by a small black sign under the chin of the face

>> The canopic jars were originally placed in pairs in black painted wooden cabinets set in the narrow gap between the outer sarcophagus and the wall of the burial chamber, but moisture caused the wood to rot away

97 Procession of demons on the inner sarcophagus of Iufaa

Basalt; sunken relief. Late Period, end of the 26th to beginning of the 27th Dynasty. Abusir West – burial chamber of the tomb of Iufaa (AW 2), discovered after the opening of the double sarcophagus in 1998.

A procession of almost seventy demons and protective gods runs along both sides of the outer upper edge of the bottom half of Iufaa's inner sarcophagus from the head almost to the knees. The earliest example of a similar group of protective gods and demons is to be found on the sarcophagus of the 19th Dynasty pharaoh Merenptah, reused roughly three centuries later for the burial of the pharaoh Pasbakhaenniut (Smendes, 21st Dynasty), and apart from this example in Abusir it appears only on a few coffins and sarcophagi of the 1st millennium BC. The gods and demons are often depicted in threatening positions (including *en face*, which is relatively unusual in Egyptian art) and with a variety of weapons. In their terrifying character they are reminiscent of the guardians of the gates of the underworld described in Chapter 144 of the Book of the Dead, which we also encounter in the decoration of the neighbouring burial chamber of the tomb of Menekhibnekau (see also no. 105). (LB)

Part of the long procession of underworld protective demons that runs along the upper section of the lower half of Iufaa's basalt sarcophagus. The demons are turned towards the head of the deceased, where they concentrate their attention for various reasons including the need to protect its form

98 Relief of "dancing cows" on the wall of Iufaa's burial chamber

Limestone; low relief with no trace of polychromy. Late Period, end of the 26th to beginning of the 27th Dynasty. Abusir West – south wall of the burial chamber of Iufaa's tomb (AW 2), discovered in 1996.

The walls of Iufaa's burial chamber and both of his sarcophagi were almost completely covered in texts and scenes intended to alleviate the earthly suffering of this long ailing priest and at the moment of his death to ensure his safe transition to the next world and his eternal blissful life there. Symbols played an important role, including those that are hard for us to understand such as these strange beings with the heads and bodies of cows (animals associated with maternal protection in the beliefs of the ancient Egyptians) and other features supposed to have magical protective power, like the rearing sacred cobras. For many years these hybrid creatures remained an isolated iconographic mystery, but a few years ago the same beings were found painted on the bandages of a mummy about two to three centuries younger, and this discovery confirmed their protective function. (LB)

These symbols, resembling dancing cows, are part of the decoration of the south wall of Iufaa's burial chamber. The texts and reliefs on this wall were intended primarily to provide the soul of the deceased with everything needed for a happy eternal existence in the other world

99 "Snake Encyclopaedia" from the burial chamber of the priest Iufaa

Limestone; low relief with no trace of polychromy. Late Period, end of the 26th to beginning of the 27th Dynasty. Abusir West – burial chamber of Iufaa's tomb (AW 2), discovered in 1996. Number AW4 CWA.

The arched section of the west wall of Iufaa's burial chamber is filled with eight texts separated by lines. Six of these are accompanied by illustrations showing snakes or creatures similar to snakes. These texts form a kind of encyclopaedia of secret knowledge relating to mythical snakes and they all have a similar structure. Most start with the phrase, "As for this snake" and continue with a description of its earthly and sacred form, its location and the ritual activities that need to be carried out for it. Where the name of the snake is not kept secret, it is given, for example one of the snakes here is called, "He who calls those who are in their fire". Some snakes also have dietary taboos relating to meat or grain, for example. Almost all are accompanied by a note to the effect that this is a being that comes forth on the first day of the new year. On the opposite arch of the east wall is a similar text and a depiction of the god Tutu, whose task was to master the demons released into the world at the end of each year by one of the belligerent goddesses. Evidently the snakes could help Tutu in this struggle. In this motif too we see the theme of battle against disease, which to judge by the condition of his mummy tormented Iufaa for most of his life. There are many indications that the text was originally an initiatory aid created by a magician, healer and priest of the scorpion goddess Selkis, who was responsible for the treatment of snakebite among other conditions and from whose circle there has survived an encyclopaedia of the real snakes of ancient Egypt. (RL, JJ)

The god Tutu in the form of a striding sphinx with a tail ending in a snake head is one of the dominating images on the east wall of Iufaa's burial chamber. This god, already appearing in texts in the middle of the 2nd Millennium BC, appears here for the first time in all his beauty

The semicircular arched upper part of the west wall of Iufaa's burial chamber is almost completely filled with the description and depiction of a group of protective beings in serpent form, and it is only a slight exaggeration to call it a "Snake Encyclopaedia"

100 Purification ritual from the tomb of the priest Iufaa

Limestone: low relief with no trace of polychromy. Late Period, end of the 26th to beginning of the 27th Dynasty. Abusir West – burial chamber of the tomb of Iufaa (AW 2), discovered in 1996. Numbers AW 4 CN, AW 4 CE.

The whole north wall of Iufaa's burial chamber and a large part of the east wall is covered with the text of a purification ritual with a total of four accompanying myths. The text of the ritual was earlier known only from one papyrus of the Graeco-Roman Period, and then only in part. Iufaa's version expands the known text by roughly two thirds. It is only in Iufaa's tomb that we find a heading for the whole text: "(How) to wash a mummy and carry out its purification". This title was clearly created secondarily during the adaptation of the whole ritual from its originally royal context, where its purpose was to purify the ruler before his coronation, to its non-royal and mortuary context, where it was performed on a mummy. In the Late Period this adaptation of originally royal texts for non-royal mortuary uses was quite common. The accompanying myths explain why this particular ritual appears in Iufaa's tomb. It is because originally the ritual related to the purification of the sun god before the creation of the world, and it is with the sun god that Iufaa identifies most often in his tomb. In addition to the original purification myth, with the sun hidden in the circle of a uroboros, we also find the myth of the origin of divine awe and protective gods in the form of sea serpents. (RL)

The uroboros, a snake in a circle biting its own tail, was a widely used symbol in ancient Egypt. In this particular case it refers to the purification of the deceased Iufaa as an important part of preparations for his transition to the next world

As the first people to enter Iufaa's burial chamber for 2,500 years, initially the archaeologists could see only the upper section of its lavish relief, for example this detail of the north wall, with one of the ushabti cabinets still lying in front of it

101 Texts against Apophis from the tomb of the priest Iufaa

Limestone; sunken relief. Late Period, end of the 26th to beginning of the 27th Dynasty. Abusir West – burial chamber of the tomb of Iufaa (AW 2), discovered in 1996. Numbers AW 4 ToSo; AW 4 ToNi.

The most important scene in Iufaa's tomb is that of the rising sun in the arch of the east wall of the burial chamber. According to most of the texts Iufaa aspired to join the sun god and be reborn with him in the east into eternal life. The snake demon Apophis was the greatest enemy of the sun god, and each night would attack him in an attempt to prevent his coming forth into the new day. This makes it logical for Iufaa to have wanted texts on the defeat of Apophis and the victory of the god Re in his tomb, and even twice over – on both the inner and outer sides of the outer limestone sarcophagus. Because the text is very close to the body of the deceased it does not speak directly of the fight with Apophis, but of his defeat and the moment of the triumph of the sun god and with him of Iufaa. The whole text starts with the cry, "It is decided! I am the victor!" It is interesting that the text also includes the wish that in the next world Iufaa should be protected against longterm confinement to his bed, which was the state that he had suffered towards the end of his life. The determinative of the snake in Apophis's name represents a snake already defeated, with knives stabbed into his coils. Hence neither the text nor the image could in any way threaten Iufaa. (RL)

The inside of the lower half of Iufaa's limestone outer sarcophagus was also decorated with a quantity of texts and pictures, which is rather unusual for this form of burial. What is more, the texts and images were not only carved in relief, but coloured in

102 Chest with vessels for sacred oils from Iufaa's burial chamber

Two types of wood of different colour (lighter and darker); l. 44 cm, w. 35.5 cm, h. 61 cm. Late Period, end of the 26th to beginning of the 27th Dynasty. Abusir West – in the layer of sand by the west wall of the burial chamber of Iufaa's tomb (AW 2), discovered in 1996. Find number 51/R/96.

Iufaa's quite rich funerary equipment was placed in the narrow passage between the walls of the burial chamber and the sides of the massive double sarcophagus. It included a luxurious inlaid wooden chest on four legs, originally with a two-section lid closed from above. The high humidity in the chamber caused the bottom of the cabinet – like its lid – to disintegrate, and its contents fell out onto the stone block on which it had originally stood. At the moment of discovery, therefore, beneath the remnants of the cabinet lay a heap of almost thirty faience and ceramic vessels for sacred oils and unguents (usually with the contents indicated on the outer side) and among them a larger bronze vessel, two model offering tables, a few amulets and small magic bricks, and a few dozen bent copper wires in imitation of the copper ingots used for millennia as the forerunners of coin. (LB)

Although the wooden coffin protecting Iufaa's mummy inside the double sarcophagus had almost completely disintegrated as a result of the humidity, this small wooden chest, originally standing just inside the entrance, had survived in good condition

103 | Texts for the magical protection of the body of the deceased

Basalt and greywacke; l. 236 cm, w. 76 cm (Iufaa); l. ca. 240 cm, w. 106 cm (Menekhibnekau). Late Period, end of the 26th to beginning of the 27th Dynasty. Abusir West – burial chamber of the tomb of Iufaa (AW 2) and the tomb of Menekhibnekau (AW 5).

In the shaft tombs of the priest Iufaa and the general Menekhibnekau archaeologists found two almost identical versions of a previously unrecorded religious-magical text that was supposed to provide magical protection for the body of the deceased and allow him a smooth passage to the next world. In both cases this new textual composition was placed on the lid of the inner sarcophagus, as close as possible to the body of the deceased, either on the bottom of the sarcophagus (in the case of Iufaa's burial, top photo) or its upper side (in Menekhibnekau's sarcophagus). This still isolated, strangely structured text is more like a table than a usual text in appearance. It starts by glorifying the universal authority of the sun god Re, describing the functions and power of the 14 parts of his body from head to feet. It then enumerates all potential opponents of Re's authority, from the gods and the blessed dead to ordinary people and other creatures, and warns them all against any actions directed against Re and the parts of his body. In the end the deceased himself enters the scene to assure the sun god that he will protect him against any dangers. For this service the deceased will be rewarded in the same way, by the greatest possible protection in the sense of the magical linkage of the fate of the individual parts of his body with the fate prepared for the god Re himself in the next world. On this basis the deceased seeks to make sure of an easy entry into the kingdom of the blessed dead and an unshakeable position within it. (JJ, DB)

Unlike Iufaa's double sarcophagus, which remained completely intact, thieves in antiquity severely damaged Menekhibnekau's sarcophagi (the exterior limestone and the inner, carved from greywacke) in order to drag out the mummy of the deceased

104 Wooden Book of the Dead of Nekau

Cedar wood; originally 6 small tablets with dimensions 34–40 cm × 13–20 cm. Late Period, end of the 26th to beginning of the 27th Dynasty. Abusir West – tomb of Iufaa (AW 2), burial chamber of the priest Neferibreseneb called Nekau, opened in 2003. Find number 181/R/03.

This tablet is part of an extraordinary find – the only known example of the Egyptian Book of the Dead written on small wooden tablets. The usual material for these kinds of texts was a papyrus scroll, or sometimes the mummification bandages or the linen shroud of the deceased. This small wooden tablet together with another five were inscribed with a selection of shorter spells from the Book of the Dead and were placed in the tomb of Neferibreseneb known as Nekau, which was hewn into the west shaft of the tomb of Iufaa in Abusir. All the wooden tablets were discovered in 2003 between Nekau's outer and inner coffins, by the left hand of the deceased. They comprised a set of six tablets each 34–40 cm in length and 13–20 cm in height. In the case of four of the tablets the texts from the Book of the Dead were written directly onto the wood, on both sides. The texts of the two others were written on a thin layer of white stucco pasted onto the wood and covering up the imperfections of the surface of the tablets. In the end these little tablets were used as a very unusual material for Nekau's own Book of the Dead, which with its wooden "pages" (unlike the usual scrolls) became the first and as yet the only known real *book* of the Dead of ancient Egypt. (JJ, RL)

Removal of the wall blocking the entrance to the long low burial chamber of the priest Nekau opened up a view of his double wooden coffin and cabinet with ushabti

< While the outer coffin of the priest Nekau was rectangular, in its shape and decoration the inner coffin recalled a mummy, or the form of the traditional ruler of the dead, the god Osiris

105 Demonic protectors from Menekhibnekau's tomb

Limestone; sunken relief with no traces of polychromy. Late Period, end of the 26th to beginning of the 27th Dynasty. Abusir West – burial chamber of the general Menekhibnekau, discovered in 2007. Number AW 5 CS.

The south, entrance wall of Menekhibnekau's tomb is covered in the text of chapter 144 of the Book of the Dead containing the names of the seven gates to the underworld and their guardians. The ancient Egyptians believed that after death they would have to overcome a series of obstacles, which included not only the judgment of their souls but negotiating the gates with their guardian demons. The deceased had to address each gate and each guardian by his name. Depicted here, for example, are three demons of the 5th gate of chapter 144 of the Book of the Dead, named "He who nourishes himself by maggots", "Burning" and "With a ghastly face and crushing blow". The ancient Egyptian Book of the Dead was not simply a guide to the underworld but above all a kind of compendium of the sacred knowledge needed by the deceased if he or she were to pass over successfully into eternal life. The vignettes of chapter 144 of the Book of the Dead usually depict the different gates as well as the demons. In Menekhibnekau's tomb the entrance to the tomb represents the "gate" with the text of the chapter written around it, and so the demons are symbolically guarding not only the underworld gate but the burial chamber as well. As on the papyrus scrolls, chapter 144 of the Book of the Dead is accompanied by the chapter 148, in which the deceased turns to the ruler of the underworld and his seven cows and to the oars of the sacred barks. (RL)

The south wall of Menekhibnekau's burial chamber, in which the entrance lay, was entirely covered with texts and depictions of the guardians who made sure that no one entered the next world without permission. Egyptologists call this text with its accompanying illustrations chapter 144 of the Book of the Dead

106 Personifications of the hours of the day and night in the burial chamber of Menekhibnekau

Limestone; sunken relief, some parts with sporadic traces of polychromy. Late Period, end of the 26th to beginning of the 27th Dynasty. Abusir West – lower part of the arched ceiling. Menekhibnekau's burial chamber (AW 5, hours of the day on the east side and hours of the night on the west side), discovered in 2007.

The personifications of the hours of the day and night are abbreviated symbolic expressions of the rituals associated with the eternal cycle of time, and figuratively life itself. They are one of the iconographic forms of the daily journey of the sun, which was believed by the ancient Egyptians to be reborn every day in the east, and then to travel across the sky and set in the west so as to return during the night to the eastern horizon. Female figures representing the twelve day and twelve night hours are supplemented with short texts giving their names. We have evidence for the idea of the twelve hours of the day and twelve nightly hours in Egypt from the 3rd millennium BC, but we first encounter it in iconographic form in the mortuary complex of the queen Hatshepsut in Deir el-Bahri and the tombs of the pharaohs of the New Kingdom in the Valley of the Kings. Only in the 1st millennium BC does it also appear in non-royal tombs, in Western Thebes and here in Abusir. (LB)

Unlike in the tomb of Iufaa, in which the ceiling was left entirely plain, in Menekhibnekau's burial chamber the decoration extended to the vaulted ceiling. The side walls of the arch offered a suitable place for a procession of figures personifying the hours of the day and night

107 | Mummification deposit at the tomb of the general Menekhibnekau

Hundreds of large and small pottery vessels with the remains of various materials. Late Period, end of the 26th to beginning of 27th Dynasty. Abusir West – network of corridors around 10-metres deep forming the letter "E", running from the south shaft (S1) in the burial complex of the general Menekhibnekau (AW 5), discovered in 2003.

This huge deposit of pottery buried in a 10-metre deep network of corridors was located near the south-west corner of the limestone enclosure wall of the large shaft tomb of the Saite dignitary in western Abusir. It contained around 320 large transport amphorae that had been used to deposit not just the materials but also the vessels (pottery and faience) used by the embalmers in the whole process of mummification. This comprised bandages of different kinds, remnants of resin, oils, myrrh, charcoal, and abundant filling material (straw, sawdust, chaff, sand, linen bandages). The close connection between the embalming process and the subsequent funeral ritual is illustrated for example by the find of the disintegrated remains of the cedar funeral bier on which Menekhibnekau's mummy was carried, and a pair of faience offering vessels by the entrance to the underground deposit. (KS)

At the time of excavation no one had any inkling that this inconspicuous small shaft, enclosed with mudbricks, would lead to one of the biggest and most important caches of mummifying material ever found in ancient Egypt to date

108 Menekhibnekau's mummification manual

Pottery vessels with text written in black. Late Period, end of the 26th to beginning of the 27th Dynasty. Abusir West – shaft tomb of the general Menekhibnekau (AW 5), south shaft SI, discovered in 2003.

The mummification deposit in the tomb of the general Menekhibnekau, discovered in 2003 (see no. 107), included larger and smaller vessels bearing inscriptions in hieratic script with some early demotic signs. Closer analysis of these amphorae, bowls and beakers has shown that the inscriptions indicated the materials and substances that were originally stored in them and used in the mummification of the deceased (e.g. loose natron, little linen bags full of natron, myrrh, oil, colouring and so on). This in itself was a very important find, but what made the discovery unique was that the 15 inscriptions on the vessels turned out also to indicate the particular day on which the substances had to be used in the mummification process. This means that Menekhibnekau's mummification deposit enables us to reconstruct, almost step by step, one of the greatest mysteries of the ancient Egyptians: the embalming ritual and process of mummification. (RL, JJ)

The study and documentation of hundreds of large storage vessels, often containing smaller vessels and other artefacts, required several years of tireless work but brought unique results

109 | Phoenician vessel

Pottery; h. 59 cm, diameter 25 cm. Late Period, end of the 26th to beginning of the 27th Dynasty. Abusir West – shaft tomb of the general Menekhibnekau (AW 5), south shaft S1, discovered in 2010. Find number 826/S/10.

Under the 26th and 27th Dynasties Memphis was one of the most important cities of the ancient world. Written records and evidence of material culture show that not only Egyptians but also people speaking Aramaic, Carian or Phoenician lived in Memphis. Herodotus in the second book of his Histories (II, 112) mentions Phoenicians from Tyre. On this Phoenician vessel we find a total of four inscriptions, although some have only survived in a fragmentary state. Three are written in Phoenician and one in Aramaic script. Palaeography has dated all the inscriptions to the 6th and at the latest the early 5th century BC. The three Phoenician inscriptions, written in black ink, state the original contents of the vessel to be "new wine" and identify individuals associated with its production and distribution. The inscription in cursive Aramaic script, probably written by the resin suppliers, was the only one made in Egypt and gives two Egyptian names: Wahibpare/Wahibre and ?-Ptah. At the time of the find the vessel was sealed and contained a mixture of light blown sand and Nile mud. (JM)

It was obvious at first sight that all kinds of different texts were written on some of the vessels in the mummification cache, but with one exception they were all written in Egyptian

< Large storage vessels containing remains of materials used for mummification were placed in the cache entirely without arrangement or order. On some of them there are remnants of the woven baskets or nets in which they were carried there

110 | Statue of the goddess Hathor in the form of a cow

Basalt; largest piece (torso): l. 62 cm, w. 20 cm, h. 56 cm. Late Period, end of the 26th to beginning of the 27th Dynasty. Abusir West – sand just below the current surface of the desert ca. 7 m east of the original east wall of the superstructure of Menekhibnekau's tomb (AW 5), discovered in 2008. Find number 734/S/08.

Like some other goddesses associated with maternal and protective functions Hathor was often depicted in the form of the animal most identified with such functions, the cow, in both reliefs and free-standing statues. In the case of a statue, a smaller effigy of the protected person usually stood in front of it. In the New Kingdom this was always the pharaoh (e.g. in the well-known group statue from the reign of Thutmose III in the Egyptian Museum in Cairo) but in the 1st millennium BC it could be a high-ranking dignitary as well, although here nothing remains of the small figure of Menekhibnekau but the tip of his kilt. The statue of Hathor probably originally stood in the chapel at the very centre of the superstructure of the tomb, but was thrown away and broken as a "pagan idol" in the period around the middle of the 1st millennium AD, when the burial chamber was probably robbed as well. The statue was broken into several pieces, but in 2017 the fragments were reassembled and the statue restored to its current form. (LB)

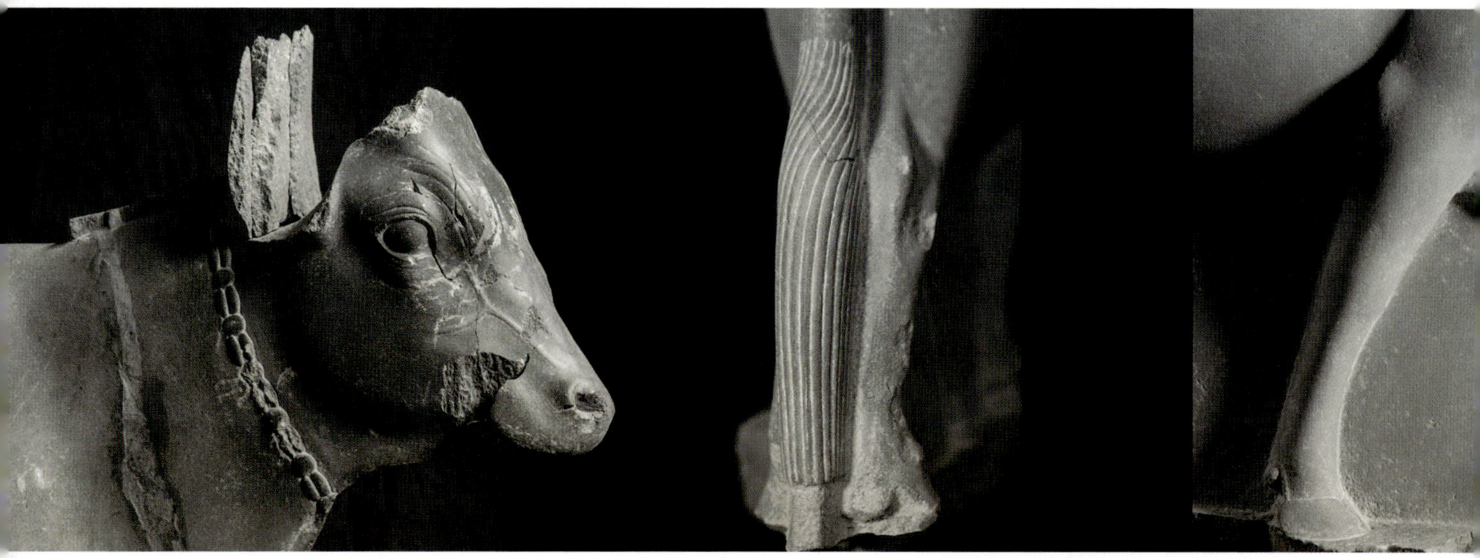

The discovery of the torso of a statue of the goddess Hathor (depicted in the form of a cow) during survey of the wider surroundings of the tomb of Menekhibnekau was all the more delightful for being so unexpected

111 Cemetery seal

Egyptian faience; 4.8 × 3.1 cm, thickness 2.3 cm. Late Period, end of the 26th to beginning of the 27th Dynasty. Abusir West – filling of the small shaft by the south wall of Menekhibnekau's burial chamber (AW 5; the small shaft between the south wall of the chamber and the double sarcophagus was part of the system for lowering the lid of the outer sarcophagus), discovered in 2007. Find number 685/S/07.

The ancient Egyptians had a passion for bureaucracy and so it is no surprise that the running of cemeteries involved quite an extensive administrative operation in which one important element was the sealing of the entrances to tombs or cult interiors, and also of cabinets, chests and vessels for all kinds of funerary equipment or objects used in the mortuary cult. The image on this quite small seal, i.e. the god Anubis, protector and guide of the deceased, in the form of a recumbent jackal and below him three rows of three captive enemies of Egypt (Libyans, Asians and Nubians) is documented from at least as far back as the 2nd millennium BC – its most celebrated instance is its imprint on the originally walled up entrance to the tomb of Tutankhamun in the Valley of the Kings. Several imprints in soft Nile clay found in the cache of mummification material close to Menekhibnekau's tomb (see also no. 107), show that this seal was actually used. (LB)

Reis (foreman of workers) Ahmad el-Kereti during excavation of the small shaft inside Menekhibnekau's burial chamber, where one of the finds was the cemetery seal

112 Ushabti of Padihor

Egyptian faience, pale blue-green glaze; h. 12.1 cm, max. w. 6 cm. Late Period, end of the 26th to beginning of the 27th Dynasty. Abusir West – tomb of Padihor (AW 3), discovered in 2001. Find number 131/R/01.

An ushabti in the form of Osiris, i.e. as a mummy with long-tipped or three-section wig, long plaited beard and hands crossed on breast (the right hand over the left). In his right hand he holds a hoe and pick, together with a bag hung over the left shoulder. The figure has a back pillar with inscription and trapezoid base. At the time of discovery the ushabti was broken in two pieces, which were later put together again. Under the glaze on the back pillar is an engraved column of text with numerous errors: "Oh Osiris Padihor, (if) Osiris Padihor (is called) to any kind of work in <'the land of the god'>; say: 'here <I am>'". (FC)

Fragments of Padihor's ushabti were found both inside the burial chamber and in the sand around his tomb, where they were thrown by tomb robbers in antiquity. They were primarily interested in objects made of precious metals and tiny faience figurines were simply in their way

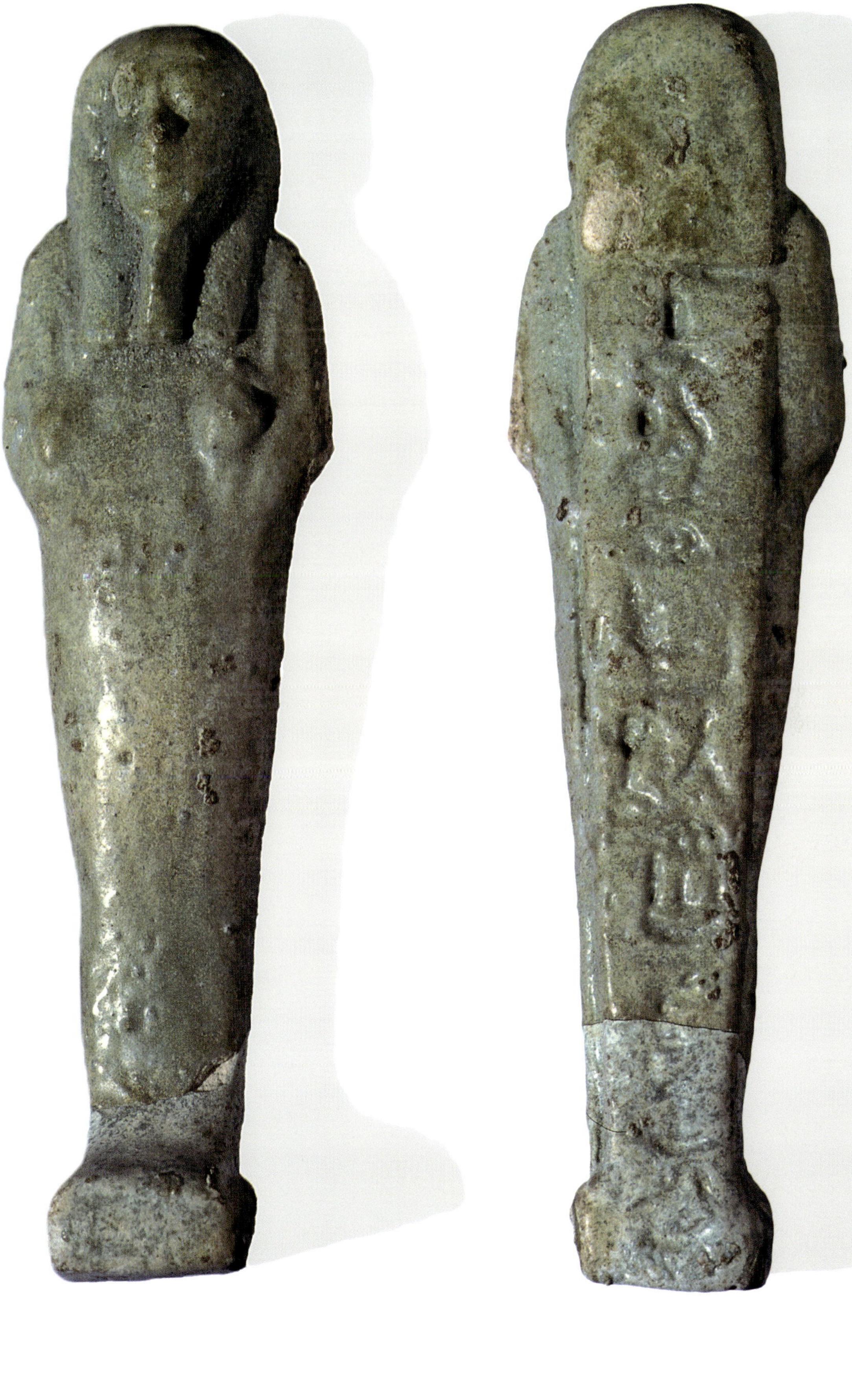

113 Corrections in the burial chamber of Padihor

Late Period, end of the 26th and beginning of the 27th Dynasty. Abusir West – burial chamber of the tomb of Padihor (AW 3), discovered in 2001.

One of the most remarkable features of the inscriptions on the walls of Padihor's burial chamber is the fact that many of the signs were corrected or accentuated in black ink not long after they were carved. This happened after the walls of the burial chamber were covered with the carved texts but before the actual burial. The black annotations can be observed on all four walls and can be divided into two groups: the highlighting of a few insufficiently carved signs and corrections of badly carved signs. Minor corrections of a similar kind have been found in other tombs, but the corrections in Padihor's burial chamber are among the most extensive. (FC)

The entrance to Padihor's burial chamber was only just big enough for the wooden coffin with his mummy to be pulled right into it. The coffin was evidently let down from above through the entrance shaft leading to the burial chamber

South Saqqara

MOHAMED MEGAHED

The royal cemetery in South Saqqara was founded at the end of the 5th Dynasty by King Djedkare, who had his pyramid complex built a few kilometres south of the royal cemetery in Abusir. Djedkare thus established a whole new royal cemetery in the Memphite necropolis, where rulers would be interred right up to the end of the Old Kingdom.

< The pyramid complexes of Djedkare and his queen

Moving the site of his pyramid complex away from Abusir might indicate that Djedkare was not of the same family as the rulers buried there, or was from a secondary branch of the royal line. However, the reasons for his decision may well have been more practical than familial, perhaps due to the lack of suitable space left for another big pyramid complex in the Abusir cemetery.

Just as in the case of other pyramids, the modern inhabitants of the area around Djedkare's monument gave this one its modern name: "El-Shawaf El-Qibli" or "Southern Sentinel". This distinguishes it from "El-Shawaf El-Bahri", which is the modern name

Detail of a depiction of King Djedkare; the eye was once inlaid with another type of stone and copper

for the neighbouring 6th Dynasty pyramid complex of Pepy I. The name "El-Shawaf" refers to the watch stations built on elevated places to ensure advance warning to the inhabitants of the Saqqara village of raids by Bedouin from the desert.

Djedkare's pyramid complex is unique in many architectural features, and the pyramid complex of Djedkare's queen, which stands north-east of the king's complex, is one of the most interesting monuments of queens from the whole Old Kingdom. It not only represents the largest of all queens' pyramids from the period, but contains architectural elements that were only reserved for ruling monarchs.

Modern excavation of Djedkare's pyramid complex, which lay forgotten for millennia, was initiated in 1945 by the Egyptian archaeologist Abdel Salam Hussein. It was interrupted by Hussein's premature death but in 1952 it continued under the direction of Ahmed Fakhry for one short season. Djedkare and his monument fell back into oblivion for almost sixty years, until 2010 when a new project was started with the aim to clean and document the pyramid complex section by section. In the course of this work archaeologists found hundreds of fragments of relief decoration from the mortuary temple. They also explored some previously unexcavated parts of the complex that were used as a non-royal burial ground during later periods by many who wanted to rest in the shadow of Djedkare; like Djedkare they wished to be remembered after death and to enjoy a happy existence in the afterlife.

Djedkare's pyramid complex is surrounded by an extensive cemetery from the late 5th and 6th Dynasty, which has not been explored although the outlines and shapes of individual tombs can be seen under the surface of the desert. The importance of this cemetery and its great potential to provide us with important information about the end of the 5th Dynasty, was confirmed in 2019 when exploration of one of the non-royal tombs started.

> The Pyramid of Djedkare. Beyond it in the distance is the outline of the centuries-older Mastabat Faraun and pyramids in Dahshur

114 Painted pottery vessel

Pottery; h. 42.1 cm, max. diameter 31.6 cm. Late New Kingdom, 20th Dynasty. South Saqqara – Djedkare's mortuary temple, discovered 2018. Find number DJ/F121/2018.

This type of vessel is known to have been made in ancient Egypt from the late New Kingdom onwards, when pottery was decorated with motifs of birds and lotus flowers painted in red and black. The decoration of this particular jar features wide black and red bands on the neck, while the broader area of the shoulder of this vessel shows a wider band filled with crossed black and red lines, then another band with birds, and yet another band of lotus flowers. The paintings are simple but full of life, and show the great skill of the ancient Egyptian artist. This pot was found together with other, undecorated vessels in a pottery deposit buried to the north of Djedkare's mortuary temple. (MM)

One of the pottery deposits with remnants of a plundered burial found to the north of Djedkare's mortuary temple

115 | Amulets and rings

Faience and copper; max. h. 2.1 cm, max. w. 2.8 cm, New Kingdom to Late Period. South Saqqara – Djedkare's mortuary temple, discovered 2018. Find number DJ/F124/2018.

Amulets were used by the ancient Egyptians for protection in life but also in funerary equipment and on the bodies of the deceased to protect them in the afterlife. These amulets were found together with a simple burial placed in the precinct of Djedkare's mortuary temple many centuries after the king himself had been laid to rest in his pyramid. The four amulets in the shape of solar disks with horns were supposed to ensure the protection of the goddess Hathor, whose diadem was precisely this shape, while the amulet in the shape of solar disk with horns on a bark invoked the protection of the god Re. The two rings bear hardly legible hieroglyphic signs and they had perhaps been used during the owner's lifetime. (MM)

Archeological works in the north-east sector of Djedkare's mortuary temple

116 Amulets and scarab

Faience; Tweret: h. 3 cm, w. 1.2 cm; Bes: h. 2.9 cm, w. 1.4 cm; scarab: h. 7 cm, w. 1.1 cm. New Kingdom to Third Intermediate Period. South Saqqara – Djedkare's mortuary temple, discovered 2018. Find number DJ/F129/2018.

This set of amulets in the shape of the goddess Tweret and the god Bes were discovered in the area immediately north of Djedkare's mortuary temple. They were found on the remains of a burial, above which another burial of an infant had been placed in a wooden chest. The two burials may be related. The goddess Tweret was associated with childbirth and the protection of women during labour. Usually she was depicted in the form of a female hippopotamus and together with Bes she was honoured as a protector of mothers and children in ancient Egypt. The faience scarab is inscribed with the name of the god Amunre. (MM)

View of the unexplored area immediately north of Djedkare's mortuary temple before the start of excavations; in the background is the smaller pyramid of the queen

117 Amulet in the form of the goddess Tweret

Bone; h. 3 cm, w. 1.8 cm, thickness 0.5 cm. New Kingdom to Late Period. South Saqqara – Djedkare's mortuary temple, discovered 2018. Find number DJ/F131/2018.

Amulets were intended to provide protection from evil forces or to ensure the favour of a particular deity. This amulet in the form of the goddess Tweret, the consort of the god Bes, with two heads was found together with a body of a woman. The goddess was invoked as a protector against evil forces during childbirth. The body of the deceased was placed in a simple structure made of irregular stones and dates from a time when Djedkare's pyramid complex was already destroyed and its walls had long ago collapsed. (MM)

Simple burial partially surrounded by pieces of limestone and quartzite

118 Amulet in the form of Heqet

Red stone (carnelian?); base: 6 x 6 mm, h. 5 mm, w. 5 mm. New Kingdom to Late Period. South Saqqara – Djedkare's mortuary temple, discovered 2018. Find number DJ/F143/2018.

This amulet in the shape of a frog symbolises the goddess Heqet. It was found with the remains of an infant who was buried in a basket made of reeds. The amulet was placed on the baby's chest together with a few stone beads. Its base is decorated with an incised *ankh* sign, the symbol of life. Often depicted in the form of a frog, or female goddess with a frog head, the goddess Heqet assisted with the formation of babies in their mothers' wombs and oversaw their birth. In funerary context, she guaranteed the re-birth of this baby. Although this amulet is very small, the artist has brilliantly captured the shape of the frog. (MM)

Burial of an infant in a reed basket under the protection of the goddess Heqet

The bottom of the basket in which the infant was buried has survived in good condition

119 | Motif of offerings

Painting on limestone wall. Old Kingdom, 6th Dynasty. South Saqqara – tomb of Pepyankh, burial chamber, discovered 1952.

This detail is from the painted burial chamber of Pepyankh Setju, who perhaps lived at the end of the 6th Dynasty and had his tomb built attached to the west end of Djedkare's causeway. Among the many ways in which the deceased could be helped to enjoy a happy and peaceful existence in the afterlife, the provision of enough offerings of food in the tomb was particularly important. These offerings could be real, ritually presented foods or foods painted on the walls of the tomb. This scene shows the variety of offerings of food and drink that were painted on the walls of the burial chamber of Pepyankh Setju. Here we can make out various types of vessels and skins full of drink, bowls and platters lined up on wooden tables, vegetables and fruits and offerings of meat. No good food was to be missing in Pepyankh's afterlife. (MM)

Pepyankh's painted burial chamber with a part of the south wall missing

120 Red granite column of Djedkare's queen

Red granite; max h. 3 m, max diameter 0.77 m. Late 5th Dynasty. South Saqqara – pyramid complex of Djedkare's queen, discovered 2018.

The monument of Djedkare's queen, which is situated at the north-east side of the king's mortuary temple, was exceptional among Old Kingdom queens' pyramid complexes. Not only its large size but also some royal features indicated that the owner of this complex played a very important role in the late 5th Dynasty, but her identity remained a puzzle for the scholars for many decades. The queen's name and titles remained unknown until 2018, when several relief fragments and remains of her funerary temple were uncovered in the area immediately north of Djedkare's mortuary temple. The most complete inscription identifying the queen as the king's wife is preserved on a column of red granite that once supported the ceiling of the portico of her funerary temple. The queen's name Setibhor, which means "Pleasure of Horus", refers to the king himself. (MM, HV)

The pyramid of Queen Setibhor, wife of King Djedkare, as seen from the ruins of the king's mortuary temple

–5000 –4000 –3000 –2000 –1000 0 1000

121 Offering list of Khuwy

Painted low relief on a limestone wall. South Saqqara – tomb of Khuwy, discovered 2019.

In 2019 the discovery of the decorated underground chamber of Khuwy at Djedkare's royal cemetery at south Saqqara attracted the attention of the entire world. The decoration of Khuwy's underground chamber is exceptionally well preserved, with bright colours that give the impression of having been painted only yesterday, not 4,500 years ago. More importantly, Khuwy's decorated chamber is one of the earliest attested examples of its kind and shows a very high quality of artistic work. The elaboration of the individual hieroglyphic signs in this offering list is breathtaking, with such intricate details as feathers in the bird-signs or little leaves in the plant-signs. The individual columns of the offering list contain the names of various offerings of food and drink. Each item ends with a determinative of a kneeling male offering bearer, who is holding in his hands the offering listed in the respective column. The decoration in Khuwy's tomb features a larger variety of colours and shades than can be usually found in non-royal tombs of the period. (MM, HV)

The south-east part of the tomb of Khuwy shows the remains of the entrance to his chapel. In the background are the queen's and the king's pyramids

122 Khuwy enjoying the afterlife offerings

Painted low relief on a limestone wall. South Saqqara – tomb of Khuwy, discovered 2019.

The decorated underground chamber of Khuwy contains some rather unusual motifs, which are usually not found in tomb substructures. These include above all two scenes of Khuwy sitting at the offering table, with heaps of food and drink offerings depicted in front of him. In the Old Kingdom such scenes feature in above-ground chapels, into which priests and relatives brought offerings for the soul of the deceased. The appearance of this motif in the substructure is very unusual. In addition, the bottom registers show the tomb owner Khuwy in one of altogether four boats in an unusually active pose adjusting the sail. The boats are headed to the west, to the land of the dead. (MM, HV)

Detail of hieroglyphic signs of one of Khuwy's titles

123 Inlaid eyes of statues of Khuwy

Copper frame with stone inlays. Size max. h. 1.8 c m, max. w. 5 cm, max. thickness 2.2 cm; South Saqqara – tomb of Khuwy, discovered 2019.

The superstructure of the tomb of Khuwy included the offering chapel, badly damaged by ancient stone robbers, and a serdab that once contained large statues of the tomb owner Khuwy. The statues seem to have been made of wood, which almost entirely disintegrated leaving only small fragments. This group of eye inlays was found inside the serdab and they represent the only surviving evidence on Khuwy's statues. Their different sizes indicate that various types of figures were once placed in Khuwy's serdab, and the high quality of their manufacturing technique underlines his high social status (MM, HV)

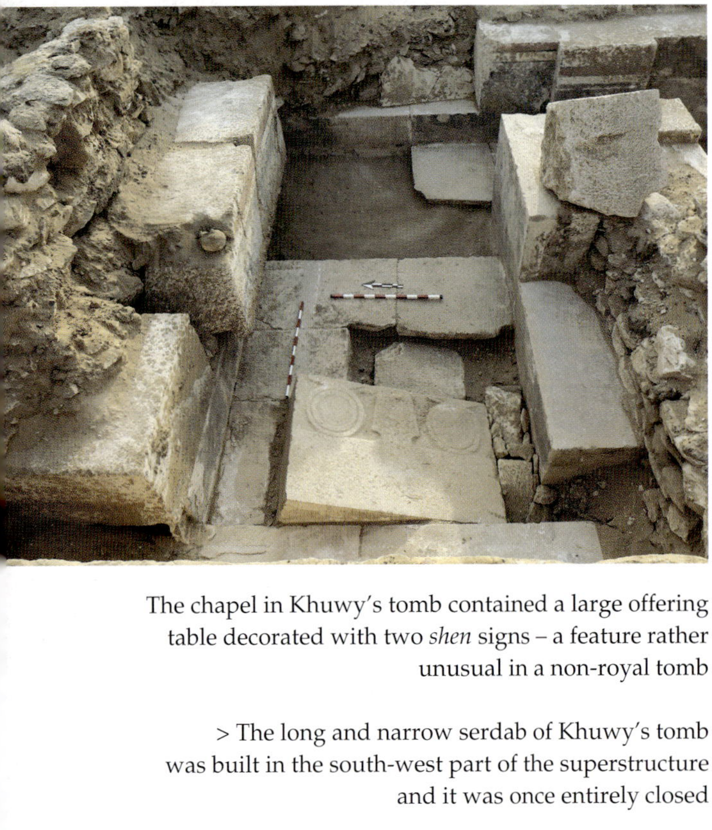

The chapel in Khuwy's tomb contained a large offering table decorated with two *shen* signs – a feature rather unusual in a non-royal tomb

> The long and narrow serdab of Khuwy's tomb was built in the south-west part of the superstructure and it was once entirely closed

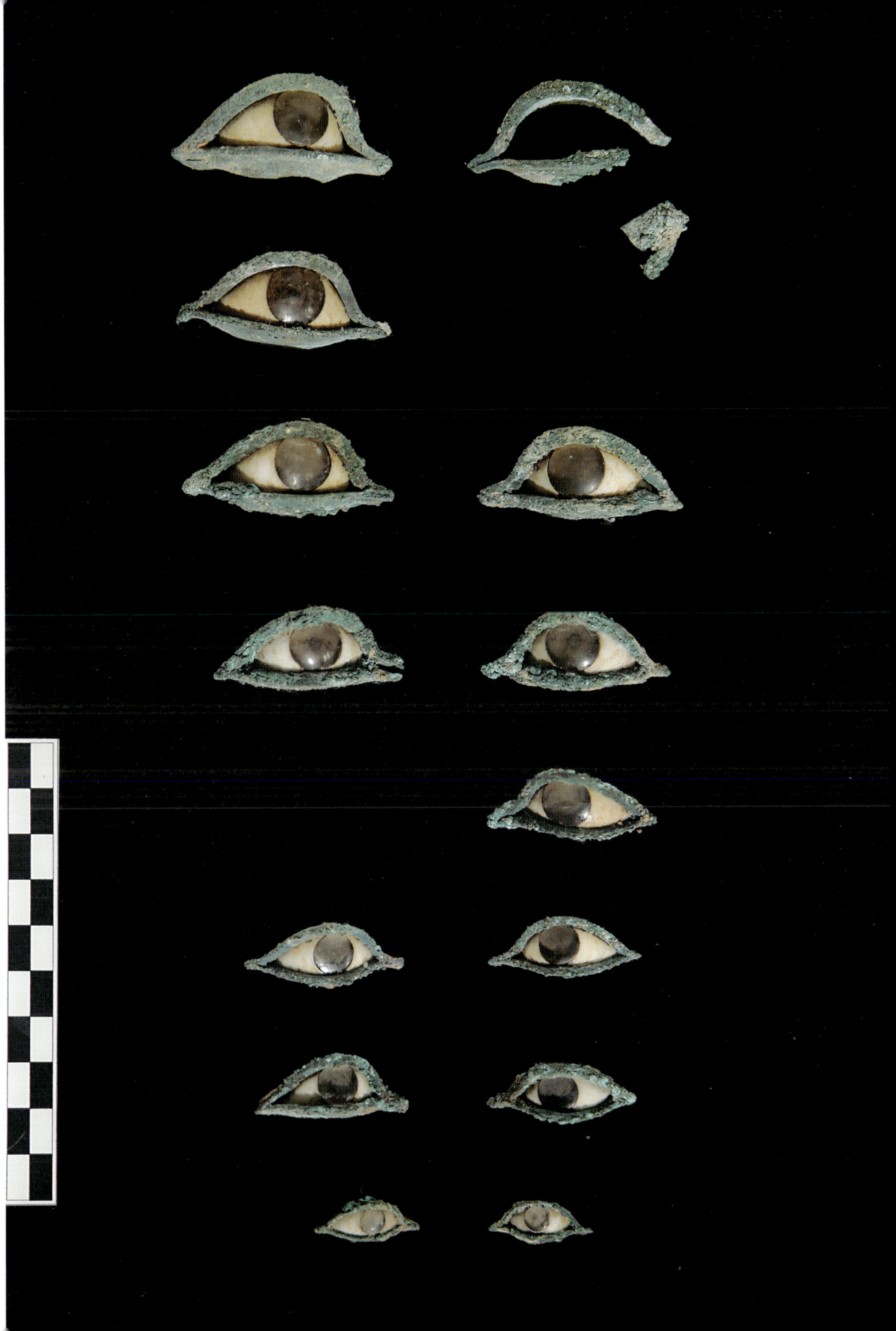

El-Hayez – the Egyptian Pompeii

MIROSLAV BÁRTA

Hidden in the seemingly endless expanses of Egypt's Western Desert, the El-Hayez Oasis lies roughly 350 kilometres south-west of Cairo. It is actually the southern part of the extensive Bahariya Oasis, which was an important centre of ancient Egypt particularly in the Late Period and the following Graeco-Roman Period. Alexander of Macedon stopped here on his way back from the Siwa Oasis and had a temple built in his own honour. The institute's research in the El-Hayez Oasis was initiated in 2003. Its preliminary purpose was to document the potential of this large territory of several hundred square kilometres in combination with targeted archaeological excavations of selected sites. It soon became clear that the territory contained important archaeological and historical sources illuminating the history of the area and climate changes over the past 10,000 years. To this should be added the discoveries of sites from the Early, Middle and Late Stone Age. Dating from the earlier Holocene, 9–7 thousand years BC, there were smaller settlements of seasonal type, most of them situated on the banks of what were then lakes (this was a time when the Sahara was only just beginning to

< The Egyptian Black Desert in El-Hayez

The start of excavation of the shaft leading to an underground irrigation canal – the workmen bringing a rope ladder to allow the smallest of them, Shaban, who later worked as a reis (foreman) in Abusir, to climb down

dry out). With regard to later periods, sites from the Graeco-Roman Period clearly predominate.

One of the most important places from this late stage in ancient Egyptian history is El-Riz, dominated by a church probably consecrated to St. Bartholomew and a big fortress with an enclosure wall rising to a height of 10 metres. In its time the surrounding settlement was one of the largest of all. Another major site is at Bir Shawish (which translates as "The Policeman's Well") where Czech excavations found sections of underground

irrigation tunnels (known as "manawars"), cemeteries and above all a settlement and industrial area where individual residential houses had survived to a height of several metres with two to three storeys hidden under the surface of the desert. These houses have been the source of unique finds of various kinds of object or ostraka (sherds with texts written on them) of the early Christian communities that lived here up to the beginning of the 5th century. The whole network of settlements ceased to exist some time after 410 AD as a result of deep crisis in the Roman Empire and the onset of climate changes.

View of the mountain in the shape of a step pyramid that guards the entrance to the El-Hayez Oasis. It is possible that the ancient Egyptians found the inspiration for the construction of their pyramids in natural desert formations of this type

124 Historical ostrakon from El-Hayez

Black pigment on pottery; 9.8 × 9.8 cm. Inscription dated the 9th of May 402 (?) AD. El-Hayez, Bir Shawish – house 3, room 12, discovered in 2007. Find number 43/BS/07.

Preserved in the El-Hayez Oasis are a whole range of inscriptions that provide very important evidence of the character of the communities there, including the names of their members and information on some of the transactions that formed the basis of economic life in this area in the 4th and the beginning of the 5th century AD. This was primarily a matter of deliveries of cotton, wine, wheat and barley, dates, chickens, eggs, chopped straw, pottery and metal objects and so on. The inscription in the photograph informs us that the heirs of a certain Timothy received a pig from Abraham, the son of Jacob, a farmer working on land belonging to an unnamed woman. The inscription is also interesting for the fact that it concerns payment of a three-year old debt. (MB)

Reconstruction of the possible appearance of the Bir Shawish site at the beginning of the 5th century. It was a real oasis with fields, palm groves and fruit orchards

125 | Stone digging pick

Chert; l. 20 cm.
4th Century AD. El-Hayez, Bir Shawish, surface find.

Stone instruments have not always been confined to cultures with a very low technological level and were not just a feature of the prehistoric age. The example of this stone-digging pick shows that stone tools were often used in the Roman era too. It is a pick weighing roughly a kilogram, which was used by the early Christian community in El-Hayez to dig underground irrigation tunnels, known as "manawars". Its weight meant that the digger had to use both hands. This type of tool can be found scattered on the surface of the desert to this day, and also in tombs from Late Antiquity, where they found a place in funerary equipment as one of the basic tools of everyday life. Water and irrigation canals were the alpha and omega of the life of the communities in the oasis. (MB)

View of two long branches of the underground irrigation canals. The mouths of shafts at regular intervals and mounds of dug-out clay indicate their course on the surface of the desert

126 Figurine of Bes from Bir Shawish

Faience; h. 3 cm. 4th century AD. El-Hayez, Bir Shawish – tomb no. I, discovered in 2004. Find number 7/BS/2004.

The god Bes was a popular deity in Ancient Egypt. He was the god of dissolute celebrations, but also the protector of children and women in childbirth, and was therefore an important household god whose figurine every family needed in the home. He was also often depicted on amulets, whose owners carried them everywhere for protection and safety. This particular find is one of many indications that although the inhabitants of Bir Shawish were Christians at the time, they still retained remnants of ancient Egyptian customs and beliefs. All the same, the spread of Christianity was very rapid. We can estimate that while at the beginning of the 4th century around 20–30 percent of the population was Christian, just half a century later at least half was Christian. (MB)

Entrance into the underground part of one of the rock tombs in the cemetery in Bir Shawish. At the bottom of the shaft is an entrance into a room cut into the rock massif that contained many simple burials of members of the early Christian community – men, women and children

127 | Bowl with cross

Pottery; 12.7 × 2.2 cm. End of the 3rd to beginning of the 4th century AD. El-Hayez, Bir Shawish – house no. 3, room 12, discovered in 2007, find number 34/BS/07.

Shallow pottery bowl with red painted decor on the inner surface, dominated by a large entirely symmetrical cross on the bottom of the bowl. The inner sides of the bowl are decorated with regular vertical lines with dotted edges. This bowl with a cross is eloquent evidence of the faith of the inhabitants of Bir Shawish at the end of the 3rd and beginning of the 4th century AD. That this was one of the earliest Christian communities is further suggested by the many personal names like James or Joseph preserved on ostraka and oil lamps. (MB)

Early Christian church (apparently of St. Bartholomew) in el-Riz on the day of a sand storm, the so-caled khamaseen

128 | Wine amphora

Pottery; h. 23.5 cm, max. w. 15.5 cm. 4th century AD. El-Hayez, Bir Shawish – house no. 3, discovered in 2007. Find number 37/BS/07.

Wine was always a mark of luxury in ancient Egypt. Finds of the vessels in which it was transported and stored are testimony to its popularity and prestige. The most valued was naturally wine that was imported, above all from the Syro-Palestinian area, but the Egyptians were already cultivating the grapevine and making their own wine from the Old Kingdom at the latest. In the Roman Period wine was also produced in the oases, including El-Hayez. This double handled vessel dates from the 4th century comes from the Roman settlement at the Bir Shawish site. The three names on the amphora – Petrus, Paulus and Papnutious – presumably indicate the three men who once enjoyed its contents. (MB)

Archeological research on house no. 3 – the workmen have just been digging through the layers of the second floor of the several-storey house, which probably belonged to a man called Apollo and his family

129 Roman fibula

Bronze; 7 × 3 cm. Roman Period, beginning of 5th century AD. El-Hayez, Bir Shawish – house no. 3, discovered in 2007. Find number 217/BS/07.

The fibula with onion-shaped buttons, which was found in one of the large houses at the Bir Shawish site in the El-Hayez Oasis, is a late Roman artefact that was imported into Egypt from the Danube basin and shows the high degree of mobility of people and objects a millennium and a half ago. The fibula is made of bronze and is an isolated find of this type at this particular site. The pin has not survived. These fibulae were used to fasten the upper parts of clothing at the shoulder. Although it was primarily a functional article, its high artistic standard is obvious. (MB)

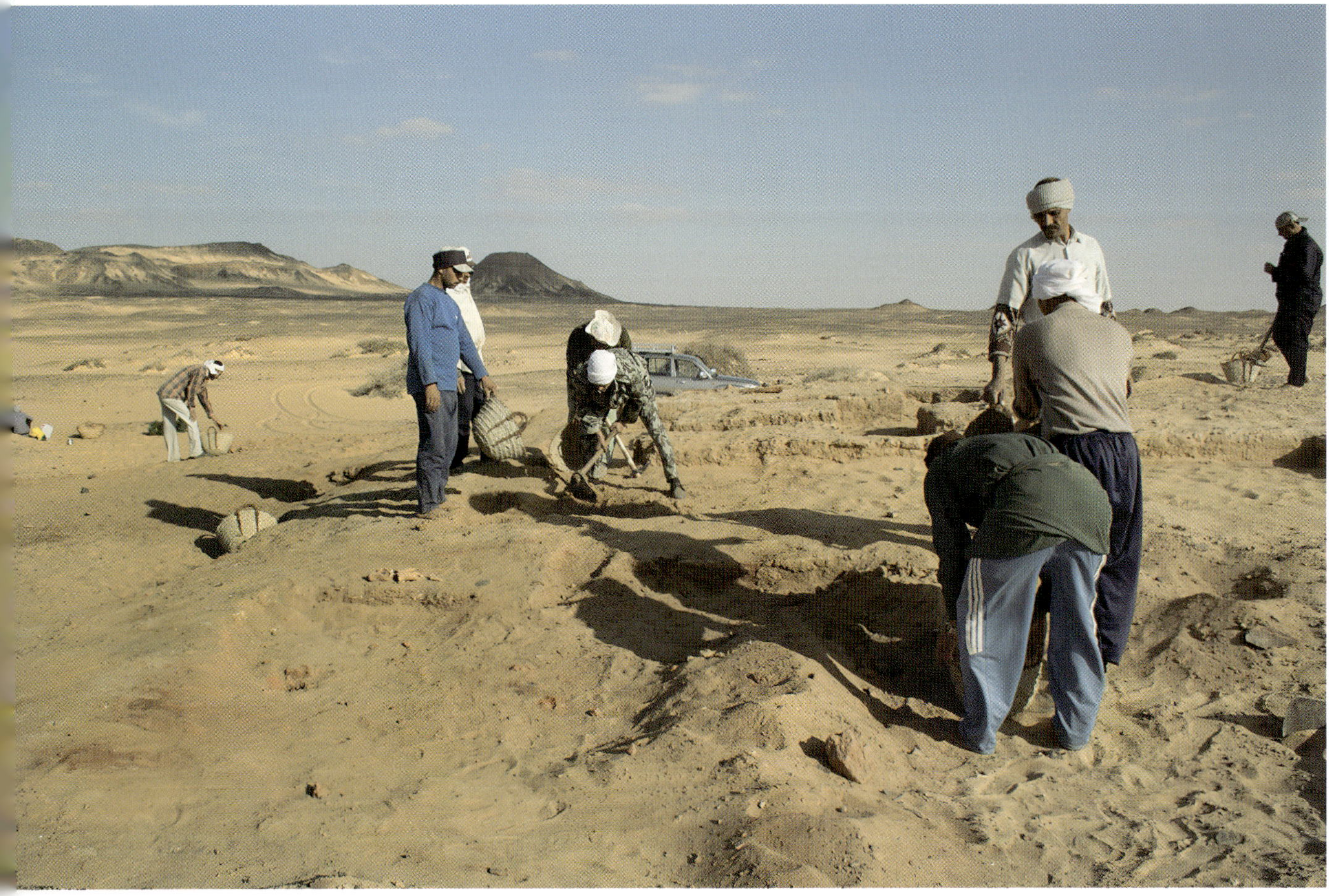

The beginning of archaeological excavations on the surface of the desert. Only a few centimetres under the surface the outlines of one of the houses of the community of early Christians start to emerge

130 | Terracotta lamp

Terracotta; h. 3.5 cm, max. w. 10.3 cm. 4th century AD. El-Hayez, Bir Shawish – house no. 3, discovered in 2007. Find number 54/BS/07.

Oil lamps which used to light dwellings represent very frequent finds at the Bir Shawish site. Just in part of the excavated house no. 3 there were as many as sixty. On its side the lamp has an inscription that was engraved even before firing – this is the personal name Apollo, probably the name of the man who ordered the lamp and therefore the possible owner of house no. 3. This possibility is supported by the appearance of the same name on several ostraka found in the same house. (MB)

House no. 3 in the Bir Shawish site after cleaning and the completion of excavation work. It has survived to this day up to a height of at least three storeys

131 Basalt figurine

Basalt;
2.7 × 4.8 × 3.7 cm.
El-Hayez, Bir Shawish – house no. 3, room II, context 02, discovered in 2007. Find number 9/BS/07.

Found in one of the dwellings in the Bir Shawish site, the figurine is an anthropomorphic torso that to judge by the style represents an ancient Egyptian god or ruler. It may, for example be the ancient Egyptian god Horus, protector of rulers and precursor of the Christian St. George slaying the dragon. The body of the figurine has its left leg forward and arms hanging straight down its sides. The man is dressed in a short pleated kilt with a middle section. At the back the figurine rests on a pillar. Unfortunately the inscription, which was most probably on the pedestal, is missing. In view of the location of the find there are grounds for thinking that it was an object venerated in the house and may have been intended to protect its inhabitants. (MB)

View of the extensive Bir Shovish site and beginning of an archaeological season

> Figurine at the moment of discovery

Lower Nubia

LENKA VARADZINOVÁ

The archaeological research in Abusir is definitely the flagship of the Czech Institute of Egyptology, but the team of Czechoslovak Egyptologists met its first truly major fieldwork challenge in Egypt in an area almost 1,000 kilometres further south – in Lower Nubia. This "Land of the Bow", as the ancient Egyptians called the Nile Valley between the First and Second Cataracts, was an important corridor of trade and cultural exchange between inner Africa and the Mediterranean, but it also functioned as a border and buffer zone. Over the millennia, periods of development of local cultures – what is known through archaeology as A-Group (ca. 3700–2800 BC) and C-Group (ca. 2300–1600 BC) – alternated with periods of the ascendancy of neighbouring kingdoms – the ancient Egyptian from the north and the Kerman, Napatan and Meroitic from the south. At the end of the 1950s, however, the remains of ancient civilisations here were suddenly under threat. The planned building of the High Dam at Aswan meant that they were bound to disappear forever under the waters of a huge reservoir together with the beautiful landscape in which they were set.

< The seasonally flooded valley (Arabic: *khor*) Rahma in the northern part of the Czechoslovak concession

A Nubian felucca cuts a furrow through the waters of the Nile close to Korosko East in the southern part of the Czechoslovak concession

> Korosko East turned out to be exceptionally rich in rock art from various periods of Nubian history

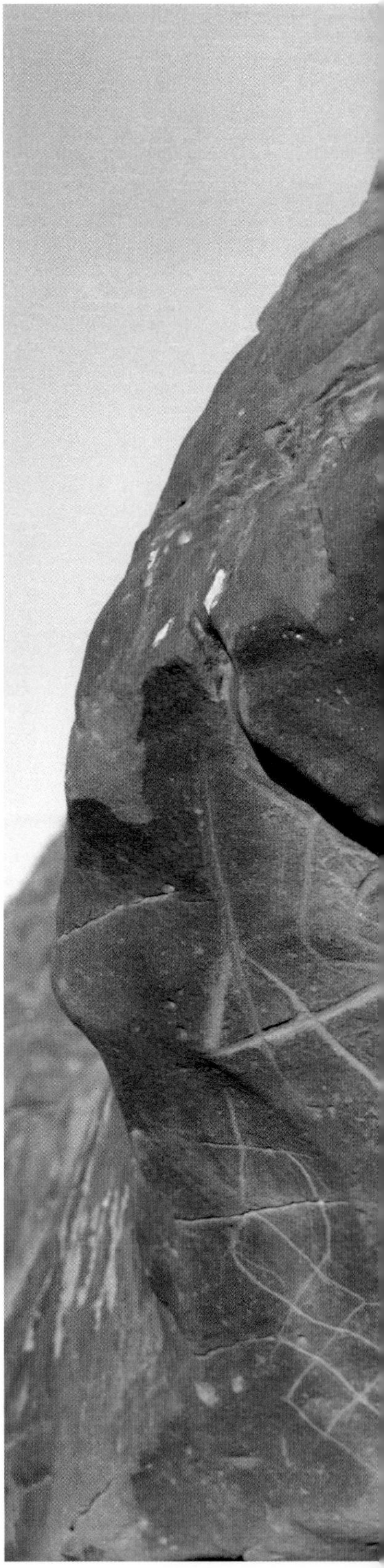

To reduce the damage to world cultural heritage, in 1960 UNESCO announced an internationally coordinated campaign of action to salvage the monuments on the Nubian territory in southern Egypt and northern Sudan that was due to be flooded by the planned dam. Czechoslovakia participated in the campaign through the newly established Czechoslovak Institute of Egyptology. Its aid was focused on the Egyptian part of Nubia, where a total of five scientific expeditions were sent under the leadership of the then director of the institute, Zbyněk Žába. These expeditions were each made up of 4 to 9 experts, accompanied by an inspector from the Department of Antiquities and workmen under a foreman, the reis. The composition of the expeditions depended on the particular tasks to be undertaken. In the years 1961–62 these tasks were the precise documentation and soundings in the area of the Southern Temple in Tafa and the so-called Roman fortress in Qertassi in northern Nubia. In 1963–65 the expedition moved further southward to carry out systematic epigraphic and archaeological exploration and research in two separate concessions.

From the archaeological and epigraphic point of view both these concessions might seem at first sight to be areas of rather marginal interest, and more or less what was left behind after the more promising sectors were taken by the other expeditions. The results achieved in a mere three seasons were for that reason all the more surprising. The quite modest corpus of rock inscriptions known up to that point was enriched by discovery of historically important evidence of the military campaigns and partial conquest of Nubia carried out by the rulers of the Middle Kingdom. A valuable set of rock art was documented to further the study of the cultural and artistic expressions of the Nubian populations, and included nine rock shelters containing rock paintings – a rare phenomenon in ancient Nubia. Finally the Czechoslovak team undertook a complete excavation of a necropolis from the 3rd to the 5th century AD in Wadi Qitna, which provided unique evidence that for many years to come defined the state of scholarly knowledge of the character of the rural population in that period.

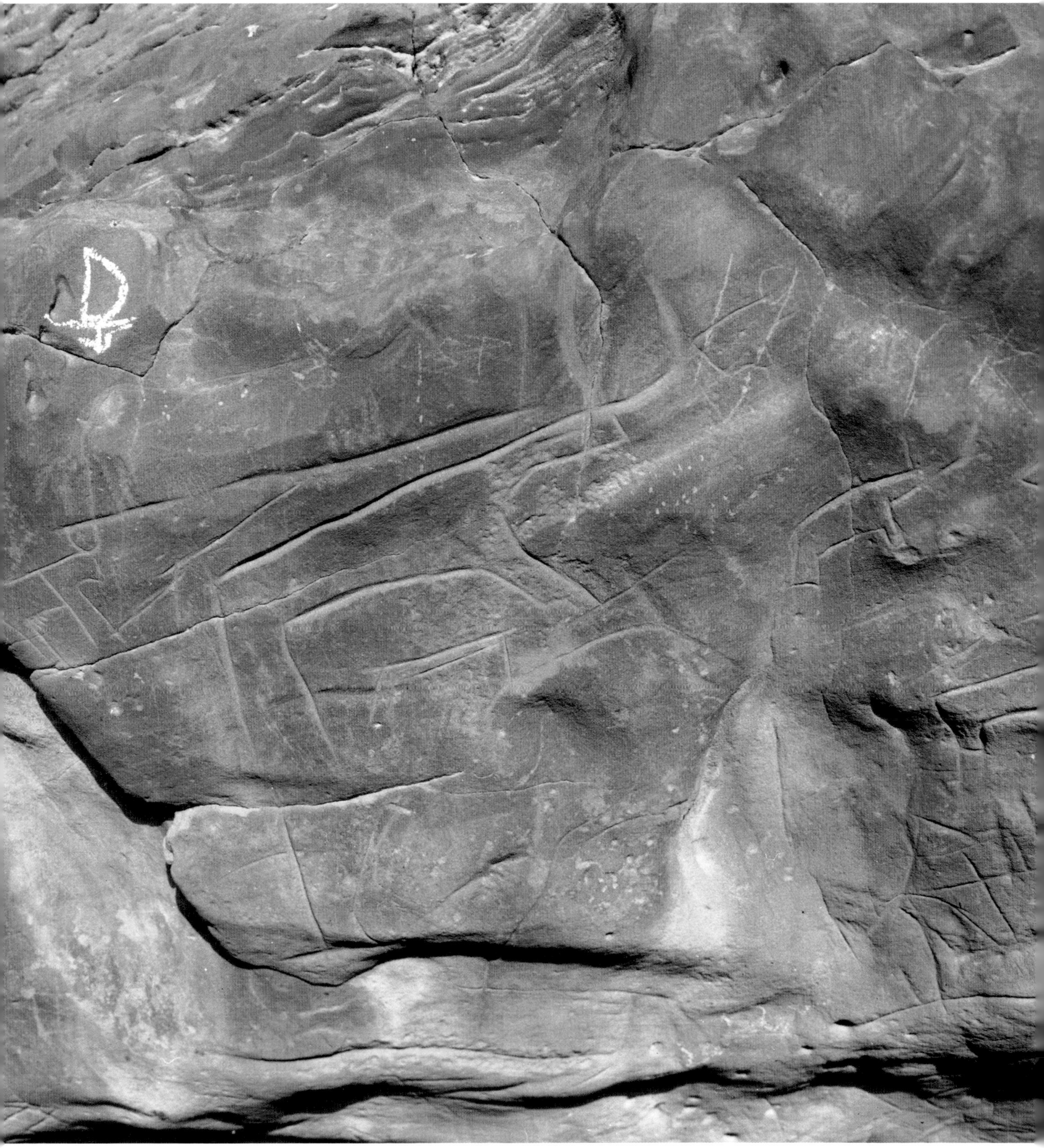

132 Historical rock inscription

Nubian sandstone (support), technique of engraving on smoothed surface; stela: w. 70 cm, h. 48 cm; inscribed surface with figure: w. 57 cm, h. 42 cm. Middle Kingdom, 12th Dynasty. Lower Nubia, on the right bank of the Nile near Gebel el-Girgawi (inscription no. 73), discovered in 1963. Field number 17 R 35.

Four thousand years ago the scribe Reniqer ("Reliable") painstakingly carved into the Nubian rock a hieroglyphic inscription celebrating the victorious military expedition led by the vizier Antefiqer. Its aim was to consolidate Egyptian supremacy in Nubia – a strategic territory containing gold mines and also cut through by a crucial trade route to black Africa. Rock inscriptions of this kind are a unique source of historical evidence. This inscription can almost certainly be dated to the 29th year of the reign of Amenemhat I (= 9th year of the reign of Senwosret I), founder of the Middle Kingdom. The "eternity" of Reniqer's inscription was ended in the 1960s, when it sank forever under Lake Nasser following construction of the High Aswan Dam. (BV)

Not far from the stela of the scribe Reniqer, Zbyněk Žába and his team documented another, previously unknown inscription created at the beginning of the Middle Kingdom in connection with the strengthening of Egyptian rule in Nubia

133 | Rock inscription with depiction of the priest Sethi

Nubian sandstone (support), technique of pecking and engraving; figure of priest: h. 32 cm; inscription: l. 13.5 cm. New Kingdom, end of the 19th Dynasty. Lower Nubia, on the left bank of the Nile about 1 km south of the Temple of Dendur by the village of Naga Khalos (inscription no. 190), discovered in 1964. Field number 32 R 26.

The rock inscription of the priest Sethi is another of the hundreds of inscriptions that were left by the ancient Egyptians on the rocks above the Nile between the First and Second Cataracts as proof of their penetration into the area south of Aswan. The name and title is accompanied by a portrait of Sethi as a kneeling priest clad in a leopard skin and a long kilt. In his right hand he holds an ostrich feather known from the depictions of "bearers of (ostrich) feathers (i.e. fan) to the right of the king" and his left hand is raised in a salute. We can trace the itinerary of Sethi from other inscriptions and images he made into the rocks of Lower Nubia, but more precise identification of this priest, who lived and travelled to Nubia towards the end of the 19th Dynasty, remains elusive. (LV)

The construction and repeated heightening of the "Old Dam" at Aswan had meant the flooding of lower-lying stretches of the Nile Valley and the moving of modern villages to safety above the continuous belts of sandstone rocks lining the Nile on both its banks. In some places, therefore, the rock inscriptions left on their walls by the ancient Egyptians could only be documented from a boat

134 Painted shelter near Korosko

Nubian sandstone (support), technique of painting in red, white and blue-black paint (cattle, human figures, boat), technique of pecking, engraving and rubbing (cattle, wild species of animals, human figures, secondary interventions); rock-art panel: l. max. 6.7 m, h. max. 2 m; cattle: l. max. 31.4 cm, human figures: h. max. 26.5 cm, boat: l. 73.5 cm. Nubian C-Group. Lower Nubia, wadi Fomm el-Atmur, approx. 2.5 km south of the village of Korosko on the right bank of the Nile, documented in 1963. Field number 17 R XIII A.

Although the motifs of cattle, people and boats are practically ubiquitous in the rock art of Nubia, the painted shelter near Korosko is an exceptional find in several respects. It differs from hundreds of other sites by the use of red, white and blue-black colours. Even the inexperienced eye is captivated by the arrangements of the figures and minor compositions into a procession as it were moving through the Nile landscape (where the natural rock layers represent water). The figural themes (above all cows with calves and cattle accompanied by herders) are characteristic of the art of the Nubian C-Group peoples. The quantity and variety of the secondary interventions in the paintings, which are probably traces of magical or ritual activities, are very unusual: for example the cutting of the throat of one of the two fighting bulls (on the opposite side below), the multiple modification of four human figures (in the middle), or the almost complete removal of other human figures (on the right). (LV)

The painted shelter was located on the right bank of the wadi Fomm el-Atmur, through which ran the famous desert route linking Korosko in Lower Nubia with Abu Hamid in what is today Sudan

135 | Coloured petroglyphs

Nubian sandstone (support), technique of engraving and relief, painting in red; panel: l. around 80 cm; figures with axes: h. max. 29.7 cm; unidentified animal: l. max. 9.6 cm. Nubian C-Group. Lower Nubia, wadi Fomm el-Atmur, about 0.5 km south of the village of Korosko on the right bank of the Nile, discovered in 1963. Field number 17 R XIX.

Three male figures dressed in close-fitting tunics and grasping battle-axes are a rare example of coloured petroglyphs, which are quite uncommon in Nubia. The basis of the execution is the technique of engraving and relief, to which is added the use of red to distinguish the exposed parts of the body (arms and lower parts of the legs) from the trunks and thighs covered in clothing, and also for finishing the axes. What is more, the figures are set onto a "base line" formed by the modulation of the rock surface, giving the impression that they are moving through a landscape. The composition, in the style associated with Nubian C-Group, is supplemented by later clumsy engraving of one seated and one standing human figure (in the second case it is an attempt to copy the warriors with axes) and an unidentified animal (some kind of herd animal) rendered in red contour. (LV)

View over the village of Naga el-Ghalban, abandoned as a result of construction of the High Aswan Dam, towards the rocky hills on the right bank of the wadi Fomm el-Atmur in which the previously unknown rock shelter with coloured petroglyphs was documented by the Czechoslovak expedition

LOWER NUBIA

136 | Magical rock art of Late Antiquity

Nubian sandstone (support), technique of painting in red (different shades); dimensions not documented. Roman to early Christian Period. Lower Nubia, on the left bank of the Nile near the village of Naga Hafir, discovered in 1964. Field number 33 R 2.

At first sight the simple geometric signs made up of points, lines and polygons might give the impression of no more than a child's painting, but in fact this is the work of specialists in magic. From the 2nd century AD these signs enjoyed a notable popularity throughout the Eastern Mediterranean world. According to ritual papyri created in Egypt in the Ptolemaic Period this was a secret script that fulfilled a function in a whole range of rituals, where it lent a protective or other power to the things that it was written on. The tangle of these marks covering almost the whole ceiling of a rock shelter near the village of Naga Hafir gives the place a strongly magical-religious atmosphere and allows us to characterise it as a simple rock shrine sought out by people for whom the temples and shrines of the official cults were for various reasons inaccessible. (LV)

The overhang of a sandstone boulder near the village of Naga Hafir provided a suitable roof for activities that have left eloquent traces in the form of geometric marks on the underside

The same type of marks adorned also another rock shelter situated a few tens of kilometres further to the south in the appealing landscape of Korosko East

Unknown temples on the territory of the Sudan – Usli

MIROSLAV BÁRTA

Usli is situated about 40 km south-west of Merowe, the capital of the Sudan's Northern Province where the ancient centre of the region known today as Gebel Barkal once stood. In Antiquity Usli was evidently known as Tare/Tele, the site of a temple of the ancient Egyptian goddess Bastet and one of the last halts of the Napatan rulers on the route to Gebel Barkal. Czech archaeological excavations were started here in 2009.

So far, the archaeological projects on the site have led to the discoveries of several sandstone temples and settlement remains from the Napatan phase of the Kushite Period (ca. 900–300 BC). A tumuli cemetery from the Meroitic (300 BC – AD 350) and Post-Meroitic (4th–6th century AD) Periods and several settlement hillocks (known as koms) dated to the Christian period (6th century – 1323/1365 AD) are also attested.

The greater proportion of ancient monuments in Usli lie close beneath the surface of the sand in a flat area of roughly 300 × 200 metres. So far archaeological work has identified concentrations of sandstone blocks and remains of the bases and drums of sandstone pillars coming from several different temples. Archaeological research on what is known as Temple 1 has shown that this temple consisted of three separate parts and its main axis was oriented from the north-west to the south-east, perpendicular to the course of the Nile here. Its floor was paved with sandstone blocks. The walls of the temple were decorated with reliefs and inscriptions but only small fragments of these have survived.

It is now clear that the arrangement of the temple is typical for ancient Egyptian temples of the New Kingdom. These consist of an entrance pylon, open columned court, large columned hall (hypostyle) and the shrine itself. The temple in Usli could have originally been 15 to 20 metres wide, and 30 to 50 metres long.

< The Usli site with remains of a stone temple before the start of archaeological research

A magnetometric survey carried out in 2013 identified a smaller (perhaps 10 × 20 m) brick temple (Temple 2) situated west of Temple 1. Detected north of the sandstone temple was an extensive and complex agglomeration of brick buildings, the most notable of which is a roughly 30 × 40 m north-south orientated structure of palace type.

Subsequent archaeological excavations in the southern wing of the agglomeration partially uncovered a grand building that may again have served as a temple (Temple 3). The most remarkable finds include dozens of larger and smaller fragments of painted plaster with predominantly geometric motifs which once decorated the building. This is a very unusual record of temple decoration. Planned future research projects should throw light on the overall decoration of the temple, and also concentrate on the structure that seems to have been a royal palace.

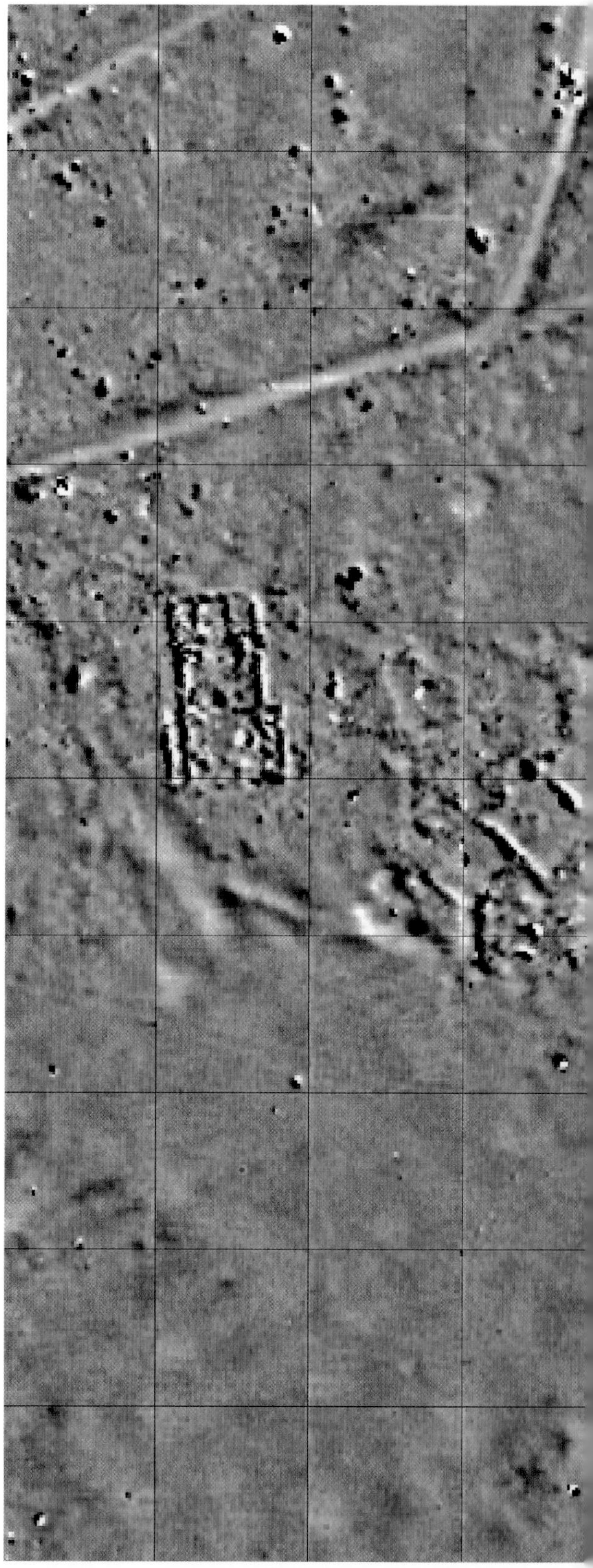

> The results of magnetometric survey in the central part of the Usli site which clearly show the remains of an extensive agglomeration of brick buildings with a centrally placed palace

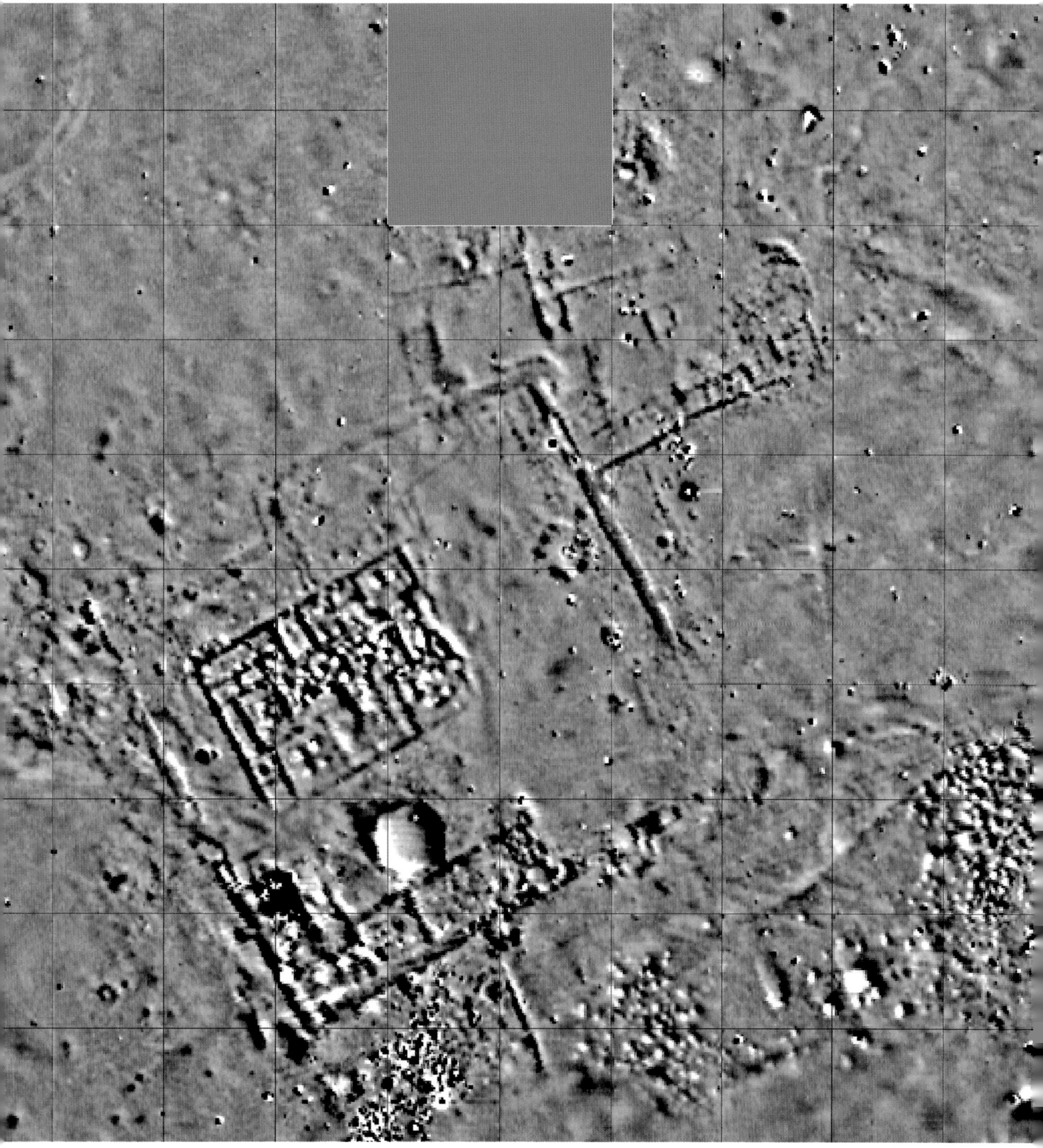

137 Fragment of the statue of a striding ruler

Granite; l. 60 cm, w. 32 cm, h. 18 cm. Kushite Period, Napatan phase. Upper Nubia, Usli, Temple I, square I, level of floor, discovered in 2009. Find number US-8-I-2009.

The most important individual finds in Usli include the fragment of a granite statue of a king in almost life-size. Large stone statues began to spread on the territory of Nubia in the context of Egyptian imperialism from the beginning of the New Kingdom. The fragment of this statue "gazing" to the south-east was found on the paved floor of Temple 1. Only the base of the statue and feet of the striding ruler up to the ankle have survived. Its back pillar bore a hieroglyphic inscription in sunken relief, of which all that remains is the final part: "beloved of (the god) Re." Although so fragmentary, the statue supports the provisional dating of the sandstone temple to the time of the Napatan phase of Kushite Period. (MB)

We still do not know the dedication of the stone temple in which the statue of the striding king was found. The fragmentary state of the statue means that the ruler too remains nameless

USLI
MAIN BUILDING
SQUARE 1
15.11.2009

138 Fragments of polychrome wall paintings

Mudbrick (support), painting in red, yellow, white and blue on coarse and fine clay plaster; w. of fragments max. 80 cm. Kushite Period. Upper Nubia, Usli, so-called southern wing of the brick palace and temple agglomeration (Temple 3), discovered in 2015. Find number US-196/2015, US-198/2015.

Fragments of painted plaster identified during excavation of what is known as the southern wing of the brick complex in Usli are remains of the original polychrome painting of the interior of the grand building. But of the building itself there remain only small remnants of mudbrick walls on which the plaster was originally set. The fragments were found in the fill covering the sandstone floor of one of the larger rooms, which once had two rows of columns supporting the roof. Just four colours – red, blue, yellow and white – were used here, creating what were geometric rather than figurative compositions. The theme of yellow stars on a blue background is identifiable, however, and this is known from the decoration of Kushite temples and palaces, where it forms either a decorative belt under the ceiling of a room, or a pattern on the robes of depicted gods and goddesses. (LV)

Apart from small fragments of brickwork, the remains of the grand building that once had walls adorned with polychrome plaster include a floor made from sandstone blocks and set into it the sandstone bases of originally wooden columns that once held up the ceiling of the uncovered room

USLI 2015
S.1 FR 41
MU2 5.3.

USLI 2015
S1 FR43
MU2 5.3.

The Sabaloka Mountains

LENKA VARADZINOVÁ

The volcanic Sabaloka mountain range rises like a rocky island out of the flat monotonous landscape 80 km north of Khartoum, the capital of the Sudan. The Nile runs through the middle of the mountain, dividing it into two parts. Where the river leaves the massif it goes through the smallest and most southerly of the six stretches of cataracts that interrupt the otherwise calm flow of the Nile between Khartoum and Aswan in Egypt. Together with the adjacent Sabaloka Mountains this section of the Nile Valley was characterised by modern travellers as the "pearl of the Sudan" and the most beautiful of the cataracts. From the archaeological point of view, however, until the arrival of the Czech expedition in the autumn of 2009 it was a *terra incognita*.

Initial prospecting revealed the exceptional potential of the area for the study especially of prehistoric settlement and its interaction with the natural environment. This is now the main goal of research, which since 2011 has focused on the western part

< Prehistoric sites in the area of the Rocky Cities on the western edge of the Sabaloka Mountains are usually surrounded by a "rampart" of massive granite boulders

The Sixth Nile Cataract by the northern edge of the Sabaloka Mountains

of the mountain range. Here a dense network of settlements from the Mesolithic (9th–6th millennium BC) and Neolithic (5th–4th millennium BC) Periods has been uncovered. Two sites dominate in the settlement structure: Fox Hill, situated in the area of the "Lake Basin" close to the Nile, and Sphinx, located in the arid but very impressive landscape of what are known as the "Rocky Cities". The exceptional value of both sites, indicated by the density of surface finds of richly decorated pottery (which appeared in North Africa as early as the 10th millennium BC), stone and bone industry, animal bones and mollusc shells, was confirmed by excavation. In both locations cemeteries of Mesolithic hunter-gatherers with individuals of both sexes and various age groups were also, surprisingly, uncovered in the excavated trenches. These notably large hunter-gatherer cemeteries (at Sphinx the number of burials is estimated on good evidence to be around 400, and at Fox Hill the number could be similar), hitherto unknown in the Sudan and unusual even in global context, are a valuable source of knowledge of the biology, sociology and way of life of North African hunter-gatherer populations in the period shortly before the introduction of productive economy, which began spreading to the continent from the 6th–5th millennia BC.

All kinds of tumuli and graves, either isolated or forming extensive cemeteries, are a much later but unmistakeable component of the archaeological landscape in Sabaloka. Most of them date from the Post-Meroitic (4th–6th Centuries AD) or Christian (6th century – 1504) Periods, when this area was on the periphery of the Meroitic Empire and later the Christian kingdom of Alodia. Test excavations carried out by our expedition have shown that these monuments have significant potential for the understanding of the still little known way of life of these populations as well as for the study of contacts and existence of borders between the political formations of the time.

> View of the southern part of the settlement platform of the Mesolithic site of Sphinx in the course of exploration of the cemetery of hunter-gatherers there

139 | Archaeobotanical collection from the 4th century AD

Seeds, fruits and vegetative parts of plants, grains of pollen; dimensions not documented. Early Post-Meroitic Period. Central Sudan, Sabaloka Mountains (Sixth Nile Cataract), on the west bank of the Nile, Fox Hill site, Terrace 10, Tumulus I, discovered in 2011. Find number FH-0382 (macro-botanical remains); FH-0120, FH-0123_b (pollen spectra).

More than 2,000 macro-botanical remains collected in the tomb of an archer at Fox Hill have drawn attention to a hitherto unexploited source of information about the life and death of people living in the little known period of transition between pagan "antiquity" and the Christian "middle ages". These are the remains of wild plants, of which some are edible. The absence of domesticated plants among these macro-botanical remains, and even in pollen found inside a beer jar and the digestive tract of the archer opens up the question of the scale of consumption of wild plants in the place and the time concerned. The type of the tumulus, made by heaped earth over a semi-circular stone core, suggests that this archer lived either on the periphery or beyond the border of what was once the Meroitic Empire. The iron weapons and faience beads, on the other hand, indicate some form of contacts with the Meroitic political centres of the time. (LV)

The semi-circular stone core and the ring of stones along the outer perimeter of the tumulus suggest affinity with the southern tradition of tumuli that so far have been found only outside the settlement area of the Meroitic Empire

The objects found close to his body indicate the individual's status as an archer – iron arrowheads with remnants of wooden shafts, a spearhead and a stone ring used to protect the thumb during archery

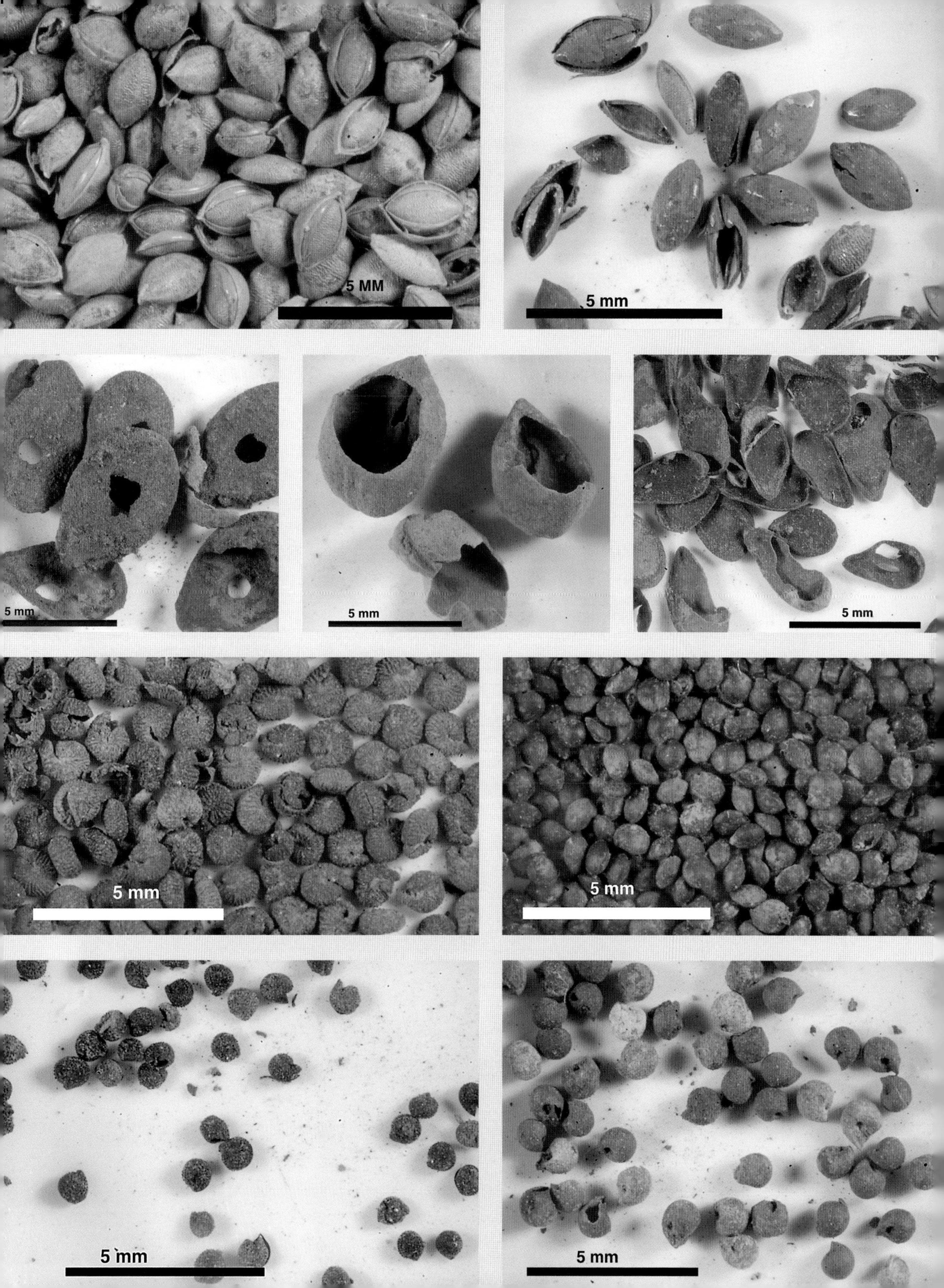
5 MM
5 mm
5 mm
5 mm
5 mm
5 mm
5 mm
5 mm
5 mm

140 Virtual reconstruction of a vanished type of architecture in the Sabaloka Mountains

Granite, technique of drilling probably with a wooden drill, possible use of an abrasive; depth of the drilled holes max. 50 cm, diameter of the mouth 4–5 cm. Dating unclear – Mesolithic, or Meroitic up to Islamic Period. Central Sudan, Sabaloka Mountains (Sixth Nile Cataract), on the west bank of the Nile, Sphinx site – central/northern part, documented in 2015. No find number.

This group of holes drilled in the rock arranged roughly in an arch are the only remains of one of the two light skeletal buildings that once stood at the site of Sphinx. They were created using bent wooden poles solidly fixed to the rock wall that formed part of their interiors. Lengthwise sticks were fastened to the vertical poles that had one end stuck into the drilled holes and the other pushed into the earth, and the whole skeletal framework was covered in roofing made of grass, mats, hides and suchlike. The dating of the drilled holes, which can be found in other places on the western edge of the Sabaloka range, and of this already vanished type of architecture, is unclear. The creators of these buildings could have been Mesolithic hunter-gatherers, or pastoralists from the Meroitic up to the Islamic Period. (LV)

The position of both reconstructed buildings on the settlement platform of the Sphinx site coincides with the only two places in this site that remain in the shade for the whole day

The arrangements of the artificial drilled holes along the edge of two granite boulders and their different depths and orientation enable us to reconstruct a relatively large dome-shaped semi-circular structure

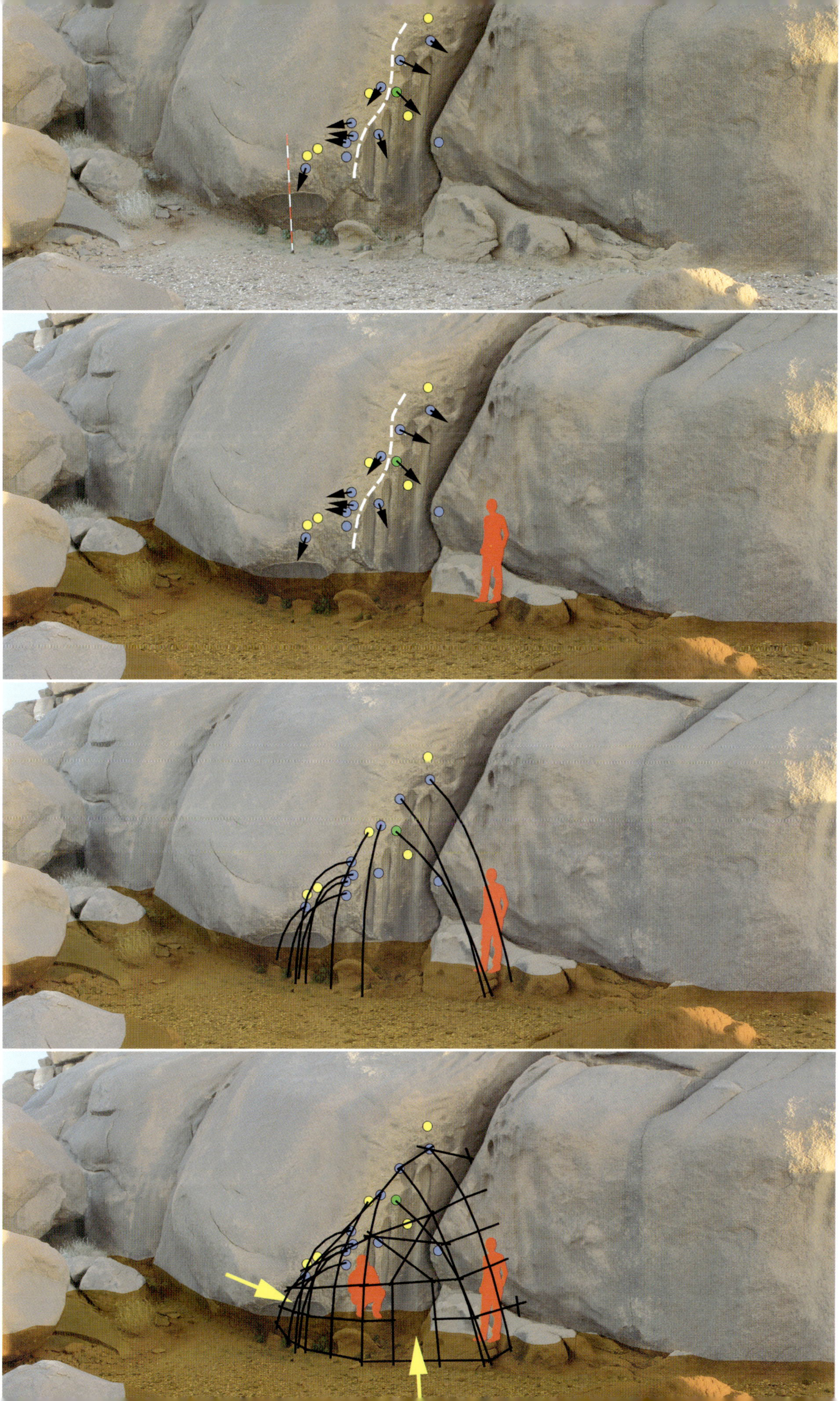

Glossary

JAROMÍR KREJČÍ

Mastaba of the vizier Ptahshepses in Central Abusir. View from the Old Portico into the chapel with three niches

akh – Eg. "radiant"; the transfigured form of human (and divine) beings, endowed with magical abilities, which the deceased assumed in the next world. The other parts of personality were →*ba*, →*ka*, name, shadow and body. The *akh* was a mighty deceased, who did not remain among the dead (*mutu*) after death, but became one of the blessed in the hereafter.

akhet – Eg. "horizon", but also the name of one of the three seasons of the year, the season of inundation. The horizon was the link between heaven and earth and also the place where the sun was resurrected and from which the gods and the *akhu*, the mighty dead (pl. of →*akh*) came into the world.

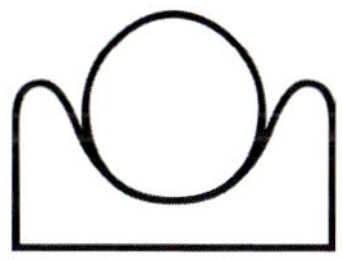

akhet

Amduat – Eg. "The Book of What is in the Underworld". One of the sets of religious texts known as guides to the Hereafter, which from the New Kingdom onwards formed part of the decorative programme of royal (and later also non-royal) tombs. They explained what happens to the sun (and the dead) in the underworld.

amulet – object with the magical power to protect its bearer. Egyptians carried amulets on their bodies in life and in death. During the embalming and bandaging process amulets were placed on the bodies of the deceased.

Amun – one of the most important of Egyptian gods. His name means "hidden". Although he was usually depicted as a seated (sometimes also standing) man with a crown of two tall feathers on his head, and a short kilt, the Egyptians believed that his true form was unknown not only to men but even to the rest of the gods. He is first mentioned in the Pyramid Texts, but it was not until the 11th Dynasty, when Egypt was reunited under a Theban royal dynasty, that his cult grew and flourished. In the era of the New Kingdom Amun was a state god and considered the king of the gods. At the same time he was joined to the sun god →Re as Amon-Re. Amun's wife was the goddess Mut ("Mother") and his son was the moon god Khonsu. Their temples in Karnak form a single immense complex. Amun's principal sacred animal was the ram.

Amun

ankh – a hieroglyphic sign in the form of a "cross" with a loop in the upper part, symbolising life. It is often depicted in the hands of Egyptian gods, in gestures expressing the giving of (eternal) life. Egyptian Christians (→ Copts) retained the *ankh*, adapting it into the form of what is known as the Coptic Cross.

ankh

Anubis – the protector god of cemeteries, mummification and the entrance of the dead into the afterworld. He was venerated from the Archaic Period onwards and was represented as a jackal or man with a jackal head.

architrave – a lintel or beam, made of stone or in some cases wood, which rests horizontally on columns, pillars or walls.

ba

ba – one of the components of human (and divine) personality. The others were →*akh*, →*ka*, shadow, name and body. It is usually translated as "spirit" or "soul". It expresses the form of divine beings or the dead that could travel between the earthly and the other world. It was represented as a saddle-billed stork or falcon with the head of the deceased.

Bes – a god in the form of a grimacing dwarf. Together with the goddess Tweret he was a protector of children and pregnant women and could ensure a successful safe childbirth. Bes brought family happiness and prosperity. In the form in which he holds a knife in his hand he would drive snakes and scorpions out of dwellings. He was also associated with music and entertainment.

Book of the Dead

Book of the Dead – the modern title given to the set of heterogeneous religio-magical texts originally entitled "The Book of the Coming Forth by Day". The main purpose of the Book of the Dead was to ensure for the dead a safe passage to a blissful life in the next world. Individual incantations (or chapters) drew on the →Pyramid Texts and the →Coffin Texts and were sometimes accompanied by illustrations (known as "vignettes").

canopic jar – one of the four (normally stone) vessels intended for storage of the mummified internal organs (stomach, liver, lung and intestines) of a deceased person or sacred animal. During the New Kingdom the lids of these vessels started to be shaped into the form of the Egyptian protective gods known as the sons of Horus (Amset, Hapy, Kebehsenuf and Duamutef).

Cartouche

cartouche – oval frame in the form of coiled rope in which two of the five names of an Egyptian ruler would be written: his throne and birth name. The frame thus magically protected the ruler whose name was written inside. See also royal titulary.

cataract – rapids on a river. In Antiquity the first Nile rapids at present-day Aswan represented the southern border of the Egyptian state.

Coffin Texts – the modern name for the set of religious texts that some consider to have developed from the →Pyramid Texts in the course of the First Intermediate Period. It is possible, however, that the Coffin Texts originated in the same period as the Pyramid Texts, as some written sources suggest. They were used primarily in the decoration of coffins until the end of the Middle Kingdom, but parts of them appear in funerary context right up to the Ptolemaic Period. Like the Pyramid Texts or the later →Books of the Dead, the Coffin Texts were intended to ensure that the deceased had a safe passage into an eternal blessed life in the next world.

concave cornice – an architectural element that copies in stone the concave curved top edge of reed matting when the rest is stretched on a wooden frame to create walls. Together with the torus (the wooden supporting framework for the reed-matt walls converted into stone) it formed what is known as the Egyptian gorge.

concave cornice

concession – generally a (state) permission to undertake particular activities; in Egyptian and Sudanese archaeology it is a license to conduct archaeological research on a precisely defined territory under conditions stipulated in advance. A written agreement on research is part of a concession.

Copt – Christian inhabitant of Egypt (today also Ethiopia) belonging to the Eastern (Orthodox) Christian tradition. Coptic was the last developmental stage of the Egyptian language and today is only a liturgical language. Coptic script consists of the capitals of the Greek alphabet supplemented by seven Demotic signs.

cosmogony – a set of ideas about the genesis and foundation of the world. In ancient Egypt several cosmogonies existed alongside each other, and were bound up with local traditions, natural conditions and cults. The most important cosmogonies were associated with the cities of Heliopolis (Iuni), Hermopolis (Khemenu), Memphis (Mennofer) and Thebes (Waset).

demotic – a type of script and language used in Egypt from the 7th century BC to the 5th century AD. Demotic (Greek for "of the people") script developed out of hieratic script and is a very simplified cursive form. From the linguistic point of view Demotic is the fourth phase in the evolution of Egyptian.

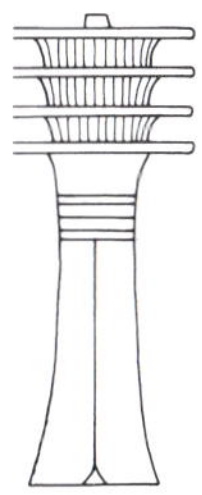

djed

djed – fetish in the shape of a column with plant patterns in the upper part. It was a symbol of permanence and stability and was one of the attributes of the Egyptian gods. It often also appears as an amulet, or pendant.

Double crown – the conjoined →White and →Red royal crown. It was the symbol of the unified Egyptian state.

dynasty – term for a historical period defined by a succession of directly related rulers. The term was introduced by the Egyptian priest Manetho (who lived in Egypt in the 3rd century BC), when he divided Egyptian history into thirty royal dynasties. This division is still used in Egyptology today and provides the basic chronological framework of research.

engaged statue – statue that is not separated from its background. It is usually to be found on the facade of a building, or the walls of a chapel or →naos. Ancient Egyptian engaged statues may also be regarded as high bas-relief.

engaged statue

faience

Ennead – the group of nine gods who were born at the beginning of the world and created the world over a few generations. The numeral nine is based on the symbolism of the number three as the sign of plurality and multiplicity, and hence refers to an absolute plural, i.e. the community of all the principal gods. The oldest Ennead came from the centre of the solar cult in Heliopolis, whereas we find records of different Enneads in other important religious centres.

faience – in Egyptology a term for a ceramic made of powdered quartz grains and covered in blue green and green glaze. Egyptian faience was used for the production of amulets, jewellery, →ushabti and other objects.

false beard – part of the royal insignia and an attribute of high status. It was fastened to the chin with strings or leather bands tied behind the ear. It was worn by kings and high-ranking dignitaries, and in some scenes by Egyptian gods.

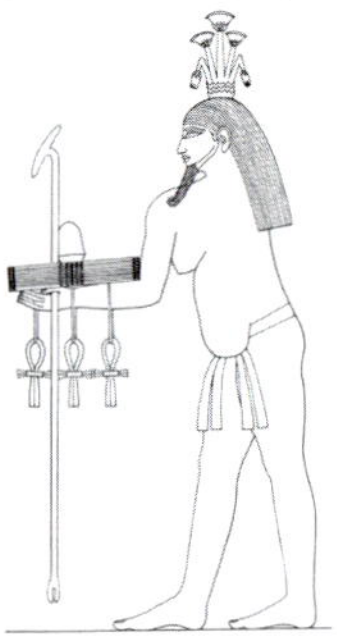

Hapi

false door – a stone (sometimes wooden) stela representing the entrance to a house. It was normally set into the west wall of the main offering chapel of a tomb. The false door is usually decorated with texts including the name, titles and stylized representation of the deceased. It connected the world of the living and the world of the dead, and relatives or priests entrusted with the task would present offerings in front of it to the owner of the tomb, with the incantation of magic formula, so as to ensure his or her welfare in the next world.

Hapi – a god associated with the Nile floods that brought nutrient-rich mud to the fields. He was depicted as a fat man with bulging stomach and breasts, a loin cloth, and a crown of water plants on his head. Hapi lived at the symbolic sources of the Nile, for example in caves close to the first Nile →Cataract.

Hathor

Hathor – a goddess depicted as a woman with cow's ears and horns or as a cow. Her name – in translation "seat of Horus" – links her directly with the god of the sky and the royal office →Horus. She was considered the symbolic mother (and also wife) of the king. In the form of a cow she was venerated in the New Kingdom as "Lady of the West" in the cemeteries of Western Thebes as protectress of cemeteries. As "Lady of the Sycamore" Hathor ensured the supply of offerings for the dead. But she was also the goddess of love, music, dance and sex. One of her attributes is a sistrum, a percussion instrument on the principle of the rattle, which can often be seen included in images of Hathor's head with cow ears.

heqa

head-rest – support for the head of a sleeper. It was shaped in a curve held up by a short leg on a pedestal. It often appears in funerary equipment, sometimes just as a model. Head-rests were made of wood, travertine, limestone or ivory.

heqa – type of the sceptre of the Egyptian king or a god, one of the royal insignia. It was a stick with a bent top resembling a shepherd's crook.

Herishef – a god whose name mean "he who is above his lake". This sacred lake was situated in what today is called Ehnasya el-Medina (in Greek Herakleopolis) in Middle Egypt, Herishef's main cult centre. His cult experienced a flowering at the end of the Old Kingdom and in the Fist Intermediate Period when the northern part of Egypt was governed by the local royal line known as the Herakleopolitan Kings. Herishef was depicted as a man with a ram head, *atef* crown and short kilt.

---

hieratic – a cursive (written) type of hieroglyphic script. It was written with a rush pen or brush on papyrus and other materials. →demotic was an even more simplified version of cursive writing.

hieratic

---

hieroglyphic script – the overall name for Egyptian logophonetic script consisting of signs that expressed either a sound value (phonograms), a whole word (logograms), or explained the meaning of individual groups of signs (determinatives). From its origins in the 2nd half of the 4th millennium BC to the 4th century AD it was used principally for royal records, but also for other official and religious texts on the walls of temples and tombs, on stelae, obelisks and other important objects.

Horus – the god of the sky, sun and light, and also closely bound up with ancient Egyptian kingship. His name can be translated as "High" or "Distant". He was represented in the form of a falcon or man with a falcon head and was one of the most important of Egyptian gods. The cults of other, local gods, including as various forms of the sun god, were incorporated into the cult of Horus.

Horus

Horus name – part of the royal titulary; the oldest of the five names of the Egyptian king. It was written into what was known as a →*serekh*, on which the god →Horus perched in the form of a falcon.

House of Life – a venerable institution, centre of learning and scriptorium, with functions that developed over time. Houses of life were parts of temple districts; Egyptians not only housed but created papyrus scrolls there. Houses of Life were also places where writing was taught, and religious-philosophical discussion conducted. They contributed to religious, political and economic life in Egypt by educating priests and officials for the state administration.

Hyksos – a Greek expression derived from the Egyptian *hekau khasut*, "rulers of foreign lands". It refers to the Asian nomads who in the course of the 1st half of the 2nd millennium BC gained control of the northern part of Egypt, where they founded the 15th Dynasty.

---

hypostyle – hall with a ceiling supported by columns or pillars.

Isis

Isis – a goddess closely connected with the gods →Osiris (as his partner) and →Horus (as his mother), and so also with the royal ideology. She was the symbolic mother of the ruler and at the same time had immense magical skill and power. She appears as an almost omnipotent magician and healer particularly from the Late Period. Her name was written using the hieroglyphic sign for throne, which also often appears as an attribute on her head. Sometimes, however, like →Hathor, she is adorned with cow's horns and a solar disk.

ka

ka – one of the components of human (and divine) personality. The others were →*akh*, →*ba*, shadow, name and body. It was regarded as a creative life-giving force and a symbol of the continuation of life. It was an important aspect of both the earthly and the posthumous life of the individual.

lotiform columns – like →papyriform columns imitated the shape of one lotus plant, or more often a bunch of lotus stems. The capital of the column was composed of open and partially closed flowers or of buds.

lotiform column

Lower Egypt – the territory of the Nile Delta and the part of the Nile Valley in the north of Egypt. The southern border with →Upper Egypt lay south of the former capital city of Egypt, Memphis (Eg. Mennofer), i.e. south of what today is Saqqara. The duality (of Upper and Lower Egypt) was reflected in the ideology of the office of king and maintained up to the Roman period.

Maat – goddess representing the all-embracing order of the world known as *maat*. This was established by the gods and meant the proper alignment of the world, society and nature, but also truth, justice, moral blamelessness, ethical values and culture. Maat was depicted as a woman with an ostrich feather on her head. This feather can sometimes represent her in iconography, for example in scenes of what was known as the weighing of the heart of the dead in the court of the underworld. Maat was also closely connected to the judicial system.

Maat

macro-botanic remains – vegetative and reproductive parts of plants. Their analysis provides information on the ecological and climatic conditions in which the plants grew, and on what happened to them after they died away.

manawar (or kanat – both from Arabic) – name for an artificial underground canal by which water in desert areas is brought from a water source simply by the exploitation of gravity. The main part of a manawar is a gallery dug underground with a very shallow slant, so that the water in it flows very slowly and does not damage the side walls. It is accessed via vertical shafts.

mastaba – a type of non-royal tomb. The term is derived from the Arabic word for a bench. The mastaba has a superstructure on a rectangular plan with slanting side walls. The body of the deceased was interred in an underground burial chamber accessed by either a vertical shaft or a descending corridor.

Morning House – a special room where the ruler underwent ritual purification. Even though divine in his essence, without this purification the king could not meet the gods during important religious rituals and in the exercise of his office. During the Old Kingdom, activities in the Morning House were considered so important that viziers and other high-ranking officials were involved in them.

---

mortuary temple – 1. temple building usually standing at the foot of the east wall of a royal →pyramid. It was here that religious rituals took place to renew the strength of the monarch (see also →*sed*) and his mortuary cult; 2. temple complex called "House of the Millions of Years". These temples were built during the New Kingdom in western Thebes as cult additions to the rock tombs of the rulers in the Valley of Kings. Their operations included not just the mortuary cult of the king concerned, but also the cults of some gods (in particular Theban→Amun and Memphite →Ptah).

mortuary temple

---

mortuary cult – set of rituals ensuring the continued and blessed life of the deceased after death. Its basis was an effort to conserve the body of the deceased, by mummification, and the construction and decoration of a tomb that would include his or her biographical details and the placing of the funerary equipment and offerings into a burial chamber together with the mummified body. The mortuary cult and regular presentation of offerings continued even after the end of the funeral ceremonies. Formally they were supposed to be presented by the eldest son of the deceased, but often special priests were hired instead.

---

mummy – an expression that in Egyptian archaeology means the dead body of a person or sacred animal that has been preserved naturally or using artificial techniques. The Egyptians believed in the importance of the existence of the material body even after death (see also →*ba*, →*akh*, →*ka*), and so tried to preserve it as effectively as possible. Using embalming and mummification they imitated the natural process of drying out that bodies underwent when interred in burial pits dug into the desert sand.

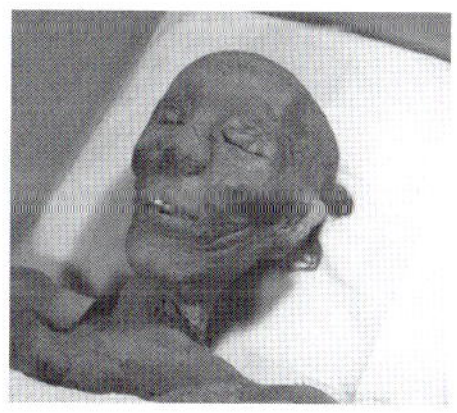

mummy

---

naos – a shrine that can be closed, usually in the form of a large cabinet, and is used to house cult statues. It was made of wood or hard types of stone and placed in the most sacred room of temples and tombs, which is why this room is sometimes also known as a naos.

---

natron – a natural mixture of sodium carbonate decahydrate and bicarbonate of soda which was mined principally in Wadi Natrun, a valley north-west of today's Cairo. Natron was used above all for drying out the bodies of the deceased during mummification, but also for ritual purification and fumigation during cult ceremonies in temples and chapels.

---

necropolis – cemetery (Greek "city of the dead"). In archaeology generally it is a term for any larger or more important group of tombs, but in Egyptology particularly for a royal cemetery.

Neith – the goddess of hunting and war, and protectress of Egyptian kings. The main centre of her cult was in the city of Sais in the Nile Delta. Neith was represented with the crown of →Lower Egypt on her head, and her attribute was a shield with crossed arrows.

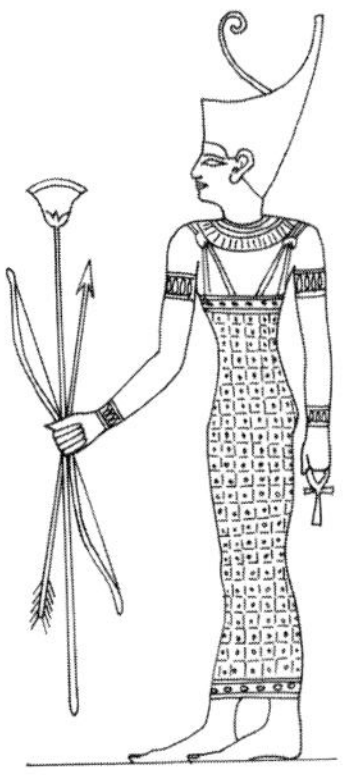

Neith

Nekhbet – the protective goddess of →Upper Egypt, depicted in the form of a vulture. The name means "of Nekheb" and refers to her main cult centre, situated in El-Kab (eg. Nekheb) in Upper Egypt.

nemes – a head covering, part of the royal insignia. It is a headscarf worn by kings or gods. It was tied into a "braid" at the back using a thin cord, while at the front its flaps hung down as far as its bearer's chest.

Nekhbet

Nephthys – "the Lady of the House", a goddess usually depicted as a woman with the hieroglyphic signs of her name above her head. She was the protectress of the living and the dead, assisted in childbirth and during funerary rituals, and together with her sister →Isis acted as a guide for the dead.

nisut-bity – Eg. "he of the sedge and bee", i.e. "king of →Upper and →Lower Egypt"; one of the five titles of the Egyptian ruler. See also royal titulary, cartouche.

Nephthys

nomarch – governor of a region, who represented the ruler in a →nome.

nome – a division of local government. Starting under the 3rd Dynasty Egypt was divided into nomes or regions; in→Upper Egypt there were 22 and in →Lower Egypt there were 20, but their numbers changed slightly in the course of history. Local gods were venerated in the administrative centres of the individual nomes.

Nun – god personifying the primeval waters from the divine creator emerged on the primeval mound and from which the world also rose up.

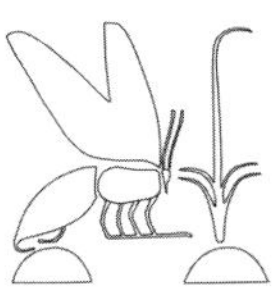

nisut-bity

Nut – one of the most important goddesses of the sky, the personification of the vault of heaven. She is depicted as a woman, but sometimes also as a cow. As partner of the god of the earth Geb and mother or grandmother of five preeminent gods (including →Osiris, →Isis and →Horus) she played a significant role in the Heliopolitan →cosmogony. As mother of the sun god she protected the divine order of the world, *maat*, from the incursions of the forces of chaos and was associated with ideas of rebirth and entrance to the other world. In the →Pyramid Texts she appears as a protectress of the soul of the ruler and is identified with his sarcophagus.

Nut

obelisk – a four-sided pillar, tapering towards the top and terminating in a →pyramidion. In most cases it was made from a stone monolith, in a few cases they were built of separate construction blocks. It is one of the symbols of the sun god, his power and continual regeneration.

Opening of the Mouth – an important ritual often conducted as part of funerary ceremonies. It involves the priest touching the mouth or eyes of statues, mummy or coffins of deceased with ritual instruments in order symbolically to open them, i.e. to revive the senses and organs of the deceased for life in the next world, or to animate the statue of a god to enable him or her to take part in the temple cult on earth.

obelisk

Osiris – god of death and resurrection, the ruler of the dead and the underworld. He was depicted as a man dressed in a close-fitting robe, who holds in his hands the symbols of the royal office (the sceptre and flail) and on his head has an *atef* crown adorned with ram's horns and ostrich feathers. Osiris was one of the main figures of almost all texts concerned with life in the next world, and he presided over the judgment of the dead. At the same time, however, he represented the continuity of royal power and government, while also being the god of fertility and crops. The main centre of his cult was Abydos, where mystery plays were probably held to worship him and for the initiation of believers.

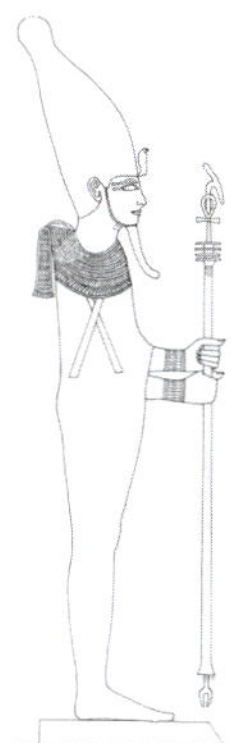

Osiris

ostrakon – sherd of pottery or chip of stone (usually limestone). Ostraka were used for writing or drawing (or sketching), as a substitute for the much more expensive →papyrus. Ostraka carried mainly everyday texts (letters, accounts, school and literary texts etc.).

palmiform columns – type of column with capital in the shape palm leaves lashed to a pole – a cylindrical shaft. The palm leaves are bound with rope, creating the lower border of the capital.

palmiform column

papyriform column – type of column imitating the shape of one papyrus plant, or a bunch of papyrus stems. The capital of the column was composed of open or partially closed inflorescences.

papyrus – a writing material obtained from the pith of the papyrus sedge (*Cyperus papyrus*). It was made by pressing together two layers of thin strips cut of the pithy stems of sedge laid criss-cross. This created long belts of material rolled into scrolls, on which scribes wrote as a rule in →hieratic script. Papyrus was also an emblem of →Lower Egypt.

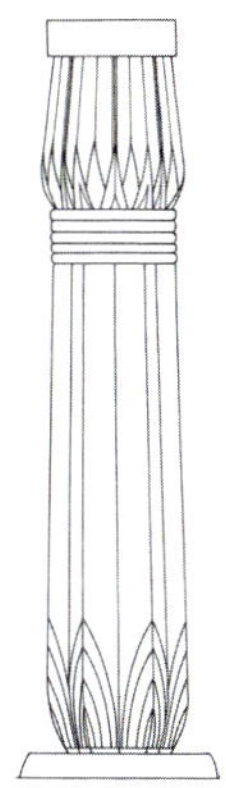

papyriform column

peret (Eg.) – the season of emergence or growth; the season following →*akhet*.

petroglyph – sign or image created on the surface of stone by cutting, hollowing, chiseling and other techniques.

pharaoh – name for the Egyptian king, which derives from the Egyptian word for the royal palace, *per aa* –"great house". It was used from the New Kingdom to mean the ruler himself. It has found its way into modern languages from biblical Hebrew.

portico – one or more rows of columns or pillars in front of the entrance to a building. Later it was also the name for a columned hall situated in front of the entrance, primarily in Ptolemaic buildings.

Ptah – one of the most important of the Egyptian gods. Ptah was represented as a man dressed in a close-fitting robe and cap, and holding in front of him the symbol of power, life and continuity – the *was* sceptre combined with the →*ankh* and →*djed*. In addition to his central position in the Memphite →cosmogony, where he appears as the creator and ruler of the world, he was also the protector god of craftsmen. His main cult centre was Memphis and the name of the biggest temple there, Hutkaptah (house of Ptah's "ka") was the basis for the Greek expression Aigyptos, from which the name Egypt later derived.

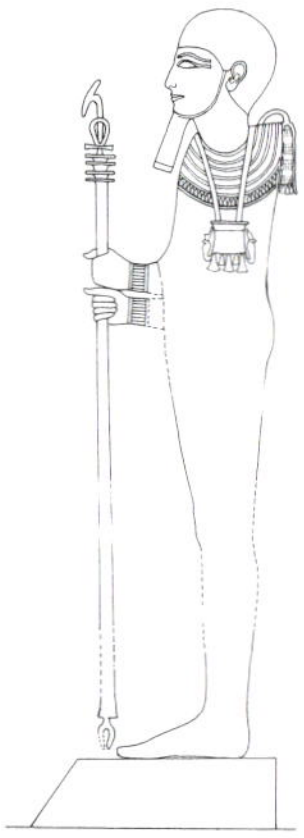

Ptah

Punt – the Egyptian name for a still not precisely identified area of East Africa (most probably today's Somalia). Egyptians had trading relations with Punt as early as the Old Kingdom and it was the source of imported myrrh, incense, ebony wood, ivory and the skins of big cats, and also monkeys and hunting dogs.

Pylon

pylon – monumental entrance to temple with two wide tapering towers on the sides. Between the towers was a lower section enclosing massive doors usually covered with metal plate. The overall shape is resembles the sign for the word *akhet* (horizon).

---

pyramid – square pyramid, i.e. polyhedron with four triangular sides on square base, the monumental superstructure of royal tombs. In Egypt the pyramids date mainly from the period of the Old and Middle Kingdom, and in Sudan from the 8th century BC to the 4th century AD. At the beginning they had a stepped shape, but this evolved into a straight-sided, true pyramid. In the period of the New Kingdom small pyramids appear even in non-royal context.

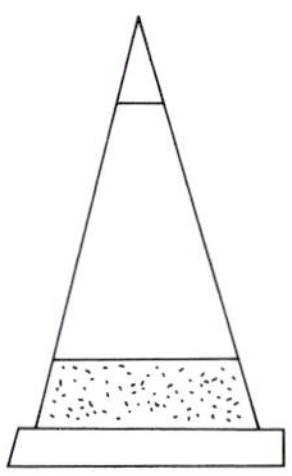

Pyramid

---

pyramidion – the very top of →pyramids and →obelisks. In pyramids this was the highest section of their stone casing, and in obelisks the tip of their monolithic (or faced) shaft. Pyramidia were often covered with gold, electron or copper plate.

---

pyramid complex – set of cult buildings with the →pyramid as their central focus. In standard form it was composed of valley temple, causeway, →mortuary temple, pyramid and satellite pyramid. The main purpose of the complex was to carry on the king's mortuary cult, thus renewing his strength and eternal life in the other world.

Pyramid Texts

Pyramid Texts – the modern name for a set of religious texts of various different kinds connected with funerary ritual and ideas of the life of the Egyptian ruler in the next world. These texts appear in the decoration of the interiors of the pyramids of the Egyptian kings and queens from the end of the 5th to the 8th Dynasty. The oldest Pyramid Texts are documented in the pyramid of the 5th Dynasty King Unas.

pyramid town – dwelling complex situated in the immediate proximity of a royal →pyramid complex of the Old or Middle Kingdom. The pyramid town was founded by central royal offices and its inhabitants (priests, officials and other staff) would take part in the running of the king's mortuary cult in the pyramid complex. For their services they would receive payment in kind from the state administration.

Re – one of the forms of the sun god, other forms were Khepri (the morning sun) and Atum (the evening sun). Re was represented in many forms: as the solar disk (the noonday sun), in human form, sometimes with a falcon head. The concept of the cycle of day and night as the diurnal and nocturnal journey of the sun, both taking 12 hours, and made by the sun in the solar bark, is the synonym for the eternal repetition of creation and regeneration. Re was the creator god (in Heliopolis, where his main temple was situated) and the first king, and he so was associated with the royal office (as one of the royal titles, "Son of Re" indicates).

Re

Red Crown – one of the royal insignia. In shape it broadened out from the brow and rose at the back into a tapering tip. It was adorned in front with a spiral that coiled backwards. It was one of the main symbols of →Lower Egypt.

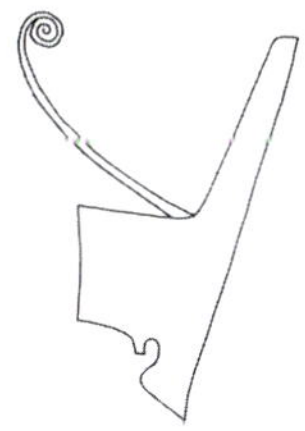

Red Crown

register – in Egyptology this is a term for a horizontal strip of decoration on the wall of a tomb or temple that is separated from other registers above or below it by a line or narrow belt. Egyptian artists used registers to express space and perspective.

reis – Arab. "head", or "chief": in the context of archaeological excavations in Egypt it is the title given to the foreman of the workers who takes care of the practical side of field research.

reis

royal titulary – the king's set of titles and names; from the beginning of the 5th Dynasty it normally consisted of five titles and five names. The oldest title was the →Horus name, then followed the titles Two Ladies, Golden Horus, king of →Upper and →Lower Egypt, son of →Re. Each of these titles was followed by the corresponding name. The names set out after the last two titles were inscribed in →cartouche.

sarcophagus – stone receptacle either of rectangular box or anthropoid shape for the interment of the body of the deceased in a burial chamber.

scarab – the scarab beetle (*Scarabeus sacer*) was considered a symbol of self-generation and renewal and as the embodiment of the morning form of the sun god. The scarab was the most popular type of amulet. The heart scarab was supposed to help the individual pass the test of judgment after death in the underworld. Quite large commemorative scarabs were made to mark all kinds of important events.

sed – festival of the king's jubilee, ideally after thirty years on the throne. The several-day ceremonies were supposed to ensure the renewal of the king's physical and magical powers. This ancient festival also played an important role in the royal mortuary cults.

sed

serdab – Arab. "cellar", term for a small, closed cult chamber in a tomb in which statues representing the deceased (usually at different ages and in different functions) were placed. In the substructure of the royal pyramids of the 5th and 6th Dynasty the serdab comprised three rooms east of the vestibule and arranged like the teeth of a comb.

serekh – stylised representation of the facade of a royal palace with entrance. It formed a rectangular, vertically orientated frame for the inscription of a →Horus name. The god →Horus was often depicted in the form of a falcon sitting on this framework.

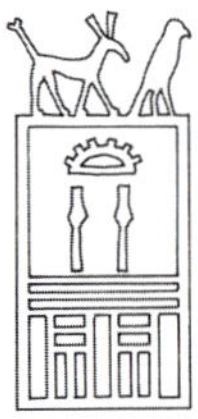

serekh

Seth or Set – god of the desert, storms, darkness, the sea and war, the lord of chaos. He was the opposite of the gods →Osiris and →Horus, but at the same time the ally of the sun god →Re against the protagonist of disorder, the serpent Apophis, and he was the protective god of →Upper Egypt. He was depicted as a man with the head of his sacred animal, but the animal has never been clearly identified. His battle with Osiris for domination over Egypt and the world became (above all from the Later Period) a symbol of the eternal struggle between order and chaos.

Seth

shelter – a rock overhang used in the past for dwelling purposes.

shemu – the time of harvest; a summer season characterised by high temperatures and low water on the Nile. It came after the season →*peret*.

Sokar – god depicted as a falcon, a man with a falcon head, or also a low hillock on which a falcon head or a bark with a falcon rests. In the Memphis area he was venerated as the god of burial, resurrection and lord of the necropolis. Sokar's important festival culminated in a procession carrying his divine *henu* cult bark.

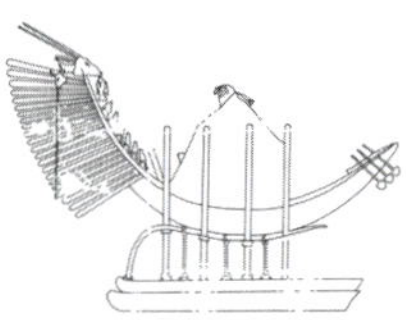

Sokar

speos – temple hollowed out of a rock face. One sub-type of a speos is a hemispeos, with an extension built onto the front of the rock part.

sphinx – the term in Egyptology for a statue with a lion's body and the head of a king or sacred animal. Connection with a lion's body expressed the strength and power of a king or god.

sphinx

substructure – the underground part of a building (e.g. a tomb).

superstructure – the above-ground part of a building (e.g. a tomb).

Tweret – goddess, protectress of women during childbirth and nursing mothers. In most cases she was depicted as a pregnant hippopotamus standing on her back legs, with hanging breasts, lion paws and a crocodile tail.

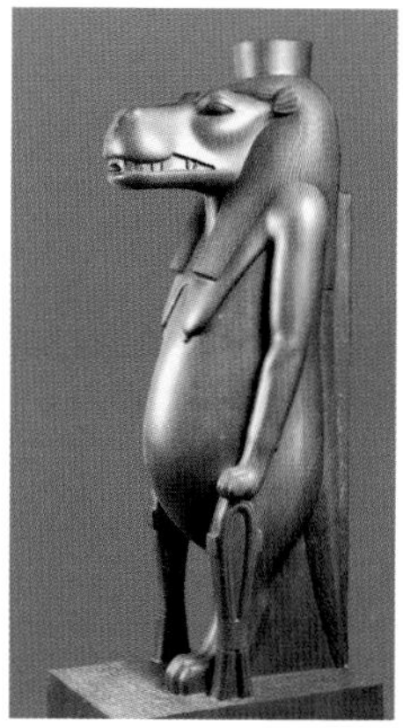

Tweret

Upper Egypt – the part of the Nile Valley lying roughly between Saqqara and Aswan, or the First Nile Cataract. The dynasty of rulers that gained control of all Egypt and unified it around the year 3100 BC came from Upper Egypt, from the Abydos region.

uraeus – the rearing cobra with outspread hood depicted on the brow of the ruler and a symbol of the fiery, i.e. protective power of the sun god.

ushabti – small figurine of a servant or workmen (mostly made of →faience, but sometimes made of wood or stone). From the First Intermediate Period onwards ushabti were added to funerary equipment. Originally they may have been "substitute" bodies for the dead, but gradually they took on the role of servants. They were not conceived as working for the deceased in the hereafter but on his behalf, i.e. working for the general good in his stead.

vizier – a modern term (coming from Persian) for the title of the highest official in the land. The vizier intervened in all areas of government; he had the deciding judicial power, directed royal building works and so on.

wadi – Arab. "valley"; the term is also used for the desert and semi-desert valleys whose dry courses turn into ephemeral streams in periods of torrential rain.

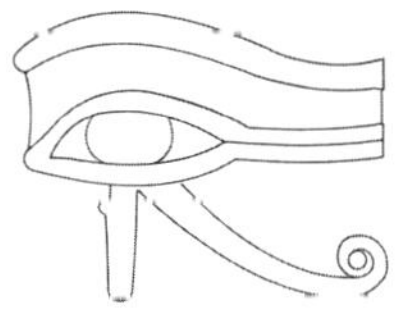

wedjat

Wadjet – protective goddess of →Lower Egypt depicted in the form of a cobra or woman with cobra head. The double town of Pe and Dep (in Greek Buto, today Tell el-Farain) in the north-west of the Delta was the centre of her cult.

wedjat – Eg. "intact, healing"; the eye of the falcon god →Horus, of which he was deprived in a mythical battle by his antagonist, the god →Seth. But his eye was found, healed and returned to Horus, and so became one of the most popular symbols of health, regeneration and resurrection.

White Crown

White Crown – one of the royal insignia. It was cone-shaped, narrowing towards a round top. It was one of the main symbols of →Upper Egypt.

The face mask of a lavishly decorated coffin emerges from the sand in the area east of Werkaure's mastaba.

Chronological table (Egypt)

Compiled by Martin Odler

Note: For the most ancient human settlements, we follow the chronology presented in Tassie (2014, Appendix One, Chronological Tables). For the time between the 4th and 3rd millennia BC, absolute dates are based on only a few radiocarbon dates. The most detailed model has been presented by Dee et al. (2013), and the first table is based on this work. The second table follows Hornung–Krauss–Warburton (eds.) (2006, 490–498), the datings of the 1st and 2nd Dynasties so far partially overlap and the related problems can only be solved by future research. The 3rd Dynasty is here taken to belong to the Old Kingdom.

Palaeolithic	ca. 300,000–8500 BC
Helwanian (Pre–pottery Neolithic B)	ca. 7100–6100 BC
Neolithic – Merimdian	ca. 5000–3900 BC
Neolithic – Omarian	ca. 4600–4000 BC
Neolithic – Faiyumian	ca. 5500–4200 BC
Chalcolithic – Maadian	ca. 3900–3350 BC
Chalcolithic – Badarian	ca. 4400–3700 BC
Chalcolithic – Naqada culture (phases I–IIIB)	ca. 3700–3100 BC
1st Dynasty / Naqada culture (phase IIIC)	ca. 3100–2900 BC

Early Dynastic Period	ca. 2900–2590 BC
1st Dynasty / Naqada culture (phase IIIC; sequence of rulers: Narmer, Aha, Djer, Djet, Den, Adjib, Semerkhet, Qaa)	ca. 2900–2730^{+25} BC
2nd Dynasty / Naqada culture (phase IIID; sequence of rulers: Hetepsekhemwy, Raneb, Ninetjer, Peribsen, Sekhemib, Sened, Khasekhemwy)	ca. 2730–2590^{+25} BC
Old Kingdom	ca. 2590–2120^{+25} BC
3rd Dynasty (sequence of rulers: Netjerykhet/Djoser, Sekhemkhet, Khaba, Nebka, Huni)	ca. 2592–2544^{+25} BC
4th Dynasty (sequence of rulers: Snofru, Khufu, Radjedef, Rakhef, Bawefra (?), Menkaure, Shepseskaf)	ca. 2543–2436^{+25} BC
5th Dynasty (sequence of rulers: Weserkaf, Sahure, Neferirkare Kakai, Raneferef Isi, Shepseskare, Nyuserre Ini, Menkauhor, Djedkare Isesi, Wenis)	ca. 2435–2306^{+25} BC
6th Dynasty (sequence of rulers: Teti, Weserkare, Pepy I Meryre, Nemtyemsaf Merenre I, Pepy II Neferkare, Nemtyemsaf Merenre II, Nitocris)	ca. 2305–2149^{+25} BC

8th Dynasty (attested rulers: Neferkaure, Neferkauhor, Neferirkare)	ca. 2150–2118^{+25} BC
First Intermediate Period	ca. 2118–1980^{+25} BC
9th and 10th Dynasties (less important Herakleopolitan rulers, several named Khety)	ca. 2118–1980^{+25} BC
Middle Kingdom	ca. 1980–1760 BC
11th Dynasty (sequence of rulers: Mentuhotep I, Antef I, Antef II, Antef III, Mentuhotep II Nebhepetre, Mentuhotep III Sankhkare, Mentuhotep IV Nebtawyre)	ca. 2080–1940^{+16} BC
12th Dynasty (sequence of rulers: Amenemhat I Sehetepibre, Senwosret I Kheperkare, Amenemhat II Nebukaure, Senwosret II Khakheperre, Senwosret II Khakaure, Amenemhat II Nymaatre, Amenemhat IV Maakherure, Sebeknofru Sebekkare)	1939^{+16}–1760 BC
Second Intermediate Period	1759–ca. 1539 BC
13th Dynasty (less important rulers, e.g. Khendjer, Neferhotep I Khasekhemre, Ibiya Wahibre, Ay Merneferre)	1759–ca. 1630 BC
14th Dynasty (less important rulers, e.g. Nehesy)	?
15th Dynasty (Hyksos rulers Khaian, Apopi, Khamudi)	?–ca. 1530 BC
16th and 17th Dynasties (less important rulers, at the end of the dynasty several significant rulers: Seqenenre Tao, Kamose Wadjkheperre)	?–1540 BC
New Kingdom	ca. 1539–1077 BC
18th Dynasty (sequence of rulers: Ahmose I Nebpehtyre, Amenophis I Djeserkare, Thutmosis I Aakheperkare, Thutmosis II Aakheperenre, Hatshepsut Maatkare, Thutmosis III Menkheperre, Amenophis II Aakheprure, Thutmosis IV Menkheprure, Amenophis III Nebmaatre, Amenophis IV Neferkheprure / Akhenaten, Smenkhkare / Nefernefruaten, Tutankhaten / Tutankhamun, Aye Kheperkheprure, Haremhab Djeserkheprure)	ca. 1539–1292 BC
19th Dynasty (sequence of rulers: Ramesses I Nebpehtyre, Sethi I Menmaatre, Ramesses II Wesermaatre Setepenre, Merenptah Baenre, Sethi II Weserkheprure, Amenmesse Menmire, Siptah Akhenre, Tawosret Sitre Meritamun)	1292–1191 BC
20th Dynasty (sequence of rulers: Sethnakhte Weserkhaure, Ramesses III Wesermaatre Meryamun, Ramesses IV Heqamaatre Setepenamun, Ramesses V Wesermaatre Sekheperenre, Ramesses VI Nebmaatre Meryamun, Ramesses VII Wesermaatre Setepenre Meryamun, Ramesses IX Neferkare Setepenre, Ramesses X Khepermaatre Setepenre, Ramesses XI Menmaatre Setepenptah)	1190–1077 BC

Third Intermediate Period	ca. 1076–723 BC
21st Dynasty (sequence of rulers: Smendes [Nesibanebdjedet], Amenemnisut, Psusennes [Pasbakhaenniut] I, Amenemope, Osorkon, Siamun, Psusennes [Pasbakhaenniut] II)	ca. 1076–944 BC
22nd Dynasty (sequence of rulers: Seshonq I, Osorkon I, Takelot I, Sheshonq II, Osorkon II, Sheshonq III, Sheshonq IIIa, Pimay, Sheshonq V)	943–ca. 746 BC
23rd Dynasty (Upper Egypt) and rival rulers (rulers: Takelot II, Iuput I, Osorkon III, Takelot III, Pedubastis I, Sheshonq IV, Rudjamun)	845–821 BC
23rd Dynasty (Lower Egypt) (rulers Pedubastis II, Osorkon IV)	ca. 730 BC
24th Dynasty (sequence of rulers: Tefnakht Shepsesre, Bakenrenef Wahkare)	ca. 736–723 BC
Late Period	ca. 722–332 BC
25th Dynasty (Nubian) (sequence of rulers: Piye/Piankhi, Shabaka Neferkare, Shabataka Djedkaure, Taharqa Khurenefertem, Tanutanum Bakare)	ca. 722–655 BC
26th Dynasty (sequence of rulers: Psametik I Wahibre, Nekau II Wehemibre, Psametik II Neferibre, Haibre, Amasis [Ahmose II] Khnumibre, Psametik III Ankhkhaenre)	664–525 BC
27th Dynasty (Persian) (sequence of rulers: Cambyses, Darius I, Xerxes, Artaxerxes I, Darius II, Artaxerxes II)	525–404 BC
28th Dynasy (ruler: Amenardis)	404–399 BC
29th Dynasty (sequence of rulers: Nefaarudj I, Pasherimut, Achoris, Nefaarudj II)	399–380 BC
30th Dynasty (sequence of kings: Nectanebo I [Nakhtnebef], Djedhor, Nectanebo II [Nakhthareheb])	380–343 BC
Second Persian domination (sequence of rulers: Artaxerxes III, Arses, Darius III)	343–332 BC
Greek rulers (sequence: Alexander III the Great, Philip Arrhidaeus, Alexander IV)	332–305 BC
Ptolemaic Period (sequence of rulers: Ptolemy I Soter I, Ptolemy II Philadelphos, Ptolemy III Euergetes, Ptolemy IV Philopator, Ptolemy V Epiphanes, Cleopatra I, Ptolemy VI Philometor, Ptolemy VII Neos Philopator, Ptolemy VIII Euergetes II, Cleopatra II, Cleopatra III, Ptolemy IX Soter II, Ptolemy X Alexander I, Berenike III, Ptolemy XI Alexander II, Ptolemy XII Neos Dionysos, Berenike IV, Cleopatra VII Philopator, Ptolemy XIII, Ptolemy XIV Philopator, Ptolemy XV Caesarion)	305–30 BC

Roman Period (Roman emperors)	30 BC – AD 395
Byzantine Period (Byzantine emperors)	395–640
Arab conquest of Egypt	640

Chronological table (Nubia and central Sudan)

Compiled by Lenka Varadzinová

Lower Nubia

Palaeolithic	ca. 300,000–8500 BC
Mesolithic (Khartoum Variant)	ca. 7000–5000 BC
Neolithic (Abkan)	ca. 5500–3500 BC
A-Group	ca. 3700–2800 BC
C-Group	ca. 2300–1600 BC
Egyptian viceroyalty in Nubia (New Kingdom)	ca. 1539–1077 BC
Ptolemaic Period (northern part)	305–30 BC
Roman Period (northern part)	30 BC – AD 298
Kushite Period, Meroitic phase (southern part)	ca. 300 BC – AD 350
X-Group (Ballana culture)	4th–6th centuries AD
Christian Period (kingdoms of Nobadia, Makuria, Dotawo)	6th century – ca. 1500
Islamic Period	ca. 1500 – present

Upper Nubia

Palaeolithic	ca. 300,000–8500 BC
Mesolithic	ca. 8500–5500 BC
Neolithic	ca. 5500–3500 BC
Pre-Kerma culture	ca. 4th Millennium – 2600 BC
Kingdom of Kerma	ca. 2500–1500 BC
Egyptian viceroyalty in Nubia (New Kingdom)	ca. 1539–1077 BC
Kushite Period	ca. 900 BC – AD 350
• Napatan phase	ca. 900–300 BC
• Meroitic phase	ca. 300 BC – AD 350
Post-Meroitic Period	4th–6th centuries AD
Christian Period (kingdom of Makuria)	6th century – 1323/1365
Islamic Period	1323/1365 – present

Central Sudan

Palaeolithic	ca. 300,000–8500 BC
Mesolithic (Early Khartoum)	ca. 8500–5000 BC
Neolithic	ca. 5000–3000 BC
Kushite Period, Meroitic phase	ca. 300 BC – AD 350
Post-Meroitic Period	4th–6th centuries AD
Christian Period (kingdom of Alodia)	6th century – 1504 AD
Islamic Period	AD 1504 – present

Selected bibliography

Abusir pyramid necropolis – in the realm of the sun god

a) Selected bibliography:

Bárta, M., *Journey to the West. The world of the Old Kingdom tombs in Ancient Egypt*, Prague 2011.

Benešovská, H. – Maříková Vlčková, P. (eds.), *Abúsír. Tajemství pouště a pyramid / Secrets of the desert and the pyramids*, Prague 2006.

Krejčí, J., *Abusir XVIII. The Royal Necropolis in Abusir*, Prague 2010.

Verner, M., *Abusir. The Necropolis of the Sons of the Sun*, Cairo 2017.

b) Bibliography for individual finds:

1. Mummy of King Raneferef

Strouhal, E. – Němečková, A., "Identification of King Raneferef according to Human Remains found in the Burial Chamber of the Unfinished Pyramid", in: Verner, M. et al., *Abusir IX. The Pyramid Complex of Raneferef. The Archaeology*, Prague 2006, pp. 513–518.

2. Striding statue of King Raneferef with Upper Egyptian crown

Verner, M., *Abusir XXVIII. The Statues of Raneferef and the Royal Sculpture of the Fifth Dynasty*, Prague 2017, pp. 142–154.

3. Raneferef seated on his throne under the protection of the god Horus

Verner, M., *Abusir XXVIII. The Statues of Raneferef and the Royal Sculpture of the Fifth Dynasty*, Prague 2017, pp. 116–132.

4. Faience inlays from Raneferef's mortuary temple

Landgráfová, R., *Abusir XIV. Faience Inlays from the Funerary Temple of King Raneferef. Raneferef's Substitute Decoration Programme*, Prague 2006.

5. Builders' inscription with a date from the pyramid of Raneferef

Verner, M. et al., *Abusir IX. The Pyramid Complex of Raneferef. The Archaeology*, Prague 2006, p. 190, no. 8.

6. Decree of King Djedkare on appointment to an office

Posener-Kriéger, P., "Décrets envoyés au temple funéraire de Rêneferef", in: Posener-Kriéger, P. (ed.), *Mélanges Gamal Eddin Mokhtar*, Le Caire 1985, pp. 195–210.

Posener-Kriéger, P. – Verner, M. – Vymazalová, H., *Abusir X. The Pyramid Complex of Raneferef. The Papyrus Archive*, Prague 2006, p. 234, pl. 18.

7. Inventory of Raneferef's cult equipment

Posener-Kriéger, P., "Quelques pièces du matériel cultuel du temple funéraire de Rêneferef", Mitteilungen des Deutschen Archäologischen Instituts, Abteilung Kairo 47 (1991), pp. 293–304.

Posener-Kriéger, P. – Verner, M. – Vymazalová, H., *Abusir X. The Pyramid Complex of Raneferef. The Papyrus Archive*, Prague 2006, pp. 246–249, pl. 31.

8. Accounting record of rations for employees of Raneferef's pyramid complex

Posener-Kriéger, P. – Verner, M. – Vymazalová, H., *Abusir X. The Pyramid Complex of Raneferef. The Papyrus Archive*, Prague 2006, pp. 266–268, pls. 49–50.

9. Seal imprint bearing the name of King Shepseskare

Verner, M., "Seals", in: Verner, M. et al., *Abusir IX. The Pyramid Complex of Raneferef. The Archaeology*, Prague 2006, p. 230, no. 92.

10. Stone vessels with royal names from Raneferef's mortuary temple

Maříková Vlčková, P., *Abusir XV. Stone vessels from the mortuary complex of Raneferef at Abusir*, Prague 2006, p. 84, figs. 5.2 and 5.3.

11. Kneeling Asian captive

Benešovská, H., "Statues from the Pyramid Complex of the King Raneferef", in: Verner, M. et al., *Abusir IX. The Pyramid Complex of Raneferef. The Archaeology*, Prague 2006, pp. 408–410.

12. Ostrakon with the name of Sahure's palace, *Wetjes-neferu-Sahure*

Posener-Kriéger, P. – Verner, M. – Vymazalová, H., *Abusir X. The Pyramid Complex of Raneferef. The Papyrus Archive*, Prague 2006, pp. 332–333.

Verner, M., "Jar dockets", in: Verner, M. et al., *Abusir IX. The Pyramid Complex of Raneferef. The Archaeology*, Prague 2006, p. 276, no. 16.

13. Animal figurines from the mortuary temple of Raneferef

Benešovská, H., "Statues from the Pyramid Complex of the King Raneferef", in: Verner, M. et al., *Abusir IX. The Pyramid Complex of Raneferef. The Archaeology*, Prague 2006, pp. 426–428, figs. 2.7.69, nos. 2 and 4, 2.7.70.

14. Pillar from the mortuary temple of Khentkaus II in Abusir

Verner, M., *Abusir III. The Pyramid Complex of Khentkaus*, Praha 1995, p. 22, 80, pl. 11.

15. Description of statues of Queen Khentkaus II

Posener-Kriéger, P., "Les fragments du payprus", in: Verner, M., *Abusir III. The Pyramid Complex of Khentkaus*, Praha 1995, pp. 133–142.

16. Abusir pyramidia

Verner, M., "Discovery of an Obelisk at Abusir", Revue d'égyptologie 28 (1978), pp. 111–118.

Verner, M. et al., *Abusir IX. The Pyramid Complex of Raneferef. The Archaeology*, Prague 2006, pp. 38–39.

17. Builders' inscription from the pyramid Lepsius no. 24

Verner, M., "Builders' marks and inscriptions", in: Krejčí, J. – Callender, V. G. – Verner, M., *Abusir XII. Minor tombs in the Royal Necropolis I: (the Mastabas of Nebtyemneferes and Nakhtsare, pyramid complex Lepsius no. 24 and tomb complex Lepsius no. 25)*, Prague 2008, p. 137, fig. 4.49.

18. Model of a goose or duck from the tomb of Nakhtsare

Krejčí, J., "3. The Mastaba of Nakhtsare", in: Krejčí, J. – Callender, V. G. – Verner, M., *Abusir XII. Minor tombs in the Royal Necropolis I: (the Mastabas of Nebtyemneferes and Nakhtsare, pyramid complex Lepsius no. 24 and tomb complex Lepsius no. 25)*, Prague 2008, pp. 56–57, figs. 3.32–3.33.

19. Miniature vessels from the tomb of the courtier Kakaibaef

Krejčí, J., "Das Grab des Kakaibaef in Abusir", Sokar 27/2 (2013), p. 25.

20. Builder's inscription with name of Queen Khentkaus III

Krejčí, J. – Arias Kytnarová, K. – Odler, M., "Archaeological excavation of the mastaba of Queen Khentkaus III (tomb AC 30) in Abusir", Prague Egyptological Studies XV (2015), pp. 33–35.

21. Ritual pesheskaf knife from tomb AC 31

Krejčí, J., "Archaeological excavation of tomb AC 31 in Abusir Centre. A preliminary report", Prague Egyptological Studies XVII (2016), p. 17.

22. Wooden stand from tomb AC 31

Krejčí, J., "Nakhtsare's cemetery in Abusir Centre", in: Piacentini, P. (ed.), *Proceedings of the Seventh Conference Old Kingdom Art and Archaeology*, Milan 2019.

23. Sacrificed calf from tomb AC 31

Krejčí, J., "Archaeological excavation of tomb AC 31 in Abusir Centre. A preliminary report", Prague Egyptological Studies XVII (2016), p. 15.

24. Set of copper models of tools and vessels from tomb AC 31

Krejčí, J., "Archaeological excavation of tomb AC 31 in Abusir Centre. A preliminary report", Prague Egyptological Studies XVII (2016), p. 17.

25. Storage jars from the funerary equipment of the lady buried in tomb AC 31

Krejčí, J., "Archaeological excavation of tomb AC 31 in Abusir Centre. A preliminary report", Prague Egyptological Studies XVII (2016), p. 17.

26. Sculptural portrait of the vizier Ptahshepses

Patočková, B., "Fragments de statues découverts dans le mastaba de Ptahchepses à Abousir", in: Grimal, N. (ed.), *Les critères de datation stylistiques à l'Ancien Empire*, Le Caire 1998, pp. 227–233.

27. Sarcophagi of Ptahshepses

Verner, M., "Newly discovered royal sarcophagi from Abusir", in: Bárta, M. – Krejčí, J. (eds.), *Abusir and Saqqara in the Year 2000*, Prague 2000, pp. 568–574, figs. 5–8.

28. Statue of the royal advisor Kaires

Bárta, M. "La tombe de Kaires. Un nouveau mystère à Abousir", Dossier d'Archéologie. Égypte. Nouvelles Découvertes 393 (2019), pp. 44–47.

29. Statue of Princess Hedjetnebu

Verner, M. – Callender, V. G., *Abusir VI. Djedkare's Family Cemetery*, Prague 2002, pp. 93–94, pl. XXIII, Kf6.

30. Princess Khekeretnebty watching the bringing of offerings

Verner, M., "The Mastaba of Khekeretnebty (B)", in: Verner, M. – Callender, V. G., *Abusir VI. Djedkare's Family Cemetery*, Prague 2002, pp. 23–25, figs. B10, Bf2, Bf4.

31. Set of travertine models from the tomb of Khekeretnebty

Verner, M. – Callender, V. G., *Abusir VI. Djedkare's Family Cemetery*, Prague 2002, pp. 34–38, figs. B25–B28, pl. VI, Bf13.

32. Textile with inscription from the tomb of Princess Khekeretnebty

Verner, M. – Callender, V. G., *Abusir VI. Djedkare's Family Cemetery*, Prague 2002, p. 47, fig. B47, pl. Bf31.

33. Tisethor's false door

Verner, M. – Callender, V. G., *Abusir VI. Djedkare's Family Cemetery*, Prague 2002, pp. 30–31, pl. V, Bf9.

34. Sarcophagus of Faaf

Verner, M. – Callender, V. G., *Abusir VI. Djedkare's Family Cemetery*, Prague 2002, pp. 68–69, pl. Df5.

35. Decorated coffin of an unknown beauty

Krejčí, J., "Architecture and Archaeology of AC 26 and AC 32", in: Krejčí, J. – Arias Kytnarová, K. et al., *Abusir XXIV. Mastaba of Werkaure, Volume I. Tombs AC 26 and AC 32 – Old Kingdom strata*, Prague 2014, p. 56.

Krejčí, J. – Peterková Hlouchová, M., "Wooden coffins", in: Krejčí, J. – Havelková, P. et al., *Abusir XXVII. Tomb of Werkaure. Vol. 2. Post-Old Kingdom strata*, Prague, forthcoming.

36. Fabric with depiction of the god Horus

Březinová, H. – Wollnerová, D., "Textile finds", in: Krejčí, J. – Havelková, P. et al., *Abusir XXVII. Tomb of Werkaure. Vol. 2. Post-Old Kingdom strata*, Prague, forthcoming.

37. Faience pendant in the form of *wedjat* eye

Krejčí, J., "Finds", in: Krejčí, J. – Havelková, P. et al., *Abusir XXVII. Tomb of Werkaure. Vol. 2. Post-Old Kingdom strata*, Prague, forthcoming.

38. Wooden figurine of a woman from the mastaba of Werkaure

Krejčí, J., "Architecture and Archaeology of AC 26 and AC 32", in: Krejčí, J. – Arias Kytnarová, K. et al., *Abusir XXIV. Mastaba of Werkaure, Volume I. Tombs AC 26 and AC 32 – Old Kingdom strata*, Prague 2014, p. 54, fig. 2.33.

Cemeteries in the shadow of the Step Pyramid – Abusir South

a) Selected bibliography:

Bárta, M., *Journey to the West. The world of the Old Kingdom tombs in Ancient Egypt*, Prague 2011.

Bárta, M. – Voděra, K., *Memories of 4500 years ago*, Brandýs nad Labem 2002.

Benešovská, H. – Maříková Vlčková, P. (eds.), *Abúsír. Tajemství pouště a pyramid / Secred of the desert and the pyramids*, Prague 2006.

Krejčí, J., *Egypt v době stavitelů pyramid*, Praha 2011.

Verner, M., *Abusir. The Necropolis of the Sons of the Sun*, Cairo 2017.

Verner, M. (ed.), *Poklady z písku. České objevování civilizace na Nilu*, Praha 2011.

b) Bibliography for individual finds:

39. Hetepi's offering scene

Bárta, M. – Vymazalová, H. – Coppens, F. (eds.), *Abusir XIX. Tomb of Hetepi (AS 20), Tombs AS 33–35 and 50–53*, Prague 2010, pp. 18–21, pls. 18–23 and 31.

40. Stone bowl with name of King Huni

Jirásková, L., "Stone vessels of AS 54 at Abusir South. A preliminary report", in: Bárta, M. – Coppens, F. – Krejčí, J. (eds.), *Abusir and Saqqara in the Year of 2010/2*, Prague 2011, pp. 447–464.

41. Meidum Bowl from the anonymous tomb AS 54

Bárta, M., "An Abusir mastaba from the reign of Huni", in: Callender, V. G. – Bareš, L. – Bárta, M. – Janák, J. – Krejčí, J. (eds.), *Times, Signs and Pyramids. Studies in Honour of Miroslav Verner on the Occasion of His Seventieth Birthday*, Prague 2011, pp. 41–50.

42. Wooden boat

Unpublished.

43. Limestone stela with offering scene and two engaged statues

Odler, M. – Peterková Hlouchová, M. – Havelková, P. – Sůvová, Z. – Arias Kytnarová, K. – Jirásková, L. – Brůna, V., "Mastaba of Nyankhseshat (AS 104). A new tomb of transitional type from Abusir South", Prague Egyptological Studies XXIII, 2019.

44. Ears and beard from the burial chamber of Kaaper the Younger

Unpublished.

45. Statue of Nefer

Bárta, M. – Vymazalová, H., "Created for eternity: statues and serdabs in the late Fifth Dynasty tombs at Abusir South", in: Kuraszkiewicz, K. – Kopp, E. – Takács, D. (eds.), *'The Perfection that Endures...' Studies in Old Kingdom Art and Archaeology*, Warsaw 2018, p. 68.

46. Nefer's false door

Bárta, M. – Vymazalová, H. – Dulíková, V. – Arias, K. – Megahed, M. – Varadzin, L., "Exploration of the necropolis at Abusir South in the season of 2012. Preliminary Report", Ägypten und Levante 24 (2014), pp. 27–29, fig. 10.

47. Offerings above the burial of a child in the tomb of the dignitary Nefer

Dulíková, V., "Korálkové šperky pro onen svět. Předběžná zpráva o souborech z hrobky hodnostáře Nefera (AS 68d)", Pražské egyptologické studie XVI (2016), pp. 20–24.

48. Double statue of an ancient Egyptian dignitary

Bárta, M. – Vymazalová, H., "Created for eternity: statues and serdabs in the late Fifth Dynasty tombs at Abusir South", in: Kuraszkiewicz, K. – Kopp, E. – Takács, D. (eds.), *'The Perfection that Endures...' Studies in Old Kingdom Art and Archaeology*, Warsaw 2018, p. 64.

49. Models of burial boats

Bárta, M. – Vymazalová, H. – Dulíková, V. – Arias, K. – Megahed, M. – Varadzin, L., "Exploration of the necropolis at Abusir South in the season of 2012. Preliminary Report", Ägypten und Levante 24 (2014), pp. 33–34.

50. Naos with three high relief figures

Vymazalová, H. – Pieke, G., "Naoi in high relief statues as part of tomb design in Abusir South", in: Piacentini, P. (eds.), *Proceedings of the Seventh Conference Old Kingdom Art and Archaeology*, Milan 2019.

51. Reconstructed bead collar necklace

Dulíková, V., "Korálkové šperky pro onen svět. Předběžná zpráva o souborech z hrobky hodnostáře Nefera (AS 68d)", Pražské egyptologické studie XVI (2016), pp. 20–24.

52. Fragment of relief decoration from the tomb of the inspector of hairdressers Ankhires

Dulíková, V. – Bárta, M. – Odler, M. – Peterková Hlouchová, M. – Sůvová, Z., "Tomb at Abusir

South from a time of change belonging to Ankhires, inspector of hairdressers of the Great House (AS 98)", Prague Egyptological Studies XXI (2018), pp. 10, 13.

53. *Kherep* sceptre from the tomb of the inspector of hairdressers Ankhires

Dulíková, V. – Bárta, M. – Odler, M. – Peterková Hlouchová, M. – Sůvová, Z., "Tomb at Abusir South from a time of change belonging to Ankhires, inspector of hairdressers of the Great House (AS 98)", Prague Egyptological Studies XXI (2018), p. 16.

54. Statue of Princess Sheretnebty with son

Bárta, M. – Vymazalová, H. – Dulíková, V. – Arias, K. – Megahed, M. – Varadzin, L., "Exploration at the necropolis at Abusir South in the season of 2012. Preliminary Report", Ägypten und Levante 24 (2014), p. 25, fig. 8.

Vymazalová, H. – Dulíková, V., "New Evidence on Princess Seretnebty", Archiv orientální 82 (2014), p. 5, fig. 3.

55. Statue of Sheretnebty and her husband

Bárta, M. – Vymazalová, H. – Dulíková, V. – Arias, K. – Megahed, M. – Varadzin, L., "Exploration at the necropolis at Abusir South in the season of 2012. Preliminary Report", Ägypten und Levante 24 (2014), p. 25, fig. 8.

Vymazalová, H. – Dulíková, V., "New Evidence on Princess Seretnebty", Archiv orientální 82 (2014), p. 4, fig. 3.

56. Fragments of the false door of Princess Sheretnebty

Vymazalová, H. – Dulíková, V., "New Evidence on Princess Seretnebty", Archiv orientální 82 (2014), pp. 3, 7–10, figs. 8–9.

57. Funerary equipment of the husband of Princess Sheretnebty

Vymazalová, H., "Expoloration of the burial apartment in the tomb complex AS 68. Preliminary report of the 2013 fall season", Prague Egyptological Studies XV (2015), p. 52.

58. Statue of the dignitary Iti

Bárta, M. – Vymazalová, H. – Dulíková, V. – Arias, K. – Megahed, M. – Varadzin, L., "Exploration at the necropolis at Abusir South in the season of 2012. Preliminary Report", Ägypten und Levante 24 (2014), p. 25, fig. 8.

Vymazalová, H. – Dulíková, V., "New Evidence on Princess Seretnebty", Archiv orientální 82 (2014), pp. 5–6, figs. 3, 7.

Vymazalová, H. – Pieke, G., "Iti and his statuette from the tomb of Princess Sheretnebty in Abusir South", in Bárta, M. – Coppens, F. – Krejčí, J. (eds.), *Abusir and Saqqara in the Year 2015*, Prague 2017, pp. 451–466.

59. Decoration of the entrance to the rock chapel of Duaptah

Bárta, M. – Vymazalová, H. – Dulíková, V. – Arias, K. – Megahed, M. – Varadzin, L., "Exploration of the necropolis at Abusir South in the season of 2012. Preliminary Report", Ägypten und Levante 24 (2014), p. 24, fig. 7.

Vymazalová, H. – Havelková, P., "Notes on the tomb of Duaptah (AS 68a) at Abusir South", Anthropologie LVII/1, pp. 87–104.

60. Stopper with seal imprint from the burial chamber of Duaptah

Vymazalová, H., "Exploration of the burial apartment in the tomb complex AS 68. Preliminary report of the 2013 fall season", Prague Egyptological Studies XV (2015), p. 49.

61. Hieratic inscription in the tomb chapel of the dignitary Shepespuptah

Vymazalová, H. – Dulíková, V., "Sheretnebty, a king's daughter from Abusir South", Archiv orientální 80 (2012), p. 344, fig. 5.

Vymazalová, H. – Havelková, P., "Shepespuptah Idu according to evidence from his rock-cut tomb at Abusir South", Annals of the Náprstek Museum 37/2 (2016), pp. 102–103.

62. False door of Shepseskafankh

Bárta, M., "Tomb of the chief physician Shepseskafankh", Prague Egyptological Studies XV (2015), pp. 15–27.

63. False door of the priest Neferinpu

Bárta, M., *Abusir XXIII. The Tomb of the Sun Priest Neferinpu (AS 37)*, Prague 2014, pp. 98–99, figs. 6.37–6.38, pls. 6.1 and 13.9.

64. Burial of a mouse in the sarcophagus of the priest Neferinpu

Vymazalová, H. – Sůvová, Z., "A Story of an Ancient Egyptian Mouse", Anthropologie LIV/3 (2016), pp. 187–194.

65. Canopic jars from the tomb of the priest Neferinpu

Bárta, M., *Abusir XXIII. The Tomb of the Sun Priest Neferinpu (AS 37)*, Prague 2014, pp. 94–96, figs. 6.33–6.34.

66. Seal impressions from the burial chamber of Neferinpu

Bárta, M., *Abusir XXIII. The Tomb of the Sun Priest Neferinpu (AS 37)*, Prague 2014, pp. 98–99, figs. 6.37–6.38, pls. 6.1 and 13.9.

67. Beer jar as a gift for the afterlife

Arias Kytnarová, K., "Abusir South 2007: Preliminary ceramics report. The tomb of priest Inpunefer and the anonymous tomb AS 47. Abusír Juh 2007: Predbežná keramická správa. Hrobka Inpunefera a anonymná hrobka AS 47", Památky archeologické CII (2011), pp. 117–158.

68. Copper mirror from the tomb of Neferherptah

Jánosi, P., "The mastaba of the chief physician, *Nfr-ḥr-Ptḥ*", Prague Egyptological Studies XIX (2017), pp. 27–36.

69. Relief of the dignitary Ankhiemaptah and his wife

Vymazalová, H., "Evidence on three possible relatives of princess Sheretnebty from her tomb at Abusir South", Archiv orientální 84 (2016), pp. 1–22.

70. Stand for offerings *in situ* in front of Kaisebi's false door

Dulíková, V. – Jirásková, L. – Vymazalová, H. – Arias Kytnarová, K. – Havelková, P., "The tombs of Kaisebi (AS 76) and Ptahwer (AS 76b) at Abusir South", Prague Egyptological Studies XIX (2017), pp. 3–26.

71. Altar of Sankhuptah

Bárta, M., "An Old Kingdom book for the afterlife", in: Magee, D. – Bourriau, J. – Quirke, S. (eds.), *Sitting beside Lepsius. Studies in Honour of Jaromir Malek at the Griffith Institute*, Leuven – Paris 2009, pp. 23–38.

72. Travertine head-rest from Setib's burial chamber

Unpublished.

73. Musical scene with love song

Vachala, B., "Das älteste Liebeslied?", in: Kloth, N. – Martin, K. – Pardey, E. (eds.), *Es werde niedergelegt als Schriftstück. Festschrift für Hartwig Altenmüller zum 65. Geburtstag*, Hamburg 2003, pp. 429–431, tab. 57.

74. Block with the motif of life in a papyrus thicket

Vlčková, P., "Abusir South at the End of the Old Kingdom", in: Piquette, K. – Love, S. (eds.), *Current Research in Egyptology 2003*, Oxford 2005, pp. 163–176, fig. 7.

75. Set of vessels from the embalming deposit in the tomb of Inti

Arias, Kytnarová, K., "Ritual ceramic deposit from the tomb of prince Werkaure? A tentative interpretation", Bulletin de liaison de la céramique égyptienne 24 (2014), pp. 71–82.

Arias, K., *Social dynamics in the material culture – Pottery of the Old Kingdom from the complex of Princess Sheretnebty at Abusir* South, Prague 2017 (unpublished PhD thesis; esp. "Ritual shafts with embalming deposits", pp. 188–192).

76. Face mask

Unpublished.

77. Copper vessels and their miniatures from the burial chamber of Inti Pepyankh

Odler, M., "For the temples, for the burial chambers. Sixth Dynasty copper vessel assemblages", in: Bárta, M. – Coppens, F. – Krejčí, J. (eds.), *Abusir and Saqqara in the Year 2015*, Prague 2017, pp. 293–315.

Odler, M., "Copper Alloy Finds from the Tomb of Inti", in: Bárta, M. – Vachala, B. (eds.), *The Tomb of Inti*, Prague, in preparation.

78. Receptacles for food offerings from the tomb of Inti Pepyankh

Bárta, M., "The Sixth Dynasty tombs in Abusir: tomb complex of the vizier Qar and his family", in: Bárta, M. (ed.), *The Old Kingdom Art and Archaeology. Proceedings of the Conference Held in Prague, May 31 – June 4, 2004*, Prague 2006, pp. 45–62.

79. Copper altar and set of miniaturised and model vessels from the burial chamber of Inti Pepyankh

Odler, M., "For the temples, for the burial chambers. Sixth Dynasty copper vessel assemblages", in: Bárta, M. – Coppens, F. – Krejčí, J. (eds.), *Abusir and Saqqara in the Year 2015*, Prague 2017, pp. 293–315.

Odler, M., "Copper Alloy Finds from the Tomb of Inti", in: Bárta, M. – Vachala, B. (eds.), *The Tomb of Inti*, Prague, in preparation.

80. Scribes' palette

Unpublished.

81. Set of stone receptacles for cosmetics

Verner, M. (ed.), *Unearthing Ancient Egypt. Fifty Years of the Czech Archaeological Exploration in Egypt*, Prague 2008, pp. 176–177.

82. Set of copper model tool blades from the burial chamber of Inti Pepyankh

Odler, M., *Old Kingdom Copper Tools and Model Tools*, Oxford 2016.

Odler, M., "Copper Alloy Finds from the Tomb of Inti", in: Bárta, M. – Vachala, B. (eds.), *The Tomb of Inti*, Prague, in preparation.

83. Imported vessels for Qar the Younger

Bárta, M., *Abusir XIII. Abusir South 2. Tomb Complex of the Vizier Qar, His Sons Qar Junior and Senedjemib, and Iykai*, Prague 2009, pp. 243–259, figs. 6.3.131–6.3.136.

84. Tablet of the seven sacred oils

Bárta, M., *Abusir XIII. Abusir South 2. Tomb Complex of the Vizier Qar, His Sons Qar Junior and Senedjemib, and Iykai*, Prague 2009, pp. 267, 269–270, 357, tab. 40.2.

85. Engaged statue of Meryherishef

Vlčková, P., "Abusir South at the End of the Old Kingdom", in: Piquette, K. – Love, S. (eds.), *Current Research in Egyptology 2003*, Oxford 2005, pp. 163–176, fig. 7.

86. Hemshezemtet's lintel with green inscription

Unpublished.

87. Fan from the tomb of Hemshezemtet

Unpublished.

88. Wooden statue

Unpublished.

89. The oldest ushabti from Egypt

Unpublished.

90. Cartouche of Ramesses II

Bárta, M. – Varadzin, L. – Janák, J. – Mynářová, J. – Brůna, V., "The temple of Ramesses II in Abusir", Egyptian Archaeology 52 (2018), pp. 10–14.

Mynářová, J., "Abusir – new evidence for the New Kingdom. LA 5, tomb A, shaft 1 – blue-painted pottery", in: Bárta, M. – Coppens, F. – Krejčí, J. (eds.), *Abusir and Saqqara in the Year 2005*, Prague 2006, pp. 74–82.

91. Mask of a cow

Bárta, M. – Sůvová, Z. – Verner, M., "The second renaissance of Abusir", in: Woods, A. – McFarlane, A. – Binders, S. (eds.), *Egyptian Culture and Society: Studies in Honour of Naguib Kanawati*, Cairo 2010, pp. 267–279.

92. Aryballos-shaped lekythos with a sphinx

Smoláriková, K., "Abúsír", in: Verner, M. (ed.), *Poklady z písku. České objevování civilizace na Nilu*, Praha 2011, p. 207.

Group of shaft tombs from the middle of the 1st millennium BC in Abusir West

a) Selected bibliography:

Bareš, L., "The development of shaft tomb burials in Egypt during the Persian Period", in: Bárta, M. – Kühlmer, H. (eds.), *Diachronic Trends in Ancient Egyptian History. Studies Dedicated to the Memory of Eva Pardey*, Praha 2013, pp. 15–23.

Benešovská, H. – Maříková Vlčková, P. (eds.), *Abúsír. Tajemství pouště a pyramid / Secrets of the desert and the pyramids*, Prague 2006, pp. 162–175.

Onderka, P. – Maříková Vlčková, P. – Mynářová, J. (eds.), *Objevování země na Nilu / Discovering the land on the Nile*, Prague 2008.
Verner, M., *Abusir. The Necropolis of the Sons of the Sun*, Cairo – New York 2017, pp. 315–370.

b) Bibliography for individual finds:

93. Foundation deposits of the tomb of the admiral Udjahorresnet

Bareš, L., "Foundation deposits in the tomb of Udjahorresnet", Zeitschrift für Ägyptische Sprache und Altertumskunde 123 (1996), pp. 1–9.

94. Double sarcophagus of the priest Iufaa

Verner, M., *Abusir. The Necropolis of the Sons of the Sun*, Cairo – New York 2017, pp. 349–351.

95. Bead net on the mummy of the priest Iufaa

Onderka, P. – Maříková Vlčková, P. – Mynářová, J. (eds.), *Objevování země na Nilu / Discovering the land on the Nile*, Prague 2008, p. 87.

96. Canopic jars of the priest Iufaa

Bareš, L. – Smoláriková, K., *Abusir XVII. The Shaft Tomb of Iufaa – Volume I: Archaeology*, Prague 2008, pp. 225–226, fig. 60, tabs. 5, 28.

97. Procession of demons on the inner sarcophagus of Iufaa

Bareš, L., "Procession of deities and demons on the inner sarcophagus of Iufaa", in: Győry, H. (ed.) *Aegyptus et Pannonia IV. Acta Symposii anno 2006*, Budapest 2010, pp. 1–12.

98. Relief of "dancing cows" on the wall of Iufaa's burial chamber

Bareš, L., "Some notes on the religious texts and scenes in the tomb of Iufaa and other Late Period shaft tombs at Abusir", in: Győry, H. (ed.), *Aegyptus et Pannonia III. Acta Symposii anno 2004*, Budapest 2006, p. 9.

99. "Snake Encyclopaedia" from the burial chamber of the priest Iufaa

Landgráfová, R. – Janák, J., "The *Book of Snakes* from the Tomb of Iufaa at Abusir", in: Kóthay, K. A. (ed.), *Burial and mortuary practices in Late Period and Graeco-Roman Egypt*, Budapest 2017, pp. 111–122.

100. Royal purification ritual from the tomb of the priest Iufaa

Landgráfová, R. – Coppens, F. – Janák, J. – Míčková, D., "Myth and Ritual in the Burial Chamber of the Shaft Tomb of Iufaa at Abusir: Snakes and Snake-like Beings", in: Bárta, M. – Coppens, F. – Krejčí, J. (eds.), *Abusir and Saqqara in the Year 2015*, Prague 2017, pp. 613–626.

101. Texts against Apophis from the tomb of the priest Iufaa

Unpublished.

102. Chest with vessels for sacred oils from Iufaa's burial chamber

Bareš, L. – Smoláriková, K., *Abusir XVII. The Shaft Tomb of Iufaa – Volume I: Archaeology*, Prague 2008, pp. 61–62.

103. Texts for the magical protection of the body of the deceased

Unpublished.

104. Wooden Book of the Dead of Nekau

Bareš, L. – Smoláriková, K., *Abusir XVII. The Shaft Tomb of Iufaa – Volume I: Archaeology*, Prague 2008, pp. 148–155.

Janák, J. – Landgráfová, R., "Nekau's Book of the Dead Reopened", in: Backes, B. – Müller-Roth, M. – Stöhr, S. (eds.), *Ausgestattet mit den Schriften des Thot. Festschrift für Irmtraut Munro zu ihrem 65. Geburtstag*, Wiesbaden 2009, pp. 83–88.

Janák, J. – Landgráfová, R., "The Book of the Dead on wooden tablets from Abusir", in: Bárta, M. – Coppens, F. – Krejčí, J. (eds.), *Abusir and Saqqara in the year 2005*, Prague 2006, pp. 28–33.

105. Demonic protectors from Menekhibnekau's tomb

Landgráfová, R., "The guardians of Menekhibnekau. Chapter 144 of the Book of the Dead in the shaft tomb of Menekhibnekau at Abusir", in: Szpakowska, K. (ed.), *Demon Things*, Swansea, forthcoming.

106. Personifications of the hours of the day and night in the burial chamber of Menekhibnekau

Bareš, L., "Personifications of the day- and night-hours in the tomb of Menekhibnekau at Abusir – a preliminary notice", in: Mynářová, J. – Maříková Vlčková, P. – Tomášek, M. (eds.), *My Things Changed Things. Social Development and Cultural Exchange in Prehistory, Antiquity, and the Middle Ages*, Prague 2009, pp. 16–24.

107. Mummification deposit at the tomb of the general Menekhibnekau

Smoláriková, K., "'Embalmers' Deposits of the Saite tombs at Abusir", Göttinger Miszellen 223 (2009), pp. 79–88.

108. Menekhibnekau's mummification manual

Bareš, L. – Smoláriková, K., *Abusir XXV. The Shaft Tomb of Menekhibnekau – Volume I: Archaeology*, Prague 2011, pp. 164–178.

Janák, J. – Landgráfová, R., "How to make a mummy: A late hieratic guide from Abusir", in: Metcalfe, R. – Cockitt, J. – David, R. (eds.), *Palaeopathology in Egypt and Nubia*, Oxford 2014, pp. 107–118.

Janák, J. – Landgráfová, R., "New evidence on the mummification process in the Late Period", in: Bárta, M. – Coppens, F. – Krejčí, J. (eds.), *Abusir and Saqqara in the Year 2010/1*, Prague 2011, pp. 30–45.

109. Phoenician vessel

Dušek, J. – Mynářová, J., "Excursus 2: Phoenician and Aramaic Inscriptions on a Phoenician Storage Jar (Excav. no. 826/S/10). A Preliminary Report", in: Bareš, L. – Smoláriková, K., *Abusir XXV. The Shaft Tomb of Menekhibnekau – Volume I: Archaeology*, Prague 2011, pp. 179–181.

Dušek, J. – Mynářová, J., "Phoenician ana Aramaic Inscriptions from Abusir", in: Botta, A. (ed.), *In the Shadow of Bezalel: Aramic, Biblical, and Ancient Near Eastern Studies in Honor of Bezalel Porten*, Leiden – New York 2013, pp. 53–69.

110. Statue of the goddess Hathor in the form of a cow

Bareš, L. – Smoláriková, K., *Abusir XXV. The Shaft Tomb of Menekhibnekau, Volume I: Archaeology*, Prague 2011, pp. 31–32.

111. Cemetery seal

Bareš, L., "A seal of the necropolis from the Late Period shaft tomb of Menekhibnekau at Abusir", in: Bareš, L. – Coppens, F. – Smoláriková, K. (eds.), *Egypt in Transition. Social and Religious Development of Egypt in the First Millenium BCE. Proceedings of an International Conference, Prague, September 1–4, 2009*, Prague 2010, pp. 15–21.

112. Ushabti of Padihor

Coppens, F. – Smoláriková, K., *Abusir XX. Lesser Late Period Tombs at Abusir. The Tomb of Padihor and the Anonymous Tomb R3*, Prague 2009, pp. 73–81, pls. 8–9.

113. Corrections in the burial chamber of Padihor

Coppens, F. – Smoláriková, K., *Abusir XX. Lesser Late Period Tombs at Abusir. The Tomb of Padihor and the Anonymous Tomb R3*, Prague 2009, pp. 69–71, pl. 7.

South Saqqara

a) Selected bibliography:

Bárta, M., *Journey to the West. The world of the Old Kingdom tombs in Ancient Egypt*, Prague 2011.
Hawass, Z., *The Realm of the Pharaohs*, Vercelli 2006.
Verner, M. – Callender, V. G., *Abusir VI. Djedkare's Family Cemetery*, Prague 2002.
Verner, M., *The Pyramids. Their Archaeology and History*, London 2002.
Verner, M., *Sons of the Sun. Rise and Decline of the Fifth Dynasty*, Prague 2014.

b) Bibliography for individual finds:

114. Painted pottery vessel

Unpublished.

115. Amulets and rings

Unpublished.

116. Amulets and scarab

Unpublished.

117. Amulet in the form of the goddess Tweret

Unpublished.

118. Amulet in the form of Heqet

Vymazalová, H. – Hashesh, Z., "Secondary burial ground in the pyramid complex of King Djedkare: Preliminary report on burials with grave goods", Annals of Náprstek Museum 2019, forthcoming.

119. Motif of offerings

Jánosi, P. – Vymazalová, H., "The decorated burial chamber of *Ppy-ʿnḫ Stw* at South Saqqara. Some preliminary observations", in: Jánosi, P. – Vymazalová, H. (eds.), *The Art of Describing. The World of Tomb Decoration as Visual Culture of the Old Kingdom. Studies in Honour of Yvonne Harpur*, Prague 2018, pp. 215–234.

Megahed, M. – Jánosi, P. – Vymazalová, H., "Djedkare's pyramid complex: Preliminary report of the 2016 season", Prague Egyptological Studies XIX (2017), pp. 36–51.

Moursi, M., "Die Ausgrabungen in der Gegend um die Pyramide des *Ḏd-kꜣ-rʿ* *"Jssj"* bei Saqqara II", Göttinger Miszellen 105 (1988), pp. 65–68.

120. Red granite column of Djedkare's queen

Megahed, M. – Jánosi, P. – Vymazalová, H., "Exploration of the pyramid complex of King Djedkare: Season 2018", Prague Egyptological Studies XXIII (2019), forthcoming.

121. Offering list of Khuwy

Megahed, M. – Vymazalová, H., "The tomb of Khuwy at Djedkare's royal cemetery at South Saqqara. Preliminary report on the 2019 spring season", Prague Egyptological Studies XXIII (2019), forthcoming.

122. Khuwy enjoying the afterlife offerings

Megahed, M. – Vymazalová, H., "The tomb of Khuwy at Djedkare's royal cemetery at South Saqqara. Preliminary report on the 2019 spring season", Prague Egyptological Studies XXIII (2019), forthcoming.

123. Inlayed eyes of statues of Khuwy

Megahed, M. – Vymazalová, H., "The tomb of Khuwy at Djedkare's royal cemetery at South Saqqara. Preliminary report on the 2019 spring season", Prague Egyptological Studies XXIII (2019), forthcoming.

El-Hayez – the Egyptian Pompeii

a) Selected bibliography:

Bárta, M. (ed.), *Ostrovy zapomnění. El-Héz a české výzkumy v egyptské Západní poušti*, Praha 2009.

Dospěl, M. – Suková, L. (eds.), *Bahriya Oasis. Recent Research into the Past of an Egyptian Oasis*, Prague 2013.

Musil, J. – Tomášek, M. – Kučová, S. – Šanderová, J., "Egyptian Western Desert in the Roman Period. Al-Hayz – Bahariya: the Survey of Development of the Landscape and its Settlement", Památky archeologické CIV (2013), pp. 5–58.

b) Bibliography for individual finds:

124. Historical ostrakon from El-Hayez

Dospěl, M., *Bīr Shawīsh, Small Oasis: Ostraka and Other Inscribed Material*, Praha 2015 (unpublished PhD thesis), pp. 109–110.

125. Stone digging pick

Svoboda, J. A., "Prehistorie jižní části oázy Bahríja. Možnosti korelace klimatického a paleodemografického vývoje v Západní poušti", in: Bárta, M. (ed.), *Ostrovy zapomnění. El-Héz a české výzkumy v egyptské Západní poušti*, Praha 2009, pp. 113–142.

126. Figurine of Bes from Bir Shawish

Dospěl, M., "Oáza el-Hajez, lokalita Bír Šovíš", in: Verner, M. (ed.), *Poklady z písku. České objevování civilizace na Nilu*, Praha 2011, p. 220.

Musil, J. – Tomášek, M., "Archeologický výzkum pozdně římského osídlení na lokalitě Bír Šovíš", in: Bárta, M. (ed.), *Ostrovy zapomnění. El-Héz a české výzkumy v egyptské Západní poušti*, Praha 2009, pp. 226–227.

127. Bowl with cross

Musil, J. – Tomášek, M. – Kučová, S. – Šanderová, J., "Egyptian Western Desert in the Roman Period. Al-Hayz – Bahariya: the Survey of Development of the Landscape and its Settlement", Památky archeologické CIV (2013), p. 46, fig. 56.

Dospěl, M., "Křesťanství a křesťané v Egyptě a v Západní poušti zvlášť", in: Bárta, M. (ed.), *Ostrovy zapomnění. El-Héz a české výzkumy v egyptské Západní poušti*, Praha 2009, p. 298.
Musil, J. – Tomášek, M., "Archeologický výzkum pozdně římského osídlení na lokalitě Bír Šovíš", in: Bárta, M. (ed.), *Ostrovy zapomnění. El-Héz a české výzkumy v egyptské Západní poušti*, Praha 2009, p. 244.

128. Wine amphora

Dospěl, M., "Written, inscribed and some decorated material from Bir Shawish, El-Hayz Oasis", in: Dospěl, M. – Suková, L. (eds.), *Bahriya Oasis. Recent Research into the Past of an Egyptian Oasis*, Prague 2013, pp. 103–105.

129. Roman fibula

Musil, J. – Tomášek, M. – Kučová, S. – Šanderová, J., "Egyptian Western Desert in the Roman Period. Al-Hayz – Bahariya: the Survey of Development of the Landscape and its Settlement", Památky archeologické CIV (2013), p. 42, fig. 49.

130. Terracotta lamp

Dospěl, M., "Written, inscribed and some decorated material from Bir Shawish, El-Hayz Oasis", in: Dospěl, M. – Suková, L. (eds.), *Bahriya Oasis. Recent Research into the Past of an Egyptian Oasis*, Prague 2013, p. 95.

131. Basalt figurine

Unpublished.

Lower Nubia

a) Selected bibliography:

Verner, M. – Benešovská, H., *Unearthing Ancient Egypt. Fifty Years of the Czech Archaeological Exploration in Egypt*, Prague 2008, pp. 14–21.
Žába, Z., "Tāfa and Qertassi. Czechoslovak Institute of Egyptology of Charles University. Aswan High Dam Program. Report of Season 1961", in: Abu Bakr, A. M. (ed.), *Fouilles en Nubie (1959–1961)*, Le Caire 1963, pp. 45–51.
Žába, Z., "The Third Czechoslovak Expedition to Nubia in the Frame of the Safeguarding of the Nubian Monuments Project: Preliminary Report", in: Abu Bakr, A. M. (ed.), *Fouilles en Nubie (1961–1963)*, Le Caire 1967, pp. 217–224.
Žába, Z., "Tâfa and Rock-Inscriptions in Korosko", in: Habachi, L. (ed.), *Actes du IIe symposium international sur la Nubie (Février 1–3, 1971)*, Le Caire 1981, pp. 39–44.
Varadzinová, L., *From Aswan to Khartoum. Czech archaeological explorations between the Nile Cataracts*, Prague 2016, pp. 15–31.

b) Bibliography for individual finds:

132. Historical rock inscription

Žába, Z., *The Rock Inscriptions of Lower Nubia (Czechoslovak Concession)*, Prague 1974, pp. 98–109, fig. 151 (no. 73).

133. Rock inscription with depiction of the priest Sethi

Žába, Z., *The Rock Inscriptions of Lower Nubia (Czechoslovak Concession)*, Prague 1974, p. 187, fig. 314 (no. 190).

134. Painted shelter near Korosko
Suková, L., *The Rock Paintings of Lower Nubia (Czechoslovak Concession)*, Prague 2011, pp. 12–56, figs. 2.1–2.21, pl. 1.

135. Coloured petroglyphs
Suková, L., *The Rock Paintings of Lower Nubia (Czechoslovak Concession)*, Prague 2011, pp. 73–81, figs. 4.1–4.5.

136. Magical rock art of Late Antiquity
Suková, L., *The Rock Paintings of Lower Nubia (Czechoslovak Concession)*, Prague 2011, pp. 93–99, figs. 7.1–7.3.

Unknown temples on the territory of the Sudan – Usli

a) Selected bibliography:

Bárta, M., "Usli", in: Onderka, P. – Vrtal, V. et al., *Núbie. Země na křižovatce kultur / Nubia. A Land on the Crossroads of Cultures: Wad Ben Naga 2014*, Praha 2014, pp. 104–105.

Bárta, M. – Suková, L. – Brůna, V., "The latest explorations at Usli, Northern Province", Sudan & Nubia 17 (2013), pp. 66–69.

Lisá, L. – Bajer, A. – Brůna, V. – Varadzinová Suková, L. – Bárta, M., "Archeologie versus archeologizace: příkladová studie Usli, Súdán", Pražské egyptologické studie XIV (2015), pp. 115–120.

Varadzinová, L., *From Aswan to Khartoum. Czech archaeological explorations between the Nile Cataracts*, Prague 2016, pp. 42–47.

Żurawski, B., "Dongola Reach. The Southern Dongola Reach Survey Report on Fieldwork in 2000", Polish Archaeology in the Mediterranean XII: Reports 2000 (2001), pp. 281–290.

b) Bibliography for individual finds:

137. Fragment of the statue of a striding ruler
Onderka, P., "Spodní část královské sochy / Bottom part a of royal statue", in: Onderka, P. – Vrtal, V. et al., *Núbie. Země na křižovatce kultur / Nubia. A Land on the Crossroads of Cultures: Wad Ben Naga 2014*, Praha 2014, p. 103.

138. Fragments of polychrome wall paintings
Bárta, M. – Turek, J., "Usli. Na prahu říše boha Amona", Pražské egyptologické studie XIV (2015), pp. 104–114.

The Sabaloka Mountains

a) Selected bibliography:

Suková, L. – Cílek, V., "The landscape and archaeology of Jebel Sabaloka and the Sixth Nile cataract, Sudan", Interdisciplinaria Archaeologica: Natural Sciences in Archaeology III/2 (2012), pp. 189–201.

Suková, L. – Varadzin, L., "Preliminary report on the exploration of Jebel Sabaloka (West Bank), 2009–2012", Sudan & Nubia 16 (2012), pp. 118–131.

Suková, L. – Varadzin, L. – Pokorný, P., "Prehistoric research at Jebel Sabaloka, Central Sudan (2011–2014)", in: Sázelová, S. – Hupková, A. – Mořkovský, T. (eds.), *Mikulov Anthropology Meeting*, Brno 2014, pp. 149–153.

Varadzinová, L. – Varadzin, L., "Sabaloka (West Bank) Research Project. Exploration of the site of Sphinx (SBK.W-60): findings of the 2014 and 2015 field seasons", Sudan & Nubia 21 (2017), pp. 23–33, 48–49.

Varadzinová Suková, L. – Varadzin, L. – Bajer, A. – Lisá, L. – Pacina, J. – Pokorný, P., "Tracing Post-depositional Processes at Mesolithic Occupation Sites in Central Sudan: View from the Site of Sphinx (SBK.W-60) at Jebel Sabaloka", Interdisciplinaria Archaeologica: Natural Sciences in Archaeology VI/2 (2015), pp. 133–150.

b) Bibliography for individual finds:

139. Archaeobotanical collection from the 4th century AD

Suková, L. – Varadzin, L. – Havelková, P. – Novák, J. – Pokorná, A., "Pohřeb lučištníka z pohoří Sabaloka / The burial of an archer from the Sabaloka Mountains", in: Onderka, P. – Vrtal, V. et al., *Núbie. Země na křižovatce kultur / Nubia. A Land on the Crossroads of Cultures: Wad Ben Naga 2014*, Prague 2014, pp. 178–183.

140. Virtual reconstruction of a vanished type of architecture in the Sabaloka Mountains

Varadzin, L. – Varadzinová, L. – Pacina, J., "From holes to huts: reconstructing an extinct type of architecture at the Sixth Nile Cataract", Antiquity 91, no. 357 (2017), pp. 589–604.

Chronological tables

Dee, M. – Wengrow, D. – Shortland, A. – Stevenson, A. – Brock, F. – Flink, L. G. – Ramsey, C. B., "An absolute chronology for early Egypt using radiocarbon dating and Bayesian statistical modelling", Proceedings of the Royal Society A: Mathematical, Physical and Engineering Science 469 (2013) (DOI 10.1098/rspa.2013.0395).

Hornung, E. – Krauss, R. – Warburton, D. A., *Ancient Egyptian Chronology*, Leiden – Boston 2006.

Tassie, G. J., *Prehistoric Egypt: Socioeconomic Transformations in North-east Africa from the Last Glacial Maximum to the Neolithic, 24,000 to 6,000 cal BP*, London 2014.

Varadzinová, L., *From Aswan to Khartoum. Czech archaeological explorations between the Nile cataracts*, Prague 2016.

Welsby, D. A. – Anderson, J. R., *Sudan. Ancient Treasures. An Exhibition of Recent Discoveries from the Sudan National Museum*, London 2014.

Illustration credits

Abbreviations: CzEgI: Czech Institute of Egyptology, Faculty of Arts, Charles University, IFAO: Institut français d'archéologie orientale, NM – NpM: National Museum – Náprstek Museum of Asian, African and American Cultures; b: bottom, c: centre, l: left, r: right, t: top

Cover

CzEgI: Milan Zemina, Martin Frouz

Introduction

2–3 CzEgI: Martin Frouz. **5** CzEgI: Jolana Malátková. **6** CzEgI: Kamil Voděra. **8** CzEgI: Milan Zemina. **11** CzEgI: Milan Zemina. **12** CzEgI: Jaromír Krejčí. **14–15** CzEgI: Jaromír Krejčí. **16** DigitalGlobe, Inc. **17** CzEgI: Lucie Vařeková, Jolana Malátková.

The Pyramid Necropolis

18 CzEgI: Jaromír Krejčí. **20–21** CzEgI: Martin Frouz. **22** CzEgI: Martin Frouz. **23** CzEgI: Jaromír Krejčí. **24** CzEgI: Kamil Voděra (l), CzEgI: Jaromír Krejčí (r). **25** CzEgI: Evžen Strouhal. **26** CzEgI: Jan Brodský (l), CzEgI: Kamil Voděra (r). **27** CzEgI: Martin Frouz. **28** CzEgI: Martin Frouz. **29** CzEgI: Jan Brodský. **30** CzEgI: Kamil Voděra. **31** CzEgI: Kamil Voděra. **32** CzEgI: Miroslav Verner. **33** CzEgI: Kamil Voděra (t), CzEgI: Jolana Malátková (b). **34** CzEgI: Miroslav Verner. **35** Archiv IFAO (t), CzEgI: Jolana Malátková, Hana Vymazalová (b). **36** CzEgI: Martin Frouz. **37** CzEgI: Milan Zemina (t), CzEgI: Jolana Malátková, Hana Vymazalová (b). **38** CzEgI: Milan Zemina. **39** CzEgI: Kamil Voděra (t), CzEgI: Jolana Malátková, Hana Vymazalová (b). **40** CzEgI: Martin Frouz. **41** CzEgI: Josef Grabmüller (t), CzEgI: Jolana Malátková (b). **42** NM – NpM: Jiří Vaněk (l), CzEgI: Petr Milde (r). **43** NM – NpM: Jiří Vaněk (t), CzEgI: Milan Zemina (b). **44** CzEgI: Jan Brodský. **45** CzEgI: Jan Brodský. **46** CzEgI: Martin Frouz. **47** CzEgI: Kamil Voděra. **48** CzEgI: Petr Košárek. **49** CzEgI: Kamil Voděra. **50** CzEgI: Milan Zemina. **51** CzEgI: Martin Frouz. **52** CzEgI: Martin Frouz. **53** CzEgI: Milan Zemina. **54** CzEgI: Milan Zemina (l), CzEgI: Milan Zemina (r). **55** CzEgI: Kamil Voděra. **56** CzEgI: Jaromír Krejčí. **57** CzEgI: Jaromír Krejčí. **58** CzEgI: Jaromír Krejčí. **59** CzEgI: Milan Zemina (t), CzEgI: Milan Zemina (b). **60** CzEgI: Jaromír Krejčí (l), CzEgI: Jaromír Krejčí (r). **61** CzEgI: Martin Frouz. **62** CzEgI: Martin Frouz. **63** CzEgI: Jaromír Krejčí. **64** CzEgI: Martin Frouz (l), CzEgI: Martin Frouz (r). **65** CzEgI: Martin Frouz. **66** CzEgI: Jaromír Krejčí. **67** CzEgI: Martin Frouz. **68** CzEgI: Martin Frouz. **69** CzEgI: Jaromír Krejčí. **70** CzEgI: Jaromír Krejčí. **71** CzEgI: Martin Frouz. **72** CzEgI: Jaromír Krejčí. **73** CzEgI: Martin Frouz. **74** CzEgI: Milan Zemina (l), CzEgI: Milan Zemina (r). **75** CzEgI: Milan Zemina. **76** CzEgI: Milan Zemina. **77** CzEgI: Martin Frouz. **78** CzEgI: Petr Košárek (l), CzEgI: Petr Košárek (r). **79** CzEgI: Petr Košárek. **80** CzEgI: Milan Zemina (l), CzEgI: Milan Zemina (r). **81** CzEgI: Jan Brodský. **82** CzEgI: Martin Frouz. **83** CzEgI: Martin Frouz. **84** CzEgI: Milan Zemina. **85** NM – NpM: Jiří Vaněk. **86** CzEgI: Milan Zemina (l), CzEgI: Milan Zemina (r). **87** CzEgI: Milan Zemina. **88** CzEgI: Milan Zemina. **89** CzEgI: Milan Zemina. **90** CzEgI: Milan Zemina. **91** CzEgI: Milan Zemina (t), CzEgI: Miroslav Verner, Jolana Malátková (b). **92** CzEgI: Jaromír Krejčí. **93** CzEgI: Jaromír Krejčí. **94** CzEgI: Jaromír Krejčí. **95** CzEgI: Martin Frouz. **96** CzEgI: Jaromír Krejčí. **97** CzEgI: Martin Frouz. **98** CzEgI: Miroslav Ottmar. **99** CzEgI: Jaromír Krejčí (t), CzEgI: Jaromír Krejčí (b).

Abusir South

100 CzEgI: Jaromír Krejčí. **102–103** CzEgI: Miroslav Bárta. **104–105** CzEgI: Miroslav Bárta. **106** CzEgI: Miroslav Bárta (l), CzEgI: Miroslav Bárta (r). **107** CzEgI: Miroslav Bárta. **108** CzEgI: Miroslav Bárta (t), CzEgI: Martin Frouz (b). **109** CzEgI: Martin Frouz. **110** CzEgI: Miroslav Bárta. **111** CzEgI: Martin Frouz. **112** CzEgI: Martin Frouz (t), CzEgI: Martin Frouz (b). **113** CzEgI: Martin Frouz. **114** CzEgI: Martin Odler (l),

CzEgI: Petr Košárek (r). **115** CzEgI: Petr Košárek. **116** CzEgI: Veronika Dulíková. **117** CzEgI: Martin Frouz. **118** CzEgI: Martin Frouz (t), CzEgI: Miroslav Bárta (b). **119** CzEgI: Martin Frouz. **120** CzEgI: Martin Frouz (l), CzEgI: Martin Frouz (r). **121** CzEgI: Martin Frouz. **122** CzEgI: Martin Frouz. **123** CzEgI: Martin Frouz. **124** CzEgI: Miroslav Bárta (l, t), CzEgI: Miroslav Bárta (l, b), CzEgI: Miroslav Bárta (r). **125** CzEgI: Martin Frouz. **126** CzEgI: Hana Vymazalová (l), CzEgI: Hana Vymazalová (r). **127** CzEgI: Martin Frouz. **128** CzEgI: Martin Frouz (l), CzEgI: Martin Frouz (r). **129** CzEgI: Martin Frouz. **130** CzEgI: Martin Frouz. **131** CzEgI: Martin Frouz. **132** CzEgI: Martin Frouz. **133** CzEgI: Petr Košárek. **134** CzEgI: Petr Košárek. **135** CzEgI: Jolana Malátková (l), CzEgI: Petr Košárek (r). **136** CzEgI: Veronika Dulíková. **137** CzEgI: Martin Frouz. **138** CzEgI: Martin Frouz (t), CzEgI: Martin Frouz (b). **139** CzEgI: Martin Frouz. **140** CzEgI: Martin Frouz (t), CzEgI: Martin Frouz (b). **141** CzEgI: Martin Frouz. **142** CzEgI: Martin Frouz (l), CzEgI: Martin Frouz (r). **143** CzEgI: Martin Frouz. **144** CzEgI: Veronika Dulíková (t), CzEgI: Martin Frouz (b). **145** CzEgI: Martin Frouz. **146** CzEgI: Martin Frouz. **147** CzEgI: Martin Frouz (t), CzEgI: Martin Frouz (b). **148** CzEgI: Martin Frouz. **149** CzEgI: Martin Frouz. **150** CzEgI: Veronika Dulíková. **151** CzEgI: Martin Frouz. **152** CzEgI: Miroslav Bárta (l), CzEgI: Miroslav Bárta (r). **153** CzEgI: Miroslav Bárta. **154** CzEgI: Miroslav Bárta. **155** CzEgI: Martin Frouz. **156** CzEgI: Martin Frouz. **157** CzEgI: Martin Frouz. **158** CzEgI: Miroslav Bárta. **159** CzEgI: Martin Frouz. **160** CzEgI: Martin Frouz. **161** CzEgI: Martin Frouz (t), CzEgI: Martin Frouz (b). **162** CzEgI: Martin Frouz. **163** CzEgI: Miroslav Bárta. **164** CzEgI: Veronika Dulíková (t), CzEgI: Miroslav Bárta (b). **165** CzEgI: Martin Frouz. **166** CzEgI: Hana Vymazalová. **167** CzEgI: Martin Frouz. **168** CzEgI: Martin Frouz (l), CzEgI: Veronika Dulíková (r). **169** CzEgI: Martin Frouz. **170** CzEgI: Miroslav Bárta. **171** CzEgI: Martin Frouz (t), CzEgI: Jolana Malátková (b). **172** CzEgI: Veronika Dulíková (l), CzEgI: Martin Frouz (r). **173** CzEgI: Sandro Vannini. **174** CzEgI: Kamil Voděra. **175** CzEgI: Kamil Voděra. **176** CzEgI: Kamil Voděra. **177** CzEgI: Kamil Voděra. **178** CzEgI: Miroslav Bárta. **179** CzEgI: Kamil Voděra. **180** CzEgI: Kamil Voděra. **181** CzEgI: Martin Frouz. **182** CzEgI: Miroslav Bárta (t), CzEgI: Kamil Voděra (b). **183** CzEgI: Kamil Voděra. **184** CzEgI: Miroslav Bárta. **185** CzEgI: Kamil Voděra (t), CzEgI: Martin Frouz (c), CzEgI: Kamil Voděra (b). **S. 186** CzEgI: Kamil Voděra. **187** CzEgI: Kamil Voděra. **188** CzEgI: Miroslav Bárta. **189** CzEgI: Kamil Voděra (t), CzEgI: Kamil Voděra (b). **190** CzEgI: Kamil Voděra. **191** CzEgI: Kamil Voděra. **192** CzEgI: Kamil Voděra (t), CzEgI: (b) Kamil Voděra. **193** CzEgI: Kamil Voděra. **194** CzEgI: Kamil Voděra. **195** CzEgI: Kamil Voděra. **196** CzEgI: Kamil Voděra. **197** CzEgI: Kamil Voděra. **198** CzEgI: Kamil Voděra. **199** CzEgI: Kamil Voděra (l), CzEgI: Martin Frouz (r). **200** CzEgI: Jan Turek. **201** CzEgI: Martin Frouz. **202** CzEgI: Martin Frouz. **203** CzEgI: Martin Frouz. **204** Hana Vymazalová (l), CzEgI: Martin Frouz; (r). **205** CzEgI: Martin Frouz. **206** CzEgI: Martin Frouz (l), CzEgI: Hana Vymazalová (r). **207** CzEgI: Martin Frouz. **208** CzEgI: Ladislav Varadzin (l), CzEgI: Vladimír Brůna (r). **209** CzEgI: Jana Mynářová. **210** CzEgI: Martin Frouz. **211** CzEgI: Martin Frouz. **212** CzEgI: Miroslav Bárta. **213** CzEgI: Miroslav Bárta.

Shaft Tombs

214 CzEgI: Martin Frouz. **216** CzEgI: Květa Smoláriková. **218–219** CzEgI: Kamil Voděra. **220** CzEgI: Milan Zemina. **221** CzEgI: Milan Zemina. **222** CzEgI: Miroslav Bárta. **223** CzEgI: Martin Frouz. **224** CzEgI: Milan Zemina (l), CzEgI: Miroslav Bárta (r). **225** CzEgI: Milan Zemina. **226** CzEgI: Milan Zemina (l), CzEgI: Květa Smoláriková (r). **227** CzEgI: Milan Zemina. **228** CzEgI: Martin Frouz. **229** CzEgI: Martin Frouz. **230** CzEgI: Martin Frouz. **231** CzEgI: Martin Frouz. **232** CzEgI: Martin Frouz (l), CzEgI: Martin Frouz (r). **233** CzEgI: Martin Frouz. **234** CzEgI: Martin Frouz (l), CzEgI: Květa Smoláriková (r). **235** CzEgI: Martin Frouz. **236** CzEgI: Martin Frouz. **237** CzEgI: Martin Frouz. **238** CzEgI: Milan Zemina. **239** CzEgI: Milan Zemina. **240** CzEgI: Martin Frouz. **241** CzEgI: Kamil Voděra (t), CzEgI: Martin Frouz (b). **242** CzEgI: Kamil Voděra (l), CzEgI: Kamil Voděra (r). **243** CzEgI: Kamil Voděra. **244** CzEgI: Martin Frouz. **245** CzEgI: Martin Frouz. **246** CzEgI: Martin Frouz. **247** CzEgI: Martin Frouz. **248** CzEgI: Kamil Voděra. **249** CzEgI: Kamil Voděra. **250** CzEgI: Kamil Voděra. **251** CzEgI: Kamil Voděra. **252** CzEgI: Kamil Voděra (l), CzEgI: Kamil Voděra (r). **253** CzEgI: Martin Frouz. **254** CzEgI: Petr Košárek. **255** CzEgI: Petr Košárek. **256** CzEgI: Miroslav Ottmar. **257** CzEgI: Miroslav Ottmar. **258** CzEgI: Kamil Voděra. **259** CzEgI: Kamil Voděra. **260** CzEgI: Kamil Voděra. **261** CzEgI: Kamil Voděra.

South Saqqara

262 CzEgI: Milan Zemina. **264** Hana Vymazalová. **265** Sandro Vannini. **266–267** Hana Vymazalová. **268** Mohamed Megahed. **269** Ashraf Senoussi (t), Ashraf Senoussi (b). **270** Hana Vymazalová. **271** Petr Košárek. **272** Hana Vymazalová. **273** Petr Košárek. **274** Hana Vymazalová. **275** Petr Košárek. **276** Peter Jánosi (t), Peter Jánosi (b). **277** Petr Košárek. **278** Hana Vymazalová. **279** Sandro Vannini. **280** Hana Vymazalová. **281** Hana Vymazalová. **282** Hana Vymazalová. **283** Sandro Vannini. **284** Sandro Vannini. **285** Sandro Vannini. **286** Hana Vymazalová (l), Hana Vymazalová (r). **287** Petr Košárek.

El-Hayez

288 CzEgI: Jaromír Krejčí. **290** CzEgI: Miroslav Bárta. **291** CzEgI: Miroslav Bárta. **292–293** CzEgI: Miroslav Bárta. **294** Jiří Musil. **295** CzEgI: Martin Frouz. **296** CzEgI: Miroslav Bárta. **297** CzEgI: Miroslav Bárta (t), CzEgI: Miroslav Bárta (b). **298** CzEgI: Miroslav Bárta. **299** CzEgI: Martin Frouz (l), CzEgI: Martin Frouz (r). **300** CzEgI: Miroslav Bárta. **301** CzEgI: Martin Frouz. **302** CzEgI: Miroslav Bárta. **303** CzEgI: Martin Frouz (l, t), CzEgI: Martin Frouz (l, b), CzEgI: Martin Frouz (r). **304** CzEgI: CzEgI: Miroslav Bárta. **305** CzEgI: Martin Frouz. **306** CzEgI: Miroslav Bárta. **307** CzEgI: Martin Frouz (t), CzEgI: Martin Frouz (c), CzEgI: Martin Frouz (b). **308** CzEgI: Miroslav Bárta (l), CzEgI: Miroslav Bárta (r). **309** CzEgI: Martin Frouz.

Lower Nubia

310 CzEgI: Evžen Strouhal. **312** CzEgI: Zbyněk Žába. **313** CzEgI: Zbyněk Žába. **314–315** CzEgI: Jaroslav Novotný. **316** CzEgI: Jaroslav Novotný. **317** CzEgI: Zbyněk Žába. **318** CzEgI: Jaroslav Novotný (l, r). **319** CzEgI: Zbyněk Žába. **320** CzEgI: Zbyněk Žába. **321** CzEgI: Zbyněk Žába. **322** CzEgI: Zbyněk Žába. **323** CzEgI: Zbyněk Žába. **324** CzEgI: Zbyněk Žába (l), CzEgI: Zbyněk Žába (r). **325** CzEgI: Zbyněk Žába.

Unknown temples on the territory of the Sudan – Usli

326 CzEgI: Jan Turek. **328–329** CzEgI: Miroslav Bárta. **330–331** Robert Stanisław Ryndziewicz, Dawid Wiesław Święch. **332** NM – NpM: Jiří Vaněk (l), NM – NpM: Jiří Vaněk (r). **333** CzEgI: Miroslav Bárta. **334** CzEgI: Petr Berounský. **335** CzEgI: Lenka Varadzinová (t, b).

The Sabaloka Mountains

336 CzEgI: Petr Pokorný. **338** CzEgI: Petr Pokorný. **339** CzEgI: Jaroslav Řídký. **340–341** CzEgI: Petr Pokorný. **342** CzEgI: Ladislav Varadzin (t), CzEgI: Ladislav Varadzin (b). **343** CzEgI: Petr Pokorný. **344** CzEgI: Ladislav Varadzin (t), CzEgI: Ladislav Varadzin (b). **345** CzEgI: Ladislav Varadzin.

Glossary

346 CzEgI: Martin Frouz. **348** CzEgI: Martin Frouz. **349** CzEgI: Jolana Malátková; **350** CzEgI: Martin Frouz, CzEgI: Jolana Malátková; CzEgI: Jolana Malátková; **351** CzEgI: Jolana Malátková, CzEgI: Jolana Malátková, CzEgI: Jolana Malátková, CzEgI: Jolana Malátková; **352** CzEgI: Milan Zemina, Archiv IFAO, CzEgI: Jolana Malátková; **353** CzEgI: Milan Zemina, CzEgI: Milan Zemina, W.Budge, The Book of the Dead, pl. 11, CzEgI: Kamil Voděra; **354** CzEgI: Jaromír Krejčí, CzEgI: Jolana Malátková; **355** CzEgI: Milan Zemina, CzEgI: Jolana Malátková, CzEgI: Jolana Malátková, CzEgI: Jolana Malátková; **356** CzEgI: Jolana Malátková, CzEgI: Jaromír Krejčí, CzEgI: Jolana Malátková; **357** CzEgI: Jaromír Krejčí, CzEgI: Jolana Malátková, CzEgI: Jolana Malátková; **358** CzEgI: Milan Zemina, CzEgI: Jolana Malátková, CzEgI: Milan Zemina; **359** CzEgI: Milan Zemina, CzEgI: Jolana Malátková, CzEgI: Jolana Malátková, CzEgI: Jaromír Krejčí, CzEgI: Jolana Malátková; **360** CzEgI: Jolana Malátková, CzEgI: Martin Frouz, CzEgI: Milan Zemina, CzEgI: Jolana Malátková; **361** CzEgI: Jolana Malátková, CzEgI: Martin Frouz.

Chronological Table

362 CzEgI: Jolana Malátková

Created for eternity:

the greatest discoveries of Czech Egyptology

Miroslav Bárta | Ladislav Bareš | Jaromír Krejčí |
Mohamed Megahed | Lenka Varadzinová (editoři)

Vydala Univerzita Karlova, Filozofická fakulta,
nám. Jana Palacha 2, 116 38 Praha 1

Tato kniha vyšla s podporou projektu Progres Q11 „Komplexita a resilience. Staroegyptská civilizace v multidisciplinární a multikulturní perspektivě" a dotace dle rozhodnutí č. 1-VEG 2019, č.j. MŠMT-906/2019-6.

Předmluvy: Tomáš Zima, rektor Univerzity Karlovy,
Zahi Hawass

Autoři textů: Katarína Arias, Ladislav Bareš, Miroslav Bárta, Dana Bělohoubková, Helena Březinová, Filip Coppens, Veronika Dulíková, Jiří Janák, Lucie Jirásková, Jaromír Krejčí, Renata Landgráfová, Mohamed Megahed, Jana Mynářová, Martin Odler, Marie Peterková Hlouchová, Květa Smoláriková, Břetislav Vachala, Lenka Varadzinová, Miroslav Verner, Hana Vymazalová, Dorotea Wollnerová

Fotografie a ilustrace: Archiv Českého egyptologického ústavu FF UK (Miroslav Bárta, Petr Berounský, Jan Brodský, Vladimír Brůna, Veronika Dulíková, Martin Frouz, Josef Grabmüller, Petr Košárek, Jaromír Krejčí, Jolana Malátková, Jana Mynářová, Jaroslav Novotný, Martin Odler, Miroslav Ottmar, Petr Pokorný, Jaroslav Řídký, Květa Smoláriková, Evžen Strouhal, Jan Turek, Sandro Vannini, Ladislav Varadzin, Lenka Varadzinová, Lucie Vařeková, Miroslav Verner, Kamil Voděra, Hana Vymazalová, Milan Zemina, Zbyněk Žába), DigitalGlobe Inc., Institut français d'archéologie orientale, Národní muzeum – Náprstkovo muzeum asijských, afrických a amerických kultur (Jiří Vaněk), Tomasz Herbich, Peter Jánosi, Mohamed Megahed, Jiří Musil, Ashraf Senoussi, Sandro Vannini, Hana Vymazalová

Obálka: (s použitím fotografií Milana Zeminy a Martina Frouze) Oleg Man
Grafická úprava a sazba: Oleg Man

Vydání druhé, první anglické, Praha 2019

Tisk: SERIFA, s. r. o., Jinonická 80, 150 00 Praha 5

ISBN 978-80-7308-927-6